San Francisco

BAY
SHORELINE
Guide

P9-CDC-883

About This Guide & San Francisco Bay 1

The Bay Trail 5

How to Use This Book 6

San Francisco 8
 Map 9
 Fort Point to Aquatic Park 10
 Fisherman's Wharf to Mission Bay 16
 China Basin to Candlestick 22

North San Mateo 25
 Map 26
 Sierra Point Parkway to
 San Bruno Point 27
 Bayfront to Shoreline Park 32

South San Mateo 36
 Map 37
 Foster City to Redwood Shores 38
 Port of Redwood City to
 Ravenswood Slough 42

South Bay 45
 Map ....46 & 47
 Dumbarton Bridge & Piers to
 Moffett Field 48
 Sunnyvale Baylands Park to
 Sportsfield Park 56

Fremont/Hayward 61
 Map 62
 San Francisco Bay
 National Wildlife Refuge to
 Coyote Hills Regional Park 63
 Alameda Creek to
 Hayward Regional Shoreline 69

Common Plants 72

San Leandro/San Lorenzo 74
 Map 75
 Marina Park to Bay Farm Island 76
 Martin Luther King Jr.
 Regional Shoreline to Robert Crown
 Memorial State Beach 79

High Spots 85

Berkeley/Oakland 86
 Map 87
 North Alameda & Oakland 88
 Emeryville & Berkeley to Point Isabel ...97

Indigenous People 102

Richmond/San Pablo 104
 Map 105
 Richmond Inner Harbor
 to Cypress Point 106
 Richmond/San Rafael Bridge to
 Point Pinole 112

Northeast Bay 118
 Map ....118 & 119
 Pinole Shores Regional Park to
 San Pablo Bay Regional Trail 121
 The Carquinez Strait—
 Crockett to Martinez......................124
 Benicia to Vallejo 129

Alien Species in the Bay 134

Guide to Boats 136

Napa/Sonoma 137
 Map ....138 & 139
 Napa 140
 Sonoma 144

Petaluma/Novato 148
 Map 149
 Petaluma/Novato 150

How to Care for the Bay 156

North Marin 158
 Map 159
 Novato Creek to Gallinas Creek 160
 Point San Pedro to San Rafael Creek 164

South Marin 168
 Map 169
 Corte Madera & Larkspur 170
 Tiburon Peninsula 172
 Richardson Bay 175
 Strawberry Point 177
 Sausalito Waterfront 179
 Fort Baker 182

Reference/Resources 185

Index 188

Illustration Credits 192

San Francisco BAY SHORELINE Guide

How to use this map

This regional map is a key to detailed maps inside, each preceding a chapter. Locate the area on this map you wish to explore and refer to the page numbers shown in red to access the detailed maps and chapters for more information.

Legend

— Bay Trail

Proposed Bay Trail (now used by public)

Proposed Bay Trail (not accessible)

— Other Trails

SAN FRANCISCO BAY TRAIL

0 — 5 Km — 10 Km

0 — 5 Miles — 10 Miles

N

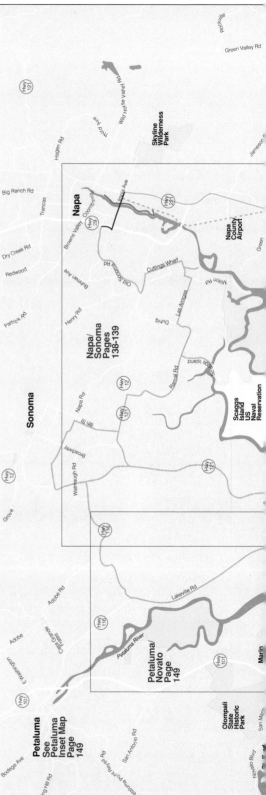

Sonoma

Napa/Sonoma Pages 138-139

Napa

Napa County Airport

Skyline Wilderness Park

Scaggs Island US Naval Reservation

Petaluma/Novato Page 149

Petaluma See Petaluma Inset Map Page 149

Olompali State Historic Park

Marin

Hwy 121
Hwy 12
Hwy 29
Hwy 12
Hwy 121
Hwy 121
Hwy 116
Hwy 116
Hwy 101
Hwy 101

Green Valley Rd
Rockville
Wild Horse Valley Rd
Third Ave
Haagen Rd
Big Ranch Rd
Trancas
Coombsville
Imola Ave
Dry Creek Rd
Browns Valley
Redwood
Burnham Ave
Old Sonoma Rd
Cuttings Wharf
Patrick Rd
Henry Rd
During
Las Amigas
Million Rd
Napa Rd
8th St
Ramal Rd
Mare Island St
Broadway
Wambaugh Rd
Grove
Adobe Rd
Lakeville Rd
Adobe
Casa Grande
E Washington
Petaluma River
Spring Hill Rd
Bodega Ave
Petaluma Pt/Pt Reyes Rd
San Antonio Rd
Novato Blvd
San Marin
Jameson C
Green

This book is your passport to San Francisco Bay and its shoreline. It was created to guide you to hundreds of beautiful places owned in common by the inhabitants of this region and the citizens of California and the United States. Few people who live nearby—and even fewer of those who visit—know that more than 40 percent of the bay's shoreline is open to the public.

For most people, San Francisco Bay means a view. Its gleaming waters are typically seen from a distance, glimpsed as a sideways blur from a fast-moving car, briefly studied from a house or restaurant window, or momentarily admired from some hilltop. The bay is out there, before our eyes, but at the same time it's invisible. Few come to know it intimately. Few realize what this great 450-square-mile estuary offers.

"San Francisco Bay is an irreplaceable gift of nature that man can either abuse and ultimately destroy—or improve and protect for future generations."
San Francisco Bay Plan, 1969

You can walk or bicycle for miles on trails that meander along the bay shoreline, tasting winds fresh off the water, spiced by the rich blend of salt and marsh grasses. You can watch thousands of migrating shorebirds, get lost in a flock of feeding terns, listen to the smacking and popping of a recently exposed mud flat, watch the water shimmer and change. You can get to know landscapes close to home that are unique, elemental, and accessible.

It's easy to get to the water's edge, once you know the way. About 173 miles of shoreline are already open to the public by means of the Bay Trail, which will eventually extend for 400 miles and enable you to circle the entire bay without once getting into a car. Many more Bay Trail segments are in the works, linking local and regional trails that have been built for walking, hiking, bicycling, and other forms of nonmotorized travel. The Bay Trail leads to places where you can fish off piers, windsurf, swim, drop a kayak or canoe into the water, picnic, or get into shape on a parcourse; to shoreline towns and historic sites, museums, nature study centers, wildlife refuges, scenic overlooks. It connects with other trails that will take you inland along creeks and streams, up into the hills, and to the edge of the Pacific Ocean, where you can pick up the Coastal Trail and move north or south. You will also be able to follow trail links to the 400-mile Ridge Trail, which is forming a second, wider ring around the bay. In fall 1994, almost 180 miles of the Ridge Trail had been completed.

In this book we show you the route that will take you around the bay along the completed and proposed segments of the Bay Trail. There are still a few gaps. To cross the Richmond-San Rafael Bridge, and move between a few other trail segments, you still need to go by bus or car. Along stretches of the proposed route, where the trail is still only a set of blue lines on a plan, you will have to use streets. Anyone ambitious enough to want to do the entire trail will probably be undeterred. Others will find ample opportunities along the Bay Trail now in place.

Anywhere you begin to explore the bay shoreline, using this book or just your eyes and ears, you are likely to be surprised and pleased at what you find. Stand a moment at the foot of Market Street in San Francisco and consider: at this spot, in 1850, you would have been half a mile out from shore. Below you now are the remains of hundreds of sailing ships, abandoned here during the Gold Rush.

Take the ferry to Oakland. As you glide under the Bay Bridge, look around for waterfowl bobbing on the water. Look up. In the girders, under the fast-moving lanes of daily traffic, peregrine falcons nest every spring. These raptors have returned from near extinction and adapted to urban life. They hunt for food in parks and streets, terrorizing citified pigeons. Under the Richmond and San Mateo bridges, double-crested cormorants raise their young. They used to nest in standing dead trees, but these have become scarce around the bay.

We share the bay with an amazing diversity of wildlife. The great shallows of the south bay, protected within the San Francisco Bay National Wildlife Refuge, which are critical habitat for

Checker lily (seed pod)

Blue larkspur

hundreds of thousands of migrating shorebirds that stop to feed and rest on their annual journey between the Far North and Central America. A couple hundred bird species live here year-round. The tidal marshes, creeksides, and grassy uplands shelter many other creatures, including the endangered salt marsh harvest mouse, burrowing owls, foxes, rabbits, and raccoons.

Human and natural history is layered along the shore. The Oyster Bay Regional Shoreline in San Leandro is just one of the shoreline parks built atop former garbage dumps. Take a picnic to this park's highest knoll and you won't see or smell any hint of its past. Visit Wildcat Marsh in Richmond, where birds and other creatures find sanctuary in a wetland that is being restored near a large oil refinery.

Along the Carquinez Strait, the sleepy town of Port Costa was once a major shipping port. Just offshore, 200-pound sturgeons still lumber along the murky bay bottom. Across the northern reaches of San Pablo Bay, thousands of canvasback ducks and scaups rest in winter months, more than anywhere else along the Pacific Coast. Go north to the Petaluma River. It's not a river at all but a 14-mile-long tidal slough. In May 1994, a young gray whale wandered all the way into downtown Petaluma, which once was a major bay shipping port.

The many wonders of San Francisco Bay are obscured by buildings, freeways, roadside sound walls, billboards, utility poles—and by the intense speed and daily routines of most of us who move along its shores. You have to slow down, turn off, stop, and look. If you get to know a stretch of shoreline nearest to your home or job, you will probably want to explore further. You will find yourself experiencing the moods and seasons of the bay, and this will help you to comprehend its past and potential future, and your own place within this landscape.

Crimson sage

How Rivers, Mountains, and the Ocean Made the Bay

The smooth shorelines and gentle hillsides around San Francisco Bay mask one of North America's most complicated and dynamic geologic puzzles. The Bay Area—and most of the Pacific Coast—rides above a break in the Earth's crust that divides the Pacific Plate from the North American Plate. Some 200 million years ago, the Pacific Plate began to scrape under the western edge of the North American Plate, moving in an easterly direction in a process called subduction. About 29 million years ago, the Pacific Plate changed course toward the northwest and began to slide past the North American Plate. It is sliding today at a rate of perhaps two inches a year. The two plates meet along the San Andreas Fault System, which extends through western California from the Mexican border to Point Arena in Mendocino County. In the Bay Area, the Crystal Springs Reservoir is on the San Andreas Fault, as are the Bolinas Lagoon, Tomales Bay, and Bodega Bay. If you stand on the western side of the fault, you are moving toward Alaska, leaving most of California behind you.

Enormous pressures at the boundaries of the two plates have fractured the surface of the Earth into countless faults, all part of the San Andreas Fault System. Rocks have been compressed, twisted, and folded.

Some 10,000 years ago, when vast glaciers capped the Sierra, the sea level was lower, and the coastal shoreline lay some 20 miles or more to the west, near the Farallon Islands. There was no San Francisco Bay as we now know it. What is now the north bay was a valley cut by a steep canyon that had been carved by the combined rivers known today as the Sacramento and San Joaquin. Their powerful combined flow created a 350-foot-deep canyon at what is now known as the Golden Gate.

Miner's lettuce

During this time, gentler rivers meandered through the landscape that became the south bay and formed the valley now named Santa Clara. The tip of the peninsula on which San Francisco stands was once mostly a dunescape, covered with river-brought sand. Cypresses, firs, pines, and junipers dominated the uplands. Mammoths, camels, horses, giant buffalo, and sloths roamed where deer, raccoons, and shorebirds live today. As the climate warmed and dried, and glaciers melted, the ocean began to rise, drowning canyons and channels to create the bay. Rivers brought sediments that accumulated along the shoreline, forming broad and fertile marshes and uplands.

The People of the Bay and the Years of Destruction

It was on the shores of this fertile embayment that the ancestors of today's Native Americans arrived from the north several thousand years ago. They lived here with grizzly bear, deer, elk, antelope, wolves, and countless birds. Offshore there were whales, dolphins, and otters, as well as enormous sturgeons and many other fish species. Salmon came upriver to spawn. Oysters and mussels covered the bay floor close to shore. Tens of thousands of people lived in villages around the bay before the Europeans arrived, and they spoke some 12 different languages. Soon after Gaspar de Portolá "discovered" the bay in 1769, a ship captain described this as a place of "inexpressible fertility."

Before long, however, newcomers felled the oaks and cut down the redwoods on nearby hills. They used oak bark to tan hides, oak wood for fuel, redwood to build the bay cities. The people of this land were killed, enslaved, or they succumbed to diseases to which they had no resistance. The grizzlies were hunted to extinction and the vast flocks of waterfowl and shorebirds were decimated. Marshes were filled and diked to make room for agriculture, industry, and cities. By the 1950s, 85 percent of the bay's

> *"For more than a century, much of the bay had been regarded as little more than ordinary real estate that happened to be inconveniently and temporarily covered by water."*
> Joseph E. Bodovitz, 1985

wetlands had been destroyed, either buried under fill, diked off and dried out, or converted to salt ponds. Freshwater inflow that was essential to maintaining a healthy bay had been diverted to other uses.

Much of what you will find in these pages seemed destined for destruction four decades ago. The photograph below and its explanation, published in the *San Francisco News* on June 18, 1958, now symbolize what seemed to be an inexorable trend.

"Two weeks ago William Manuel could stand out on the end of his 'pier' and watch the water lapping underneath his house-on-stilts at Candlestick Cove. Today his beach and the waterfront he leases have become part of the road to the new Giants Stadium. And soon his house must go."

This house did go, along with the habitat for mud flat creatures, fish, and shorebirds, as the bay shoreline was extended with fill to build the access road to Candlestick Park, the Bayshore Freeway, and other construction and development projects. Every bayshore community seemed to have plans to expand bayward. Hills near the shore were gouged and carved to provide bayfill.

In 1961, the U.S. Army Corps of Engineers published a map that showed what the bay was likely to look like in the year 2020: not much more than a river winding between new developments on fill. About four square miles of bay were being filled each year. Gigantic plans were under way for replacing bird and fish habitat with roads and houses. San Mateo County planned a freeway, parallel to the Bayshore Freeway, on some 23 new square miles of land to be created by gouging into San Bruno

Mountain. The Port of Oakland's plans included two square miles of fill from the Bay Bridge toll plaza almost to Treasure Island. San Rafael had filling plans for some 75 percent of its tidelands.

The Bay is Rediscovered

In 1962, three women changed the course of the bay's history. Catherine Kerr, Sylvia McLaughlin, and Esther Gulick, all wives of University of California officials, could see the bay, with garbage dumps burning on the shore, from their homes in the Berkeley hills. Shortly after the Army Corps of Engineers' map appeared, they called a meeting of about a dozen people whom they expected to be as concerned as they were. The Save San Francisco Bay Association was born. In 1965, through the efforts of Senator J. Eugene McAteer and Assemblyman Nicholas Petris, a bill was passed establishing the San Francisco Bay Conservation and Development Commission (BCDC) and directing it to prepare a plan for the long-term use and protection of the bay and for regulating development in and around it. The Commission was given permanent regulatory authority in 1969 and directed to carry out the essential features of the Bay Plan.

Anyone seeking to alter the shoreline now must seek a permit from BCDC (see p. 5). If BCDC grants a permit, it requires that public access be provided whenever possible. What remains of the bay's marshland today is protected, and some of what was lost is being restored, as you will find in this book.

The historic turnaround of the 1960s opened the way to new visions. Communities began to look at their shoreline as a potential public amenity. Many asked for help from the State Coastal Conservancy, which was able to craft solutions to the land use conflicts that inevitably arose and to undertake projects that realized the new visions. The Save San Francisco Bay Association evolved into a citizens' stewardship organization. It is now working not just to assure that the Bay is protected as the legislature has directed; it has launched a restoration campaign. Public agencies and a growing number of local and regional citizens' organizations are trying to restore degraded streams to health, to protect wetlands, wildlife habitat, and open spaces, and to find ways to help people live in closer harmony with the bay.

How the Bay Trail Began

A new dream was launched one autumn day in 1986, when Senator Bill Lockyer of Hayward was having lunch with a local editor in a waterfront restaurant. The end-of-session frenzy was over and he was in a reflective mood. "Let me try this idea out on you," he said to his companion. "What if we tried to develop a pedestrian and bicycle path around the bay, with access to the shoreline?" His luncheon partner applauded the idea and urged the senator to pursue it. "So I got my staff working on it," Senator Lockyer said. "The outcome was SB 100." Co-authored by all Bay Area legislators, the bill passed. It defined parameters of the planning process, designated the Association of Bay Area Governments as the lead agency, and provided $300,000 for the preparation of a Bay Trail Plan by July 1, 1989.

The Bay Trail Plan (see p. 5) shows a network of trails that meander and loop along the shore, connecting all nine surrounding counties and linking with the Ridge Trail. By late 1994 about 43 percent of both trail systems were completed and in use. This book is evidence of what can be accomplished, and what more can be done.

Dwarf plantain

The State Coastal Conservancy has been the principal funding source for the Bay Trail and is playing a major role in its development. The agency's mandate to provide maximum feasible public access to the state's coast and San Francisco Bay means more than providing pathways. People must know that the access exists, they must be able to find it, and they must realize that they have a right to use it. You may have lived on the bay for years and have no idea certain delightful shoreline spots are available for your enjoyment. Look at your maps, check the text, and be adventuresome.

"As we explore our environment, we discover special places and they become ours. We appropriate them, grateful to have found them in the public domain, leaving them undisturbed. Once we have sat alone underneath the Golden Gate Bridge, or trekked out a long, dusty back trail, that spot under the bridge, that trail become very personally and uniquely ours. By experience, we possess them."
Erick Mikiten, *A Wheelchair Rider's Guide to San Francisco Bay and Nearby Shorelines,* 1990

Most of the 6.5 million people who call the Bay Area home have come from elsewhere. But slowly, we may be coming to know ourselves as people from the San Francisco Bay/Delta region. There are those who dream of a time when the seasonal return of the salmon through the Golden Gate will again be celebrated as a major holiday, as it was with the Ohlone, uniting a diverse human population and connecting us with the bay's natural rhythms.

Today you will not likely find any "pristine" shoreline. Almost every inch has been altered by riprap, fill, levees, dikes, and various structures. And yet, more than two centuries after European settlement began, the San Francisco Bay shoreline retains an allure, a history, a diversity of people and places—and a wildness—unequaled by other settled shores. Under those power poles, surrounding those levees, hidden amongst the riprap, on top of the former dumps, and across thousands of acres of wildlife refuges and parks, amazing life abounds. It would be impossible to restore the bay's former character. But we can rejoice in getting to know what has been preserved. Consider this book as a claim check to priceless heirlooms that we almost lost but have now recovered. We offer it in hopes it will help us enjoy them and pass them on to future generations of humans and fellow creatures.

Rasa Gustaitis and Jerry Emory

The Bay Trail Is a Work in Progress

The San Francisco Bay Trail is a hiking and bicycling trail system around San Francisco Bay. It links communities, parks, piers, wildlife reserves, boat launches, and other areas open to the public along the shore. It connects with trails that lead inland, and with the Ridge Trail, which is forming a second, wider ring around the bay. About 170 miles (43 percent) of the planned 400-mile Bay Trail had been completed in mid-1994, and work was under way on numerous other segments. The creative spark for the Bay Trail came from Senator Bill Lockyer of Hayward, who conceived and introduced a bill that initiated the plan for a "ring around the bay" pedestrian and bicycle trail. Coauthored by the entire Bay Area legislative delegation, the bill passed in 1987, directing the Association of Bay Area Governments (ABAG) to develop and adopt a plan and implementation program for such a trail, in cooperation with a wide array of local and regional agencies, environmental organizations, and recreational interests. ABAG, with an advisory committee, approved the Bay Trail Plan in 1989. The route of the trail, as included in this plan and later modified by the committee, is shown in the maps of this guide. You will note that the trail is not simply "a string of pearls connecting gems," as had earlier been envisioned: It has tendrils and loops, inviting you to explore parks and open spaces and move inland, sometimes along creeks, toward the Pacific Ocean or into inland park areas.

Coordinating work planned or under way on the Bay Trail is the Bay Trail Project, a nonprofit organization housed within ABAG. It encourages and promotes diverse efforts to further this trail system's completion. Bay Trail policies and guidelines are intended to complement the adopted regulations of local management agencies. Trail segments are built by local, regional, state, and federal agencies, in partnership with citizens' organizations, business, and industry. The State Coastal Conservancy is the largest single funding partner.

The Bay Trail Project needs volunteers to help develop trail segments, review new opportunities, attend public meetings, and take part in surveys and public events. There are many ways you can participate. For more information, call 510-464-7904.

Marin Conservation Corps trail-building at China Camp

The San Francisco Bay Conservation and Development Commission

In 1965, the California legislature passed the McAteer-Petris Act, in response to urgent pleas from the Save San Francisco Bay Association, formed four years earlier by citizens who were alarmed at the rapid filling of the bay. Four square miles of bay were being lost every year. The legislation established the San Francisco Bay Conservation and Development Commission (BCDC) as a temporary state agency, charged with preparing a plan for the long-term use and protection of the bay and with authority to regulate development in and around it.

The San Francisco Bay Plan, completed in 1969, includes policies on 18 issues critical to the wise use of the bay, including fill, ports, waterfront parks, public access, appearance and design, marsh protection, and water-related recreation. The legislature adopted this plan in 1969 and gave BCDC permanent planning and regulatory authority over the bay. In 1977 the legislature expanded that authority to include the protection of the 85,000-acre Suisun Marsh, the largest remaining wetland in California.

BCDC also has the authority to use the federal Coastal Zone Management Act to carry out the provisions of the Bay Plan, the Suisun Marsh Protection Plan, and state laws. It has issued hundreds of permits for development and other projects, many with conditions requiring public access, wetland protection, and open space. Thanks in large part to the work of the commission, the State Coastal Conservancy, and local jurisdictions, as well as to the actions of vigilant citizens, public access to the bay continues to be expanded and some diked wetlands are now being restored.

Citizens who find problems on the bay, or who want more information, may contact the San Francisco Bay Conservation and Development Commission, 30 Van Ness Avenue, Suite 2011, San Francisco, CA 94102. Telephone 415-557-3686.

A few hints will help you use this guide to full advantage, and to enrich your experience of the shoreline as you follow the Bay Trail.

See Where You Are

First, spend some time getting acquainted. Glance at the table of contents and the index. Look at the pull-out map of the entire bay. Locate yourself in relation to what's around you.

The Order of Things

Read the introduction. Note that chapters are organized counter-clockwise around the bay, moving south from San Francisco and ending at the Golden Gate Bridge after Marin County. You, of course, will choose your own route of travel.

Keys to the Bay Trail

The big map is keyed to 13 regional maps, each followed by a chapter that describes specific places. Note that the red, pink, and purple lines denote trails or trail routes, not roads. Don't assume you can drive along these lines. Many Bay Trail segments are paths through parks, pre-serves, and other open spaces that exclude motor vehicles, although other segments do run alongside streets, roads, or even highways, and some are merely sidewalks or road shoulders.

Reaching the Bay Trail

The maps indicate roads, streets, and highway turnoffs, as well as BART routes that lead to places described in the guide. For detailed directions, see the text, especially the "Getting Around" sections. There are phone num-bers in the chapters, as well as in "Resources," for finding out whatever else you need to know about the places described.

The Bay Trail Is a Network

The Bay Trail is not a single trail but an interconnected trail sys-tem that links parks, open spaces, points of interest, and communities on or near the bay shoreline. It will take you all the way around the bay, but also will encourage you to loop inland toward nearby open spaces and preserves, to wander up streams, and, if you choose, to move on to the Ridge Trail, which, with the Bay Trail, forms the second of two concentric rings around the bay. In mid-1994, some 170 miles (about 43 percent) of the planned 400-mile Bay Trail had been completed.

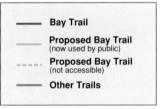

———	**Bay Trail**
-------	**Proposed Bay Trail** (now used by public)
... ...	**Proposed Bay Trail** (not accessible)
————	**Other Trails**

Red, Pink, Dashed Pink, and Purple

The solid red line on the maps indicates completed segments. Solid pink shows proposed seg-ments that are now used by the public. Some of these are yet to be adopted by the local jurisdic-tions they pass through; some lack amenities that will be added later; some are busy streets or roadways rather than trails. They are a way to go, however, if you want to move from one complet-ed stretch of Bay Trail to another, staying as close as possible to the bay's edge. Inaccessible segments of the Bay Trail route appear in dashed pink. Some of these are private property. Please do not trespass. With this guide you should be able to circle the entire San Francisco Bay shoreline.

Icons

𝝅 ♿ ⌫ 🦆 ⛵ 🚶 🚴

Within each chapter you will find sets of icons, suggesting what you can see and do at places described. The two hikers

🚶 stand for pedestrians, of course, but where you see them you can probably bicycle or rollerskate too: most of the Bay Trail is designed for varied use. Wheelchair users will find that more places are accessible than are indicated by the ♿. Only those sites and trail segments officially designated as barrier-free have the symbol. The ⚓ indicates docking or hand-launching spots available to the public. The ⌫ indicates piers and other good fishing spots.

More Colors

Green areas on the maps are public parks and wildlife reserves. Blue means water. Yellow indicates airports, mili-tary reservations, and some other public institutions.

Changes to Come

In the text we have indicated places where road and highway projects are expected to change access routes to trails and other shoreline features within the next few years.

Take Your Guide to the Shore

Once you have a sense of the book, take it along on a bayshore excursion. Get to know the stretch of shoreline closest to your home or workplace, then explore outward. You may be surprised to discover that you are only a few minutes from a shoreline park, wildlife area, or historic site. Any point on the entire bay is within two hours' traveling distance from wherever you start on the shore. So why not venture from Petaluma to the San Francisco Bay Wildlife Refuge in the south bay, or from Redwood City to the upper reaches of the Napa River? Bring your bike, your hiking shoes, and don't forget this book.

Signage

Not all access points for the Bay Trail and other shoreline features are clearly indicated by signs. Some small parks, and some trails, lack signs entirely and you may get the impression they are private, not public. Don't get discouraged. Use the guide to find your way, then call or write to tell us what is needed. Contact the access program manager at the State Coastal Conservancy, 1330 Broadway, Suite 1100, Oakland, CA 94612. Tel: 510-286-1015. Budget permitting, we will try to improve the signage.

Watching Wildlife

Always consider yourself a guest in wildlife habitat, and do your best not to disturb the residents. If you see a wild creature, freeze. Listen like a deer. Relax and look without moving. Don't try to sneak up on birds and animals, causing them to flee. They need their energy for feeding and other activities. Stay on trails to reduce human smells, sounds, and movements in the wild. Immerse yourself in nature. Leave no traces.

Dogs

Do respect regulations regarding dogs. Your pet needs exercise, but not in places where wild creatures will be disturbed. You may not see the harm in your dog's joyfully setting a flock of shorebirds to flight. But yours is probably one of many dogs to do this every day, disturbing these birds' feeding and resting patterns. Be especially careful near wildlife reserves.

Fishing & Crabbing

There are more than 40 public piers on the bay, and you don't need a license to fish from them. You do need a license for crabbing from piers, and to fish from the shoreline. To buy a license, and for more information, inquire at your local sports store, or call the Department of Fish and Game at 707-944-5500.

BIKES, BART, AND BRIDGES

Bikes & BART

Bikes are permitted on BART all day Saturday and Sunday, but only during non-commute hours Monday through Friday. Bike permits cost $3.00 and are good for 3 years. They can be purchased at the Lake Merritt BART station or by mail. Temporary permits are available at all stations. Bikes must be walked to the last car of each train for transport. To find out how to purchase a permit by mail, call 510-464-7133.

Bikes & Bridges

The Dumbarton and Golden Gate bridges have bike lanes. Dumbarton's bike lane is accessible 24 hours a day. For the biking hours on the Golden Gate, see page 184.

Caltrans operates bicycle commuter shuttles (vans towing bike trailers) on the San Francisco–Oakland Bay Bridge and the Benicia–Martinez Bridge. The Bay Bridge shuttle runs between the MacArthur BART station in Oakland and the Transbay Terminal in San Francisco. These shuttles cost $1.00 each way. To find out more, call 510-286-4444.

At the Carquinez, Richmond–San Rafael, and San Mateo–Hayward bridges, Caltrans towing services will transport recreational bikers free if contacted in advance. This is not a daily commuter service. Single bikers should call a day in advance (if possible) to make arrangements. Bike groups (two or more) should call 5 working days ahead. For more information, call 510-286-0669.

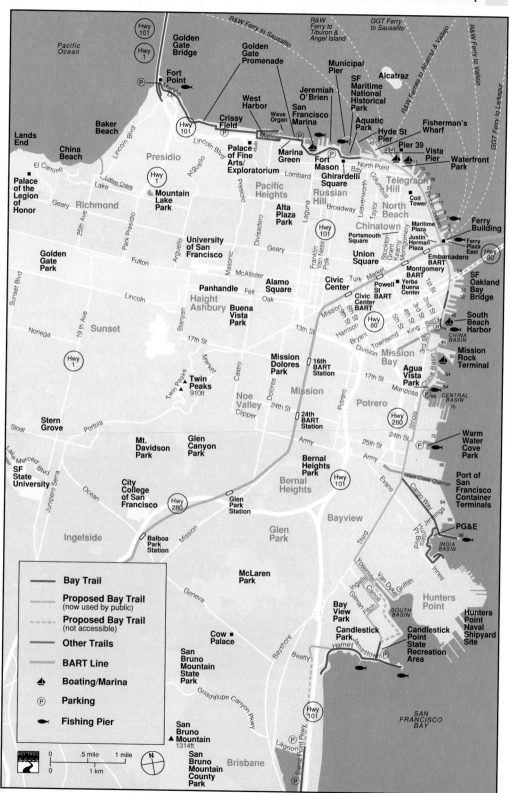

Bay Trail

Proposed Bay Trail
(now used by public)

Proposed Bay Trail
(not accessible)

Other Trails

BART Line

⛵ Boating/Marina

Ⓟ Parking

🐟 Fishing Pier

FORT POINT TO AQUATIC PARK

"Among American cities, San Francisco is that rarity, an exciting town to walk."
Margot Patterson Doss
San Francisco at Your Feet

Aquatic Park, looking toward the Golden Gate Bridge

From Fort Point to Candlestick Point Recreation Area, almost the entire San Francisco bayfront is man-made. Beneath the streets, parks and buildings lie abandoned ships, excavated hilltops, rotting piers, compacted 19th century trash, and massive amounts of rubble dumped into the bay after the 1906 earthquake and fire. Above all that, you will find one of the world's most inviting urban waterfronts.

The northern bayfront, as well as the city's ocean shoreline, is almost entirely within the Golden Gate National Recreation Area (GGNRA), the first urban national park in the United States. Walking or biking along the Golden Gate Promenade, you will pass historic forts and ships, windy beaches, the historic San Francisco Presidio, the unique cultural center at Fort Mason, and much more. Eventually you will arrive at Aquatic Park, where hardy souls swim in chilly waters alongside the historic ships.

Fort Point ♿

On a promontory directly under the Golden Gate Bridge, Fort Point stands as an intact example of pre–Civil War American military architecture. It was built in 1861 to protect San Francisco's harbor and deter foreign ventures along the coast, replacing the 1794 Spanish Castillo de San Joaquin, which stood some 80 feet upslope. Nobody ever fired on Fort Point and it was soon obsolete: its brick and granite walls could not have withstood the rifled cannons designed in the late 1860s. Today rangers lead thousands of visitors past cannons and up spiral staircases to soldiers' and officers' quarters and jail cells. Lantern tours are available on winter nights.

Outside the compound, turn north and you are directly beneath the bridge. Look up at the powerful girders and listen to the cars speeding across. Note

Fort Point

how the bridge's arches frame the fort. Below you, sea stars and numerous algae cling to rocks and can be seen at low tide or between waves. Don't climb down to them; the surging water is dangerous. Before you, one

mile across the Golden Gate, the Marin Headlands loom to the northwest, Fort Baker is tucked into the shore just east of the bridge, the city of Tiburon is to the northeast, and Angel Island stands offshore.

Coastal Trails and Beaches 🚶🚶

The Fort Point Trail winds under the bridge toward the toll area en route to the Coastal Trail and leads south to Baker Beach, China Beach, Lands End, the Cliff House, Ocean Beach, and Fort Funston. (Trail branch just above the fort is temporarily closed.) At low tide you can explore the tide pools at China Beach. But please, don't collect or trample tide pool creatures. Be careful along coastal cliffs: they are unstable and dangerous. Keep to main trails. In San Francisco, only China Beach and Aquatic Beach (at Aquatic Park) are safe for swimming, and only when a lifeguard is present. Baker Beach has a strong riptide.

Golden Gate Promenade

Golden Gate Promenade 🚻 🐦 ♿ 🐟 ⛵ 🚶🚶 🚴

Eastward from Fort Point, Marine Drive leads to the Golden Gate Promenade, a 3.5-mile bayshore trail. The pier near the start of this trail is open sunrise to sunset. Take the Promenade past Crissy Field toward Marina Green, to Fort Mason, and on to Aquatic Park and the San Francisco Maritime National Historical Park. Whether you live in the city or are visiting, you will be enriched. Watch the birds, boats, and people. Stroll in the wind, scan the bay and the skylines of San Francisco, Marin, and the East Bay.

Presidio 🚻 ♿ 🚶🚶 🚴

The San Francisco Presidio is the nation's oldest continuously active military base and has been home to the Sixth Army. Its history dates back to 1776 when Spanish Captain Juan Bautista de Anza, Padre Pedro Font, and six soldiers camped near the lagoon and freshwater springs in what was then duneland. In 1822 Mexican independence ended Spanish rule, and in 1848, when Mexico ceded California to the United States, the U.S.

Officers' family housing in the Presidio

Army took over. In response to soldiers' complaints about the harshness of conditions, more than 60,000 trees were planted in the 1880s. Now the Presidio is a forested 1,400-acre reserve, one-third larger than Golden Gate Park, rich in history, natural resources, and future potential. Among more than 800 buildings is the finest collection of military architecture in the West. At the Presidio Army Museum, artifacts and displays offer insights into the past. The Presidio Historic Trail, a 7-mile loop, passes 27 spots of historical significance. Abundant plant life includes 240 native species. Springs still supply up to 2 million gallons a day to the Presidio and until recently also served the San Francisco Exploratorium. San Francisco's last free-flowing stream, Lobos Creek, rises in the Presidio near 16th Avenue and empties into the ocean at Baker Beach. The Presidio is passing into the hands of the National Park Service, and its future is being planned with enthusiastic citizen participation.

PRESIDIO'S ENDANGERED PLANTS

In 1816 a Russian expedition set anchor near the Presidio. Adelbert Chamisso and Johann Eschscholtz, the ship's naturalist and surgeon, collected 82 species of plants. Many of California's native plants were first described from their collections: yerba buena, California poppy, wax-myrtle, and coffeeberry. Today, some 240 California native species have been recorded within the Presidio's 1,400 acres. Two endangered plants, the San Francisco campion and the San Francisco lessingia, are protected under an agreement between the U.S. Army and state and federal agencies.

San Francisco campion

Crissy Field 🪑 🦅 ♿ 🚶 🚴

The Golden Gate Promenade passes between Crissy Field and a sandy beach with dunes and a series of exercise stations. The field was built on fill as a racetrack for the 1915 Panama-Pacific International Exposition. It was converted to an airstrip soon thereafter and named after Major Dana Crissy, who was killed after taking off from this runway during a 1919 transcontinental air race. In 1920 dozens of biplanes arrived here to begin active duty as the 91st Aero Squadron. By 1936 the airstrip

View of Crissy Field with U.S. Coast Guard Station Fort Point in foreground

was no longer needed: the new Hamilton Field, in Marin County, accommodated larger and faster aircraft. So Crissy Field was decommissioned. The beach here is a popular viewing spot for air shows, such as the aerial displays of the Navy's Blue Angels during Fleet Week (October), and the Fourth of July fireworks. It also attracts kite flyers and skilled and daring windsurfers (winds and tides are extremely powerful here). The dunes are being restored.

Palace of Fine Arts

SAN FRANCISCO BAY FERRY BOATS

Before the bay had bridges it had ferries. The first ferry service on the bay began in 1850. By 1929 more than 50 ferries worked bay waters. During 1930 they transported 6 million vehicles and about 60 million passengers from San Francisco's waterfront to Vallejo, Sausalito, Tiburon, Richmond, Oakland, Berkeley, Alameda, and even Sacramento. The ferry *Eureka*, moored at the Hyde Street Pier, was capable of carrying 2,300 people and 120 autos.

Motor vehicles and the construction of the Bay Bridge (1936) and the Golden Gate Bridge (1937), combined with policies favoring auto traffic, doomed the major ferry routes. To pay off the bonds for the Bay Bridge, policies were adopted to put ferries at a disadvantage. Bay Bridge tolls were set below the price of a ferry ride; the interurban electric railways stopped service to ferry terminals in 1939 and crossed the Bay Bridge instead. Finally, the Bridge Bond Act of 1944 made it illegal to operate a ferry across the bay within ten miles of the Bay Bridge. Eventually almost all ferry crossings were replaced by bridges.

In the 1970s ferry service was revived to Sausalito, Tiburon, Larkspur, Vallejo, and eventually to Oakland and Alameda.

Tourist-oriented ferries navigate to Angel and Alcatraz islands. The 1989 earthquake proved the lasting value of ferries: they carried thousands of East Bay commuters across the water while the Bay Bridge was repaired.

Palace of Fine Arts 🪑 ♿ & Exploratorium

Hundreds of acres of bayshore in today's Marina district were filled with thousands of tons of sand and bay sediment for the 1915 Panama-Pacific International Exposition. The only building that remains is the Palace of Fine Arts. It was designed by Bernard Maybeck for a short life span but was rebuilt in 1968 and now houses the Exploratorium, founded by physicist Frank Oppenheimer. Here scientists and artists create exhibits that allow visitors to discover sensory phenomena and scientific principles through play. (Fee.)

TIDES AT THE GOLDEN GATE

Tides manifest the gravitaional pull of the sun and moon on the earth. This pull creates a "long-period wave," or bulge, which moves across the oceans, creating tides twice a day. At the Golden Gate, tides can fluctuate from 2 to 7 feet as an estimated average of 2.3 million cubic feet of salt and fresh water surge in and out of the bay. Through time, this action, together with powerful river flows, has helped scour the bay floor down to nearly 350 feet where the water enters the open ocean. In contrast, south bay waters are barely 10 feet deep.

Marina Green

Want to jog, fly a kite, fish, relax, feed the gulls, contemplate the bay, or check out the latest in exercise apparel? This is the place. On the western end of the Marina Green, a wind-sheltered patch of grass invites sunbathing. Just off the promenade, next to the Saint Francis Yacht Club and the bay, is a comfortable wood and stone rest area perfect for boat watching. East on the jetty, past a small stone lighthouse and the Golden Gate Yacht Club, is the Wave Organ, a stone sound sculpture. The San Francisco Marina is on the eastern edge of the Marina Green.

The number and variety of kites flown here on weekends are staggering. Watch the show, then try to figure out what the Magnetic Silencing Range Building does (read the placard next to the fenced-in white building on the bayside of the Green), or slide a quarter into one of the pay telescopes at the eastern end of the Green and scope Alcatraz, Angel Island, and boats on the bay. On the riprap shore here people go poke-poling after monkey-faced eels that hide in the rocks. They use bamboo poles, short leaders, and hooks baited with shrimp.

Marina Green

Wave Organ

WAVE ORGAN

Odd. Beautiful. Eerie. These are some of the adjectives you might hear visitors mutter at this "wave-activated acoustic sculpture" conceived by Peter Richards of the Exploratorium and built in 1986 by stone mason/artist George Gonzales on the jetty beyond the Saint Francis and Golden Gate yacht clubs. The walk-in sculpture is made of materials salvaged from old sidewalks, destroyed buildings, and even demolished mausoleums. Its fractured columns and granite amphitheater are arranged around a series of pipes that "play" the waves. With low moans and backwash gurglings, the Wave Organ interprets the moods of the bay for receptive audiences. If the organ doesn't perform for you, the jetty affords a fantastic view of the Golden Gate Bridge, perhaps the best in the entire bay. It is also a peaceful spot to relax and observe the busy Marina Green. On a surprising little beach on the jetty's south side, shorebirds rest and feed at low tide.

FOGHORNS

San Francisco Bay's first fog signal was a manually operated cannon ignited every half hour to guide ships through the fog. It was installed in 1857 at Point Bonita, north of the Golden Gate, but was soon replaced by a mechanized bell. By 1860, bells were added at Fort Point and Alcatraz. In 1875, a large whistle was installed at Yerba Buena Island, and eventually a boisterous mix of sirens, trumpets, bells, and whistles serenaded residents around the bay. The airhorns' soothing sound was as much a part of San Francisco as its fog until recently, when the U.S. Coast Guard replaced most of them with electronic signals. (Four are still in use on the Golden Gate Bridge.) The San Francisco–based U.S. Lighthouse Society has offered to maintain at least one recently decommissioned foghorn, on Alcatraz Island, and hopes to open a National Fog Signal Museum at Lime Point Lighthouse, in cooperation with the National Park Service.

Fort Mason

Fort Mason

From the Spanish fort Batería de San José, to Mexico's Punta Medanos de Arena (Sand Dune Point), to a strategic U.S. military base, Fort Mason (formerly Black Point) has figured in regional and national history. At Pier 3, the World War II Liberty Ship *Jeremiah O'Brien* is a quiet reminder of one of the greatest mass-production efforts in U.S. history: over 2,750 Liberty Ships were constructed between 1941 and 1945 at several bayside facilities. During World War II and the Korean War some 1.5 million soldiers embarked from the piers at Fort Mason.

Today the lower 13 acres of Fort Mason, with three covered piers and four three-story warehouses, house the Fort Mason Center, a self-supporting hub of San Francisco's cultural diversity. Over 50 nonprofit organizations occupy the former warehouses, while the piers are used for special events. The 50 acres of upper

Fort Mason meadow

Fort Mason house the GGNRA and Golden Gate National Park Association headquarters, the International San Francisco Hostel, the San Francisco Conservation Corps, offices of the Gulf of the Farallones National Marine Sanctuary, an exercise course, vast lawns, and the Black Point Battery. To move between the two areas, either use the long stairway over the 90-foot retaining wall or go to the corner of Marina and Laguna and follow the path. Resting against the retaining wall is the stern of the *Galilee*, an 1850s clipper ship that once rode the winds between New York and San Francisco.

DUNE RESTORATION

Although dune-colonizing plants endure sand blast, poor soils, and intense exposure to the sun, they are vulnerable to invasive species and to trampling. The dunes of Crissy Field may be remnants of a larger dune system, edged by salt marshes and lagoons that once covered much of today's Presidio and Marina district. The National Park Service has been temporarily fencing off sections of these dunes and revegetating them with native species, including sand verbena, seaside daisy, yerba buena, and San Francisco silver lupine. Dunes at Baker Beach and Fort Funston have also been revegetated.

Aquatic Park 🚻 ♿ 🐟 🚶 🚲

The promenade winds east through Fort Mason, up and over Black Point (the site of a Civil War–era cannon installation), then drops down toward Aquatic Park, with its small beach. The exposed shoreline face of Black Point is one of the few remnants of the city's original shoreline. In the sheltered bay off Aquatic Park devoted swimmers brave the chilly waters (55°F average) year-round. Most belong to the Dolphin Swimming & Boating Club or the South End Rowing Club. Both clubs were established in the 1870s and have sponsored rowing and swimming races in the bay for generations.

The well-worn Municipal Pier arcs 1,850 feet into the bay from the western edge of the park and attracts fishermen and crabbers. The spectacular views from the end of the pier of the Golden Gate Bridge, tankers, sailboats, and Aquatic Park are well worth the walk. The abandoned pier to the west once served Alcatraz Island. At the Hyde Street Pier, to the east, the National Park Service's San Francisco Maritime National Historical Park offers tours of six vessels. Three other ships are moored nearby. This pier, built for ferries in 1922, also houses the park's Maritime Store.

The maritime park's museum is at the foot of Polk Street, in a triple-decked art deco building that resembles a ship, built by WPA crews during the Depression. The library and archives are at Fort Mason's Building E.

Next to the museum, settle into the concrete bleachers and watch the scene: octogenarians adjusting swimming caps, enormous cargo ships entering the bay, children playing in the sand. In a quiet western corner of this park, serious games of bocce ball take place daily. On Sundays, drummers often gather for jam sessions on the bleachers. Plenty of shops and restaurants are in converted factories nearby.

Maritime Museum and Aquatic Park

Getting Around

The Bay Trail follows the Golden Gate Promenade between Fort Point and Aquatic Park. At the Saint Francis Yacht Club, a path atop a jetty leads to the Wave Organ. At Fort Mason, you can bypass the long flight of stairs connecting the lower and upper fort by following Laguna St to Bay St, then taking the paved trail past the International Hostel. A paved but steep bayside trail leads down to Aquatic Park.

BAYKEEPER

The BayKeeper organization was founded by Michael Herz in 1989 to "protect, preserve, and enhance the resources and health of the ecosystems and communities in the Bay-Delta region." Herz and BayKeeper volunteers patrol the waters and shores of the bay, looking for unauthorized dredging, pollution sources, toxic spills, and assorted illegal activities. They then report them to authorities and pursue each case. BayKeeper has an office in Fort Mason and welcomes visitors.

A citizens' patrol

FISHERMAN'S WHARF TO MISSION BAY

Along these three miles of waterfront, working fishermen unload their catches in the early morning, next to the tourist magnet of Fisherman's Wharf. Ferries leave for various destinations, weaving among rafts of sea lions and boisterous gulls. Old piers and new reach into the bay, providing vistas, fishing spots, and commerce opportunities.

Fisherman's Wharf

Fisherman's Wharf ♿ 🚶

Tourists crowding the waterfront between Hyde Street Pier and Pier 45 experience the old and the new, the sublime and the garish. This is historic Fisherman's Wharf. Bay winds blend the aroma of warm sourdough bread, glistening fresh fish, steaming crab pots, crusty pier pilings, and boat diesel into a smell unique to the waterfront along Jefferson Street. Behind neon signs and lumbering tourist buses, tradition prevails.

The true fisherman's waterfront survives on Fish Alley at the foot of Leavenworth, on Pier 47, and on Pier 45 where commercial boats unload their catches of herring, bass, and salmon under clouds of gulls. Most of the real work takes place between 3 a.m. and 9 a.m. Between November and June some 1 million pounds of Dungeness crab arrive at Pier 45 from beyond the bay. Work your way around some of the narrow byways and you'll catch a glimpse (and a whiff) of history: many of these fishermen and fisherwomen are grandchildren and great-grandchildren of San Francisco's fishing pioneers.

San Francisco's fishing industry began during the Gold Rush. Italians, and some Dalmatians and Greeks, realized their "pot of gold" was more attainable on the waters than in the gold mines. A variety of seafood was soon for sale at the expanding fisherman's wharf: salmon from the Sacramento River, bay herring, shrimp (collected almost exclusively by Chinese immigrants), oysters, mussels, and sardines

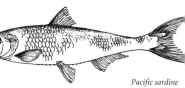

Pacific sardine

(from 1920 until the late 1940s). True to the history of this city and this industry, many recent immigrants continue to join San Francisco's fishing fleet. A World War II submarine, the USS *Pampanito*, can be toured at Pier 45. (Fee.)

Pier 39

Pier 43 to Pier 39

♿ 🐟 🚶 🚲

Just east of Fisherman's Wharf, by Pier 43, you can rest on a bench and observe waterfront activities from Vista Pier and the public pier between piers 41 and 39. The derelict Pier 43 once serviced railroad ferries that carried freight to Richmond and Tiburon. It is to be rebuilt for public access.

Pier 39 is the largest shopping complex on the waterfront, with about 20 restaurants and numerous specialty stores. A $30-million "Underwater World" aquarium is to be constructed on the south side of the pier. The pier's biggest attraction, however, may be its uninvited itinerant population of California sea lions.

Hundreds of sea lions invaded Pier 39's "K" dock in January 1990. What at first was seen as a problem soon became a tourist bonanza. Management fenced off the dock and surrendered it. Some 600 rambunctious male

Sea lions — uninvited residents

pinnipeds loll about on floating docks in midwinter. Most migrate south in June to breed at the Channel Islands and along

Mexico's Pacific shore. Docent-led talks about the sea lion are sponsored by Pier 39 and the Marine Mammal Center and are available free on most weekends. The sea lions can also be observed from Pier 41.

Between piers 41 and 43 the Blue & Gold Fleet offers boat tours of the bay. From these piers the Red & White Fleet offers other tours, as well as ferries to Sausalito, Tiburon, Vallejo (and Marine World via shuttle), Angel and Alcatraz islands, Alameda, and Oakland.

Blue & Gold Ferry returning to Pier 39

Alcatraz—The Rock

The name Alcatraz (Spanish for pelican) had been given to the island today called Yerba Buena, but in 1826 Captain Frederick Beechy mistakenly transferred it, on a map, to this rocky island with steep cliffs that were perfect for nesting seabirds. The mistake stuck. In the early 1850s the U.S. Army took command and placed artillery on the island. In 1854 the first lighthouse on the West Coast was built here. The Alcatraz Citadel was completed in 1859 and was used mostly as a military prison until 1933 when it was converted to a maximum-security federal penitentiary. Among famous inmates on The Rock, as Alcatraz is unofficially called, were Al "Scarface" Capone, "Machine Gun" Kelly, and the "Birdman of Alcatraz," Robert Stroud. The prison was shut down in 1963.

In 1964 a small group of Sioux arrived on the island to claim it on the grounds that an 1868 treaty promised Native Americans homesteading rights on surplus government lands. They were quickly

---

1850s SHORELINE

From Fort Point to Candlestick Point, the shoreline was once fringed with marshes, creeks, and coves that supported abundant shellfish, wildlife, and Ohlone villages. By the 1950s, San Francisco's 12.5 miles of bay waterfront were dominated by 42 piers with more than 18 miles of ship-berthing space. The piers, roads, and small parks along today's waterfront were all built on landfill.

Take a walk along the 1850s shoreline—North Beach to Mission Bay—and consider the previous landscape. From Fisherman's Wharf walk up to Columbus and Taylor (six blocks from Pier 45), and imagine a 1,600-foot pier shooting north into the bay from that corner. In 1850 you would have been standing on the shoreline, at the foot of Meiggs Pier. The pier was eventually enclosed by a sea wall that now forms the foundation of Fisherman's Wharf. The shoreline curved down to the corner of present-day Bay and Taylor streets then moved south, up from Embarcadero to Broadway. From there it

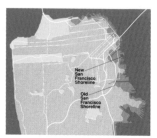

Pre–1850 shoreline, and today's.

bowed inland and formed Yerba Buena Cove, San Francisco's most important 19th century anchorage. The plaque in the sidewalk at First and Market marks the approximate historic shoreline.

Imagine standing on this spot in the early 1850s, looking toward Yerba Buena Island, and counting more than 800 sailing vessels. Hundreds of boats arrived at Yerba Buena Cove during the Gold Rush only to have their entire crews jump ship and head toward the Sierra. Some 770 ships were abandoned and subsequently used for storage or housing, or were scrapped. Over the decades the shoreline was filled and moved bayward toward today's Fireboat Dock, then continued south to Townsend, where it turned inland to form Mission Bay.

1882 view from Telegraph Hill, with Meiggs Pier

Alcatraz Island, 1980s

removed by federal marshals. In November 1969, 90 Native Americans from more than 20 tribes occupied Alcatraz in the name of Indians of All Tribes. They held it until June 1971. Each year, Native Americans and friends return for "Un-Thanksgiving Day." Since 1973, Alcatraz has been part of the GGNRA. More than 1 million people visit annually.

The Embarcadero Promenade

The Embarcadero ("boarding place" in Spanish) is a stretch of waterfront about 2 miles long, edged with both active and neglected piers and restaurants. The entire Embarcadero is built on fill and the abandoned hulls of 19th century sailing ships. In 1959, construction of the elevated Embarcadero Freeway was stopped by citizen protest. The freeway had been scheduled to connect the Bay and Golden Gate bridges, but it was stopped after slicing across the foot of Market Street in front of the Ferry Building. It carried traffic between the Bay Bridge and North Beach until 1989 when an earthquake damaged it. In 1992 it was demolished.

Immediately east of Pier 39, the Embarcadero Promenade begins at East Waterfront Park with a garden and observation deck. From Pier 33 you can take dining and dancing cruises on the bay. Across from Pier 23—the Foreign Trade Zone—is another small park with a nice lawn. Crossing the Embarcadero from piers 17, 15, and 9 (look for the working tugs docked here) is the Waterfront Historical District. Looming across the Embar-

Embarcadero Promenade

cadero is the sheer face of Telegraph Hill. During the mid-19th century, portions of the hill were excavated and used as ballast for ships and to fill Yerba Buena Cove, the first six blocks of today's Market Street.

Pier 7

Pier 7, built in 1990, is a public access pier, open for strolling and fishing. It offers views of the Bay Bridge, Treasure, Yerba Buena, and Angel islands, and the East Bay. Looking inland you see Coit Tower and the financial district. Between piers 5 and 3, notice the Santa Rosa Ferry, built

in 1927. It once carried 65 vehicles and 1,200 passengers daily, but is now used for offices, conferences, and parties. The public is welcome aboard Monday through Saturday. Southeast of Pier 1, the 1896 Ferry Building served over 100,000 commuters daily during the 1920s. Far fewer ferry riders now come here to take the Golden Gate Ferry to Sausalito and Larkspur and the Red & White Fleet's ferries to Vallejo and Tiburon. Blue & Gold docks here from Alameda and Oakland. Ferry Plaza East, with fishing spots and benches, wraps around the Ferry Building. Beneath it, BART crosses the bay. Between the Ferry Building and the Fireboat Dock (next to Pier 24 below the Bay Bridge) are concrete benches where financial district workers eat bag lunches and gaze at the bay. Across the Embarcadero is Maritime Plaza and Justin Herman Plaza, where various special events occur.

After pausing under the Bay Bridge to listen to the click-clack of cars passing overhead, check out Red's Java House, a historic working person's lunch spot. Major redevelopment plans are pending between Red's and South Beach Harbor, an area where most of the piers are abandoned or used for storage.

South Beach Harbor

South Beach Harbor, next to Pier 40, is a municipal marina. Just north of the harbor's road entrance is a schooner-turned-restaurant. The *Dolphin P. Rempp* was built in 1908 in Denmark to carry lumber, but it also saw

South Beach Harbor

action in World Wars I and II as a supply ship. To the south of the harbor, past old warehouse piers, the Third Street Bridge crosses Mission Creek. It is a drawbridge, as are the Fourth Street and Islais Creek bridges. All are raised upon request to allow boats to enter.

BAY BRIDGE

In 1955, the American Society of Civil Engineers honored the San Francisco–Oakland Bay Bridge as one of the seven "Modern Civil Engineering Wonders" of the world. Opened in November 1936, it spans more than 4 miles of water and is actually two distinct types of bridges joined at Yerba Buena Island. At first the bridge carried autos on its top deck, and trucks, buses, and two tracks for the key system rail service on the lower deck. In 1958 the rails were removed and both levels were assigned to motor vehicles.

Agua Vista Park

Mission Bay

Mission Rock Street, off Third Street, brings you to China Basin Street and the area of Mission Bay. Before it was filled, Mission Bay was a sheltered embayment edged by rich tidal marshland backed by dunes, and the site of commerce during the Gold Rush. Mission Creek emptied into the bay where King Street now meets Division Street. What we now call Mission Creek is a tidal inlet in the approximate location of the historic mouth of the creek. A houseboat community has survived here for many years. The creek itself is culverted

and incorporated into the city's sewage system. In the early days of European settlements, Mission Creek was navigable all the way to Mission Dolores. Mission Rock Terminal (Pier 50) is built atop Mission Rock, a well-known nearshore feature in the 1850s. The schooner *C. A. Thayer* (now docked at the Hyde Street Pier) unloaded lumber from the north at the thriving shipyards here in the 1890s, while several blocks to the south thousands of whalebones and tanks of whale oil cluttered the shore at the Pacific Steam Whaling Company.

Today this no-nonsense urban waterfront is occupied by heavy industry and enormous drydocks. There is a small boat launch between piers 50 and 54. Roads and sidewalks are crisscrossed by abandoned train tracks that are rough for wheelchairs and a hazard for bicycles. From China Basin Street, glimpse tankers and military ships hauled out on dry docks at piers 68 and 70, their huge propellers riding high and dry. Agua Vista Park, an open patch of waterfront just north of Mission Rock Resort, has a public pier.

YERBA BUENA AND TREASURE ISLANDS

Yerba Buena Island was known as Alcatraz in the early 1800s (see page 18) and then as Goat Island in the mid-1800s when many goats were grazed here. In 1931 it was officially renamed after a sweet smelling native plant, which the Spanish called *yerba buena*. In the late 1930s, a 400-acre island was constructed with bay dredgings to the north of Yerba Buena Island, and attached to it. The new island, named Treasure Island, was the site for the 1939–40 Golden Gate International Exposition. Some 4,000 trees and 2 million flowering plants were planted for the occasion. Many of the palms and varieties of eucalyptus are still alive. The Navy took possession of the man-made island after the fair. It will be returned to civilian use. The Treasure Island Museum (stop at guard station to ask directions) is open seven days a week and maintains exhibits on the construction of the island, the Exposition, and naval history.

Treasure Island International Exposition 1939

Yerba Buena Island Naval Barracks ca. 1900

Sea stars on piers

PIER PILING BIOLOGY

San Francisco's fertile bay waters support many kinds of fish and shellfish. On countless pier pilings, barnacles, mussels, sea stars, and anemones grip these columns of artificial habitat as crabs and fish circle about, feed among them and on them.

ANCHORED TANKERS

Just south of the Bay Bridge, enormous tankers often anchor mid-bay. They wait here either for high tides, so they can move into port, or for berths to unload crude oil or take on petroleum products. Tankers are among the largest craft that enter the bay. They often have deep drafts requiring that they be "lightered"—cargo offloaded onto barges, so they can ride higher in the water and reach port.

YERBA BUENA

Yerba buena (*Satureja douglasii*) is a mint common to the Pacific Coast of North America. Between April and September, it produces small white to lavender flowers. When the Spanish arrived, they learned that local Ohlone people placed great faith in the medicinal qualities of this plant. Accordingly, the Spanish named it "*yerba buena*," the "good herb." Ohlones, Spaniards, Mexicans, and early Californians brewed an aromatic tea from its dried leaves as a remedy for fevers and stomach ailments. Its medicinal qualities are still appreciated today.

Yerba buena

The name "Yerba Buena" appears frequently throughout San Francisco's history. In addition to gracing Yerba Buena Island, the settlement that became San Francisco was known first as Yerba Buena. The community of Yerba Buena began to form in 1835 on the shore of the anchorage the Spaniards had called Yerba Buena Cove. In 1847 the city was officially renamed after Saint Francis.

PIER MATHEMATICS

Before the turn of the century, San Francisco's piers were numbered and named for the streets at which they began. That changed when the Embarcadero was built. Now piers between the Ferry Building and Fisherman's Wharf have odd numbers, those between the Ferry Building and the northern edge of Hunters Point have even numbers. (Fort Mason's piers are separately numbered.)

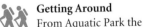

Getting Around

From Aquatic Park the Bay Trail route follows Jefferson St to the Embarcadero, continues along the Embarcadero to South Beach Harbor, then turns south on Berry St and continues on 3rd St to Mission Rock and China Basin St. At South Beach Harbor, a paved path leads to a fishing pier.

CHINA BASIN TO CANDLESTICK

The waterfront winding for some seven miles between China Basin and Candlestick Point is unknown territory for most tourists, and even for many San Franciscans. In the 1890s, this stretch of the Port of San Francisco was noisy with shipbuilding and other water-related industry. The Arctic Oil Wharf was at today's Pier 64, the Union Iron Works at Pier 68. Bethlehem Steel's shipyard

Port of San Francisco, looking north

and handsome brick buildings (still standing) extended behind Pier 70 at today's 22nd Street. The Pacific Rolling Mills and California Sugar Refinery were at Pier 72. Now port activity is less intense and many derelict structures and piers can be seen. Anyone interested in the city's waterfront history, or industrial architecture, will find it here. Some colorful eateries and several small parks and fishing piers provide views of rusty cranes and other structures that now appeal as found art.

Islais Creek

Like Mission Creek, Islais Creek was once an embayment. The creek itself flowed from Twin Peaks, meandering through marshes toward the bay. Today it is underground, trickling into a channeled tidal inlet at the Highway 280 overpass and mixing with salt water as it flows bayward under the Third Street drawbridge. Citizens are working to replace riprap along the inlet's shores with native vegetation, including holly-leaved cherries. The word "Islais" derives from the Salinan Indian word for wild cherry.

Islais Creek

Upstream from the drawbridge, see the old copra docks of the Cargill Company. Downstream are petroleum docks, a huge container facility, a wharf from which tallow is shipped to Asia, and the port's abandoned grain terminal. Fishermen use two small parks on the east side of the bridge.

Warm Water Cove Park

This small park at the foot of 24th Street is a planted patch of bayfill between the Pacific Gas & Electric Company's Potrero Power Plant and the Army Street Terminal (Pier 80). The plant releases water it has used for cooling into the channel on its north side. This water is slightly warmer than bay water, hence the name. Look north toward Pier 70 at the streetcars rusting in a corporation yard, and south, toward Pier 80, at tankers docked and anchored. Oakland is across the bay. To the west, the foot of Potrero Hill marks the original bay shoreline. This park is isolated and not recommended for solitary exploration.

India Basin and Pier 98

"Pier 98" is a landfill jetty created for the Southern Crossing Bridge, which was never built. It is now overgrown with exotic grasses and native baccharis plants and crisscrossed by informal trails. Although there is flotsam and jetsam throughout, nature is making a valiant attempt at reclamation. Many forms of algae and other life forms cling to rocks here. Fine views of birds on the water are available from the end of the spit, as well as views of Hunters Point, the Bay Bridge, and Oakland.

On the southern edge of the jetty is a small marsh. Great blue herons, egrets, and gulls feed among pickleweed, cordgrass, and eelgrass. Offshore rafts of cormorants and terns work the waters seasonally. From the base of the spit, a developed dirt trail wraps around the back of PG&E's Hunters Point Power Plant. It passes a sluice gate at the plant's water intake and a marine waterfall formed by water being discharged after doing service as coolant. At discharge the bay water is slightly warmer than it was at intake and creates a habitat for some marine species usually found farther south. Look for red sponges on the rocks below the waterfall.

The sluice gate, as well as other spots around the plant, attract fishermen who haul in jacksmelt, topsmelt, grunion, striped bass, and shiner perch. The trail continues around the plant as a dirt path to a cove with mud flats busy with a variety of birds at low tide. A scrap of the old shoreline can be seen here. Across India Basin, to the south, a cove with boats at anchor was a Chinese shrimp camp until the 1940s. To get to Pier 98, turn east off Third near Islais Creek channel, take Cargo Way to Jennings, park, and venture through the gate.

India Basin, with "Pier 98" in foreground

Double-crested cormorant

DOUBLE-CRESTED CORMORANT

Three species of cormorants can be found along the Pacific Coast, but the double-crested is most likely seen on bay waters. Cormorants live almost entirely on fish that they catch under water, sometimes at great depths. They are often seen standing atop rocks, posts, or pier pilings, drying their outspread wings. Some have nested in the understructure of the Bay Bridge.

Candlestick Point State Recreation Area

Candlestick Point State Recreation Area is a refreshing surprise for those who thought Candlestick was only for ball games and traffic jams. A reclaimed landfill that wraps around the stadium has been turned into a park with ample lawns and exercise stations. At low tide, mud flats are exposed and shorebirds arrive to feed. Fishermen try for perch, shark, jacksmelt, and flounder off two piers here.

Hunters Point Shipyards can be seen to the north. Jets from San Francisco Airport gain altitude overhead. To the west is Candlestick Stadium and Bay View Park atop the hill that was carved away and terraced to fill the bayshore. Between Candlestick Point and Hunters Point is Yosemite Creek, which is to be restored. To the southwest is San Bruno Mountain and the explanation for wind in this area: Alemany Gap, which acts as a funnel. If the San Francisco Giants or San Francisco 49ers are playing, expect heavy traffic. Windsurfers favor this site.

Learning to fish at Candlestick Point

HUNTERS POINT

In 1849 entrepreneur Robert E. Hunter tried to found a new city on this point, which the Spanish had named Punta de Concha (Shell Point). But what took hold instead was shipbuilding. An enormous stone dry dock was built here in 1868, and through the turn of the century the area was known for its construction and repair of West Coast ships. During World War I the Bethlehem Steel Company produced large cargo ships at Hunters Point, and during World War II the Navy expanded the point into the bay on fill to make room for urgent war production. Large machine shops and warehouses were

World War II Shipyards, Hunters Point

built around the dry docks. A work force, mostly African Americans, was hired and housed just upslope from the shipyards, in an arrangement similar to that at the Marinship yards and Marin City, and in Richmond.

Today the Navy is in the process of turning the facilities over to the city of San Francisco. There are many visions for the future of the area, as well as unanswered questions regarding the extent of toxic waste on the site. Some buildings are already rented out to artists and small businesses, including a mushroom farm. Community leaders from the Hunters Point neighborhood hope that the shipyards can be converted to businesses that will create jobs for local residents.

Hunters Point today

INFORMATION

BayKeeper
415-567-4401

Blue & Gold Fleet
415-781-7877

Bus Routes   415-673-MUNI

**Candlestick Point State
Recreation Area**
415-557-4069

**Dolphin Swimming &
Boating Club**
415-441-9329

Exploratorium   415-561-0360

Fort Mason Center
415-979-3010

Fort Point   415-556-1693

General GGNRA Information
415-556-0560

Golden Gate Ferry
415-332-6600
(Sausalito, Larkspur)

**Golden Gate National Park
Association**
415-776-0693

Marina Green Harbor
415-292-2013

National Maritime Museum
415-556-3002

Pier 39 Information
415-981-7437

Presidio Army Museum
415-556-0856

Red & White Fleet
415-546-BOAT
(Sausalito, Tiburon, Vallejo &
Marine World via shuttle,
Angel and Alcatraz islands)

South End Rowing Club
415-776-7372

Treasure Island Museum
415-395-5067

U.S. Park Police Emergencies
415-556-7940

USS *Pampanito*
415-929-0202

 Getting Around
The Bay Trail route moves from China Basin St to Illinois St, onto Third St, to Yosemite, then turns toward the bay until Ingalls. Right on Ingalls, then left on Carroll Ave will bring you to Candlestick Point State Recreation Area. If you take Cargo Way (off 3rd St) you will arrive at the foot of Pier 98 and at a dirt trail leading around the Hunters Point PG&E power plant to India Basin. Exercise normal caution in isolated industrial areas.

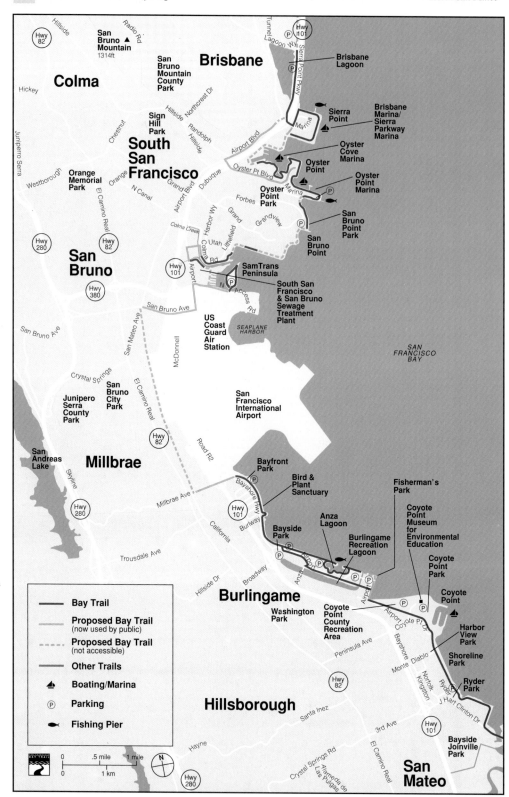

Hwy 82

Hillside

Radio Rd.

San Bruno ▲ Mountain 1314ft

San Bruno Mountain County Park

Brisbane

Hwy 101

Brisbane Lagoon

Colma

Hickey

Northcrest Dr

Hillside

Randolph

Chestnut

Hillside

San Bruno Mountain County Park

Sign Hill Park

South San Francisco

Airport Blvd

Marina

Sierra Point

Brisbane Marina/ Sierra Parkway Marina

Oyster Cove Marina

Oyster Pt Blvd

Oyster Point

Oyster Point Marina

Juniperro Serra

Westborough

Orange Memorial Park

Orange

N Canal

Grand Blvd

Dubuque

Forbes

Grandview

Oyster Point Park

San Bruno Point Park

El Camino Real

Colma Creek

Harbor Wy

Colma

Utah

Littlefield

Grand

San Bruno Point

Hwy 280

Hwy 82

San Bruno

Hwy 101

Airport

Rd

SamTrans Peninsula

South San Francisco & San Bruno Sewage Treatment Plant

San Andreas Lake

Hwy 380

San Bruno Ave

San Mateo Ave

Access Rd

N

US Coast Guard Air Station

SEAPLANE HARBOR

SAN FRANCISCO BAY

San Bruno Ave

McDonnell

Crystal Springs

Junipero Serra County Park

San Bruno City Park

El Camino Real

San Francisco International Airport

Hwy 82

Road R2

Millbrae

Skyline

Millbrae Ave

Bayshore Hwy

Bayfront Park

Bird & Plant Sanctuary

Fisherman's Park

Hwy 280

California

Burlway

Bayside Park

Anza Lagoon

Burlingame Recreation Lagoon

Coyote Point Museum for Environmental Education

Trousdale Ave

Hillside Dr

Broadway

Anza

Coyote Point Park

Coyote Point

Hwy 101

Burlingame

Washington Park

Coyote Point County Recreation Area

Airport

Coyote Pt Dr

Bayshore

Harbor View Park

Shoreline Park

Peninsula Ave

Monte Diablo

Norfolk

Kingston

Ryder Park

Hwy 82

Santa Inez

Hillsborough

J Hart Clinton Dr

Hayne

3rd Ave

Hwy 101

Bayside Joinville Park

Crystal Springs Rd

El Camino Real

San Mateo

Hwy 280

Alameda de las Pulgas

Legend:

── Bay Trail

Proposed Bay Trail (now used by public)

Proposed Bay Trail (not accessible)

Other Trails

⚓ Boating/Marina

Ⓟ Parking

🎣 Fishing Pier

0   .5 mile   1 mile

0   1 km

N

SIERRA POINT PARKWAY TO SAN BRUNO POINT

S outh of Candlestick Point, bay waters once met land farther west. The shoreline skirted the eastern foot of San Bruno Mountain, then meandered south into marshes. Almost all these wetlands have been filled and put to industrial and commercial uses. Yet there is much to discover along this stretch of bayshore: diverse opportunities for recreation as well as remnants of history and natural landscape.

San Bruno Mountain area from Candlestick Point Park

Brisbane Lagoon and Sierra Point

South of Candlestick Point and inland from Highway 101 is Brisbane Lagoon, which was a cove until the highway cut it off from the bay. Culverts under the highway still admit the tide, allowing bay fish to survive here. To reach the lagoon's northern shore, turn on Lagoon Way, or pull into the parking lot off Sierra Point Parkway. This small turnout has a dozen parking spaces and spots for fishing. It is also a good place for watching waterbirds.

Sierra Point exercise station with San Bruno Mountain in background

Sierra Point was built on fill and is now an office park. A public shoreline trail passes an exercise station (to the south) and the wooden Brisbane Fishing Pier (to the north). A typical catch here might include brown smoothhound sharks, staghorn sculpin, and various perch species. Along the point's eastern edge are the Brisbane and Sierra Parkway marinas.

Bayshore Freeway under construction southeast of Candlestick Point, 1955

San Bruno Mountain offers glimpses of the past.

SAN BRUNO MOUNTAIN

San Bruno Mountain looms out of the peninsula's urban jumble like a giant stranded whale attempting to return to the bay. Its two parallel ridges undulate for 5 miles and rise to 1,314 feet, sheltering a valley that was once a salt marsh. One of the Spaniards who first saw this marsh in 1774 described it as "teeming with geese, ducks, cranes, and herons." The marsh is gone, replaced by an industrial park and quarry, but the mountain survives as a unique island in time, offering a glimpse of the land as it was before the Europeans' arrival.

Natural scientists who know the mountain call it a botanical treasure. Its slopes and ravines support four native plant communities: grassland, coastal scrub, foothill woodland, and salt marsh. In spring, the grassy slopes come alive with wildflowers. The inner ravines are lined with live oak, California bay, holly leaf cherry, and California buckeye. On outcroppings of the green-ish-gray sandstone, called Franciscan graywacke, grow the endangered San Bruno manzanita (found nowhere else in the world) and other rare and unique plants. The endangered Mission blue butterfly feeds on lupine here. The endangered San Bruno elfin butterfly survives here and in only two other spots on the peninsula. Look for it in shady canyons, where you see moss and lichen. Today, 3,400 acres of the mountain are pre-served in parks and open space, but only after intense citizen efforts against decades of development schemes. Among serious proposals was one to level the mountain and use it to create thousands of acres of bay fill.

San Bruno elfin butterfly

From the western ridge peak—the highest point on the northern San Francisco peninsula—you can see the entire region spread out before you: ocean, bay, and the distant peaks of Tamalpais, Diablo, and Hamilton. To the immediate north, San Francisco's downtown thrusts upward. To the south, the soft lines of the coastal mountains rest the eyes. If you come here when the Pacific fog is gently pushing up into the canyons (part of the area's natural air conditioning), you might see the great "hand of God" phenomenon as giant white fingers of fog probe the ground. To reach the mountain from the Bayshore Freeway, take Bayshore Boulevard toward Brisbane and Daly City. Go west on Guadalupe Canyon Parkway and turn left on Radio Road.

SOME NATIVE PLANTS

The best season for exploring San Bruno Mountain is spring, when the wildflowers bloom. But don't hesitate to come in other seasons. Walk some of the trails and see the native plant communities that survive here almost undisturbed. Below are a few of the native plants you may find.

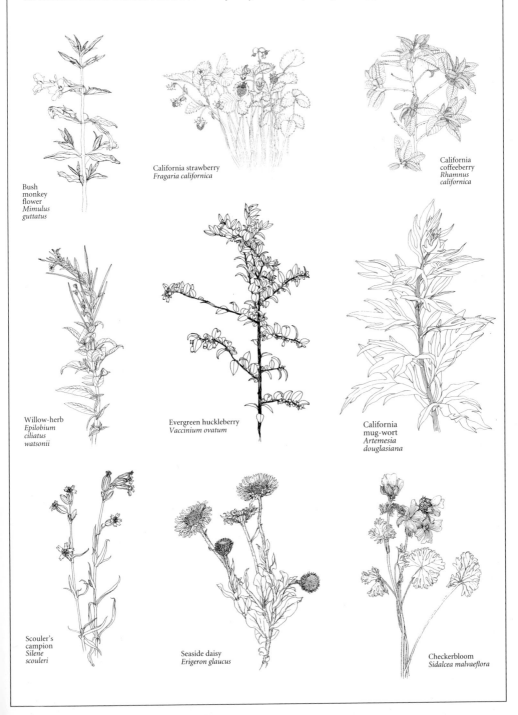

Bush
monkey
flower
*Mimulus
guttatus*

California strawberry
Fragaria californica

California
coffeeberry
*Rhamnus
californica*

Willow-herb
*Epilobium
ciliatus
watsonii*

Evergreen huckleberry
Vaccinium ovatum

California
mug-wort
*Artemesia
douglasiana*

Scouler's
campion
*Silene
scouleri*

Seaside daisy
Erigeron glaucus

Checkerbloom
Sidalcea malvaeflora

San Bruno Point

Beneath the commerce and fill-extended shore of San Bruno Point are remnants of a smaller peninsula that became known as China Point in the 1870s. It was the site of one of the largest Chinese fishing camps that formed on the bay after the completion of the transcontinental railroad in 1869 released thousands of Chinese workers. Another big camp was on today's Hunters Point. Many of the railroad workers had been fishermen in their native Guangdong Province, and they sent home for their equipment, or built it anew. Some junks (flat-bottomed ships with high poops and battened sails) would haul in about 7,000 pounds of bay shrimp daily.

Today nothing remains of these Chinese camps. (See p 165 for the sole exception, preserved in Marin County.) If you come here by car, park in the lots north of San Bruno Point Park

Chinese shrimp camp

(crowded during weekdays), then venture southward along an uneven 0.5-mile trail and old parcourse to the tip of the point and imagine a fleet of junks, in full sail, returning with tons of bay shrimp.

Southward from San Bruno Point (across an inlet and Colma Creek and before the airport) is a service area for SamTrans buses (just off North Access Road). This was a marsh at the end of Colma Creek before it was filled. Stop in the parking lot and explore the 0.5-mile perimeter

trail and parcourse. On its western side a vibrant marsh grows between abandoned World War II shipbuilding piers next to the South San Francisco/San Bruno Water Quality Control Plant. At low tide, marsh islands are exposed in the inlet, and shorebirds and ducks feed calmly despite the proximity of Highway 101, overhead jet traffic, and revving SamTrans buses. The sewage treatment plant discharges treated wastewater a mile off Point San Bruno. Sludge from the plant is used to produce soil conditioner.

SamTrans Peninsula

Oyster Point

Oyster Point did not exist until after 1900 when filling slowly began. In the 1870s the area immediately north of today's Oyster Point—Oyster Cove—encompassed a calm inlet and the site of Samuel Purseglove's Corville and Company oyster beds. Oysters were raised here for almost 40 years until bay pollution and health concerns over the eating of bay shellfish destroyed the industry. Between 1912 and 1983 Shaw Batcher Shipbuilding, Western Pipe and Steel, American Bridge, and U.S. Steel occupied the shores of the cove. Ships for World Wars I and II were built here, and piping was manufactured for the Hetch Hetchy, Grand Coulee, Shasta, and Folsom dams.

Only a few old piers and acres of rubble now bear witness to a century of enterprise. A small fringe marsh and old pilings line Oyster Cove

Oyster Point Fishing Pier

and approach Oyster Cove Marina on the point. Farther out on the point are various businesses, warehouses, a yacht club, restaurants and a hotel, and Oyster Point Park. The park's fishing pier is a favorite of shark fishermen, and in 1992 a 38-pound halibut was reeled in here. Oyster Point Marina's West Basin has a small beach with a cold-water shower.

SAN FRANCISCO INTERNATIONAL AIRPORT

San Francisco International Airport began in 1927 as Mills Field Municipal Airport. Although it is in San Mateo County, it is owned by the city and county of San Francisco. More than 32 million travelers and nearly 500,000 airplanes passed through annually in the early 1990s. The airport's 5,170 acres are mostly bay fill; about half are developed, and for now the rest are open space and tidelands, albeit a bit noisy. If expansion plans are realized, another 20 million travelers could be accommodated annually.

OYSTERS

For the local Ohlone people, shellfish was a staple food, as evidenced by the mounds of oyster and other mollusk shells that once ringed the bay and its creeks. Many European immigrants and newcomers from the East Coast loved oysters too, but found that San Francisco Bay's native oyster, with its dark meat, strong flavor, and small size (about 2 inches across), was a poor substitute for the ones they remembered.

After 1851, when it was discovered that oysters from Shoalwater Bay in Washington State (today's Willapa Bay) were similar to Eastern oysters, several Bay Area oyster companies began importing them. Some 125,000 bushels were shipped to San Francisco annually and either sold or stored in bay waters off Sausalito's shoreline to grow more.

In the 1860s and 1870s, however, hydraulic mining in the Sierra Nevada added thousands of tons of sediment to the normal silt load carried into the bay by the Sacramento and San Joaquin rivers. By 1862 the

Eastern oyster (Crassostrea virginica)

Sausalito storage area was covered with silt, and that year's entire crop perished. Oyster beds in the north bay were soon abandoned for the shallow, calmer, and relatively silt-free waters of the south bay, mostly along the western bayshore of San Mateo County. In 1869, when the transcontinental railroad was completed, Eastern oysters began to be shipped west in iced railcars to the bay's oyster beds. They quickly dominated the industry.

Between 1895 and 1904 well over 10 million pounds of oyster meat were harvested off San Mateo County's shoreline. The Morgan Oyster Company was the largest producer and eventually bought out all other oystermen on the bay. By 1923 Morgan owned 16,580 acres of tidal lands in San Mateo County (where most

Oyster harvesting ca. 1880

production took place), 13,550 acres in Alameda County, and 1,700 acres in Santa Clara County.

Oysters are filter feeders, pumping up to 6 gallons of water across their gills every hour while feeding. They consume minute organisms and organic material at the base of the bay's food chain. They process everything in the water, including the bacteria in human and animal waste, chemicals, and surface runoff pollutants. These substances accumulate and concentrate in their fatty tissues.

As early as the 1870s the outpouring of raw sewage from the city of San Francisco and other nascent cities, and heavy ferry and steamer traffic, began to pollute the bay and affect the oysters. Diversion of freshwater streams in the south bay for agriculture diminished the seasonal flushing action of winter rains. By 1905 oyster seed could no longer survive in the bay. Outbreaks of typhoid fever were blamed on contaminated oysters. By 1940 commercial oyster growing in the bay ceased, and a once vital Bay Area industry disappeared.

Getting Around

The Bay Trail runs south from Candlestick Point on Sierra Point Pkwy, but the north end of the parkway is temporarily closed. Use inland streets to reach the southern section of the parkway and Sierra Point. To visit San Bruno Mtn, go west on Guadalupe Canyon Pkwy (off Bayshore Blvd) to Radio Rd. At Sierra Point the Bay Trail, paved, curves around the point. On the south side of the point the trail is dirt as it leads partway to Oyster Point. Use Airport Blvd to reach Oyster Point. About 2 miles of the Bay Trail wind through Oyster Point. To move farther south to San Bruno Point, use streets. A portion of the Bay Trail is completed on the shores of Colma Creek. Use streets to reach its north or south shores. Another portion of the trail runs along the shore of the "SamTrans Peninsula" off N Access Rd. To reach Bayfront Park, on the south side of San Francisco International Airport, use streets.

BAYFRONT TO SHORELINE PARK

Children who aspire to be pilots, want to learn more about nature, or simply like to watch birds on the water, will find this section of shoreline fascinating: it has the best park for airplane watching, one of the Bay Area's premier natural history museums, good fishing spots, and even a sandy beach. Plenty of adults will also find things to do and enjoy here.

Mud flats and tidal marsh at Bayfront Park

Bayfront Park

Airplanes come in low over bay waters from the south and lift off to the east at San Francisco International Airport. You can watch these landings and take-offs from benches along a walkway in this park, between a manicured lawn and a marsh popular with shorebirds. The noise is tolerable since you are several hundred yards from the closest runway.

Bayfront Park

Plant and Bird Sanctuary

South of Bayfront Park on Bayshore between Mahler and Burlway roads is a small plant and bird sanctuary maintained by the city of Burlingame.

Egret

Anza Lagoon and Burlingame Recreation Lagoon

On the northern peninsula of Anza Lagoon a unique half-circle pier arcs out over the water. The entire area surrounding Anza and Burlingame lagoons (both tidal) is fill and now covered with office buildings, restaurants, and hotels. On the eastern tip of this area, Fishermen's Park offers angling, parking, and an unimpeded view of Coyote Point.

Bayside Park

Bayside Park

Eucalyptus tower at the edges of this park, windshelter for baseball diamonds, a playground, and lawns. Across the street on the bay is a small public fishing shore. A sewage disposal plant abuts the park to the south.

Anza Lagoon

Coyote Point

In 1824 Russian Captain Otto von Kotzebue sailed into the south bay to resupply at Mission Santa Clara (Mission Dolores was low on provisions). En route, he and his men rested on what the captain described as a "pleasant little island" with grassland and oak trees. He thought he was the first human to set foot on the island, but large shell mounds indicate otherwise. In the later 19th century this island was "The Coyote," separated from the peninsula by the Samphire Marsh. After the marsh was filled and the island linked to the shore, it became Coyote Point. Hundreds of eucalyptus trees have replaced the oaks, and lawns have replaced native grasses. Today this is the 670-acre Coyote Point County Recreation Area and site of the nationally recognized Coyote Point Museum.

In the museum's four-level exhibit hall, you are guided past displays on the biosphere, topographical maps of the Bay Area, and exhibits on redwood forest, oak forest, chaparral, grasslands, baylands, and coast habitats. (You start on the top floor and move down.) Here you can learn about bay circulation and pollution, and view animals found along the shore. Outside is a Wildlife Habitat Exhibit with some 25 live native animals.

Coyote Point Museum

The western edge of the county park features a large beach area (in front of the Peninsula Humane Society), which is popular with windsurfers in spring, summer, and fall. At the eastern end of the beach a ramp built for wheelchairs provides safe and easy access into the water. Picnic

Coyote Point beach area

areas, several restaurants, and a firing range are also within the park. On the eastern side of the point, where the park wraps around the county-operated golf course, are the Coyote Point Marina and Yacht Club. Eastward beyond the marina some natural and artificial islands and sand bars make for good birding and offer views of the East Bay and the San Mateo Bridge.

Coyote Point Recreation Area

COMMON BAY SHARKS

Unlike most fish, sharks and rays have skeletons made of cartilage instead of bone. Their scaly skin feels like sandpaper. Of the half dozen or so shark species common in the bay, those most frequently caught from piers are the brown smoothhound shark and the leopard shark. Many fishermen regard most sharks as "trash fish," but when properly cleaned and prepared they are delicious. Thresher sharks are known for their good taste. Sharks are most numerous in southern bay waters where they prey on small fish and scavenge dead fish and marine mammals. Some biologists believe that the shark's role as scavenger is so critical that without it portions of the bay would become excessively polluted. For fishing information on the size and catch limit of sharks and rays, call the California Department of Fish and Game.

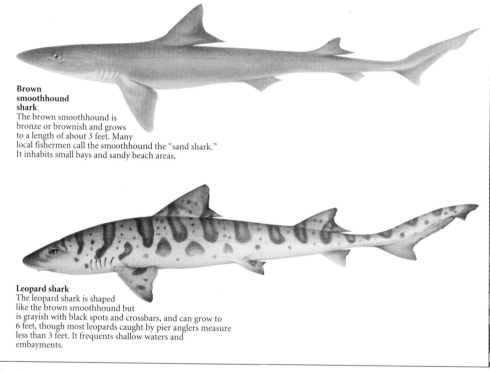

Brown smoothhound shark
The brown smoothhound is bronze or brownish and grows to a length of about 3 feet. Many local fishermen call the smoothhound the "sand shark." It inhabits small bays and sandy beach areas.

Leopard shark
The leopard shark is shaped like the brown smoothhound but is grayish with black spots and crossbars, and can grow to 6 feet, though most leopards caught by pier anglers measure less than 3 feet. It frequents shallow waters and embayments.

Shoreline Park, and More

Windswept Shoreline Park extends south from Coyote Point atop a large levee and beneath countless electrical towers looming along the bayshore (there is a substation by the golf course). The treeless landscape is stark yet beautiful—it's just you and the bay. Harbor View Park is "downslope" from the levee off Monte Diablo Avenue, connected by a trail with this half-block park with a baseball diamond, lawn, play area, and restrooms.

At the southern tip of Shoreline Park is another half-block park.

Shoreline Park

Ryder Park, with a large lawn and struggling pines, is next to the outlet of San Mateo Creek, which forms a small delta. Shorebirds visit at low tide. The park can be reached from the levee, J. Hart Clinton Drive, or Ryder Street. Beyond this park,

the former San Mateo dump is a hill ringed by a pathway. It will eventually become part of Shoreline Park. A parking area for Bay Trail access is to the south, on the bay side of Third Avenue across the outlet of Marina Lagoon.

Ryder Park

COMMON BAY RAYS

Rays are represented in California waters by the bat ray (with "wings"), three species of stingrays (circular-shaped), and six species of nonvenomous skates (square-shaped). Three of these are frequently caught off Bay Area piers and are considered delicious.

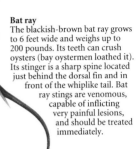

Bat ray
The blackish-brown bat ray grows to 6 feet wide and weighs up to 200 pounds. Its teeth can crush oysters (bay oystermen loathed it). Its stinger is a sharp spine located just behind the dorsal fin and in front of the whiplike tail. Bat ray stings are venomous, capable of inflicting very painful lesions, and should be treated immediately.

Big skate
Sometimes called the "barn-door skate," big skates grow to 8 feet and can weigh 200 pounds. Color varies from blackish to red-brown, but all big skates are covered with white spots and have two prominent "eyespots" on their backs.

Getting Around

Between Bayfront Park and Bayside Park the Bay Trail route passes in front of a series of hotels and restaurants (off Bayshore Hwy) on a paved path. The trail follows the shore around Anza Lagoon while another branch of the trail moves across Airport Blvd to Burlingame Lagoon. On the eastern end of Burlingame Lagoon the trail crosses a small bridge en route to Coyote Point. Numerous small pathways and trails crisscross Coyote Point. The Bay Trail route follows Coyote Point Dr, then extends as a paved path along Shoreline Park and wraps around the former San Mateo dump.

Shoreline near Anza Lagoon

I N F O R M A T I O N

Burlingame Park Department
415-696-7245

City of San Mateo Parks
415-377-4734

Coyote Point Museum
415-342-7755

Department of Fish & Game
707-944-5500

SamTrans (Buses) & CalTrain
1-800-660-4287

San Mateo County Parks (including Coyote Point)
415-363-4021

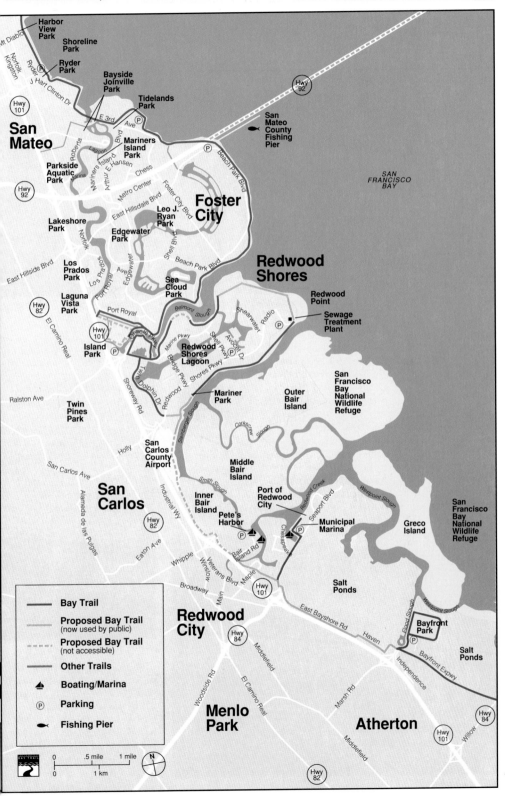

FOSTER CITY TO REDWOOD SHORES

Along this stretch of bayshore the San Mateo County Fishing Pier offers excellent angling next to the San Mateo–Hayward Bridge. Paved trails, parcourses, and parks border planned communities. The marshes of the San Francisco Bay National Wildlife Refuge extend to the south.

Looking north over multi-colored salt ponds toward the Port of Redwood City, the three Bair Islands, Redwood Shores, and Foster City

Foster City

T. Jack Foster

Developer T. Jack Foster had a vision for a new city on the shores of San Francisco Bay. It was to be completely planned before the first load of concrete was poured and to be built partly on bay fill, with every home having access to water. In 1958 he bought Brewer's Island, with 4 square miles of bayshore. In the next six years he had 14 million cubic yards of sand pumped from the bay to shape islands, peninsulas, and a sinuous 200-acre lagoon. In the process, hundreds of acres of tidal wetlands were destroyed. Many of them had been covered by lush marsh vegetation and were home to many bird species. Today Foster City has 19 parks, 4,565 homes, and about 30,000 residents. The Bay Conservation and Development Commission, as well as state and federal laws, protects remnant marshes on the bay as vital wildlife habitat. Foster City represents the 1950s version of the dream of a planned community that had earlier inspired Venice in Los Angeles as well as diverse other development projects in this country and abroad. A more recent version is Blackhawk, inland in Contra Costa County.

Birdwatchers at Foster City shore

Along the bayside of Foster City, off Beach Park Boulevard, small marshes and mud flats exposed at low tide are good spots for birding. Windsurfers use several nearby access ramps into the bay. A wider marsh, and a parcourse, border Belmont Slough. Respect the marsh as a sensitive wildlife area; keep dogs on leash.

Foster City today

San Mateo–Hayward Bridge & Pier

The 7.8-mile San Mateo–Hayward Bridge, with its 2-mile-long, six-lane western span, arches 135 feet over the bay's navigation channel, then leads eastward to southern Alameda County just above bay waters. It carries some 70,000 cars daily. This bridge was opened in 1967, replacing a two-lane bridge built in 1929.

Part of the old bridge was converted to the San Mateo County Fishing Pier—the longest pier on the bay. By the pier's parking lot, you can walk underneath the new bridge, which is only a few feet above your head here. The sound and vibrations are impressive. Moving onto the pier you can observe bay currents swirling around the bridge's massive footings, watch workers cleaning and painting the bridge, and in spring marvel at the swarms of barn swallows buzzing their mud nests on the bridge's underside.

To the south, ducks bob on the surface while cormorants rest on the electrical towers marching across the bay. Views from the end of the 4,135-foot pier are unique; nowhere else can you walk so far out over the bay at water level. Because of the pier's

Cormorants nesting on bridge

length, and the varying depth of the water (40 feet deep at the end of the pier), a good variety of fish is caught here, including sharks, rays, jacksmelt, seaperch, and sturgeon.

San Mateo Bridge and Fishing Pier at dusk

Island Park

Island Park

Island Park is a great place to relax between Foster City and Redwood Shores. Although it's next to Highway 101, the park's large lawns are close enough to Belmont Slough to attract resting shorebirds and gulls. A par-course starts here and swings around Oracle Parkway toward the Redwood Shores complex.

Redwood Shores

This planned community, built partly on former salt ponds, is a newer and much smaller version of neighboring Foster City. It is bordered by marshes and features an industrial park, seven small parks, and a variety of single-family homes and apartment complexes. Before relocating to Vallejo, Marine World operated on this small peninsula from 1968 until 1986. A gravel trail atop a levee stretches along Steinberger Slough from the South Bayside System Authority Wastewater Treatment Works, which services most of southern San Mateo County, to Mariner Park. This trail offers excellent views of the southeast bay and the Coast Range. Before sunset ducks and egrets gather at a pond between the trail and the wastewater plant.

At low tide the slough transforms into a mud flat busy with feeding shorebirds. The wildlife refuge extends to the south and offers a glimpse of what much of the south bay once looked like. Power poles run southward, providing roosts for cormorants and various birds of prey.

Levee trail along Steinberger Slough

The lone concrete building at the end of Radio Road was built by the General Electric Co. to house a shortwave radio station during World War II. Messages sent from here reached troops throughout the Pacific. Today the building (and most of the original equipment) is owned by KGEI Far East Broadcasting Co., a Christian station capable of transmitting to Moscow and China. It broadcasts in Spanish to Latin America.

Marsh beside the trail

BLACK-SHOULDERED KITE

This striking white and black marsh inhabitant (formerly known as the white-tailed kite) hovers like a hawk and soars like a gull. It eats small rodents and insects in marshes and grasslands bordering the bay. Although this kite's population plummeted throughout its range in recent decades because of pesticide contamination and habitat loss, it appears to be making a comeback. It lives mostly in California west of the Sierra, southern Texas, and southward throughout Latin America.

NORTHERN HARRIER

The northern harrier (marsh hawk) is common throughout the bay. It glides over marshes with wings in an open "V" as it searches for rodents. The white rump patch is distinctive in both sexes. Adult males are gray and white with a barred tail. Females are darker brown.

MUD FLAT VIEWING

If you work your way toward the bayshore during low tide, moving past brass buttons, pickleweed, and finally cordgrass, you'll find yourself at the edge of a glistening mud flat. What at first might appear as an odoriferous wasteland is actually one of the richest and most ecologically important habitats in the bay.

In one cubic inch of tideland mud, more than 40,000 organisms can live—from minute phytoplankton, diatoms, bacteria, and zooplankton to more visible worms, snails, shrimp, mussels, clams, and crabs. Countless shorebird species probe and peck for food at low tide in the mud flats. When the tide moves back in, so do rays, flounder, young bass, crabs, diving ducks, and cormorants, also coming to feed. In summer, an abundance of sea lettuce (a common algae) and, occasionally, eelgrass gives the mud flats a bright green sheen.

Most mud flat species are burrowers, so inspect the surface. In summer and fall, you may notice large jelly masses, which protect the eggs of lugworms. These worms make the small coils of sand you may see atop the mud. The darker sand mounds, which look like miniature volcanoes, are entrances to the burrows of pink ghost shrimp. As the shrimp strain mud for bacteria and other food, they deposit filtered sand on the surface.

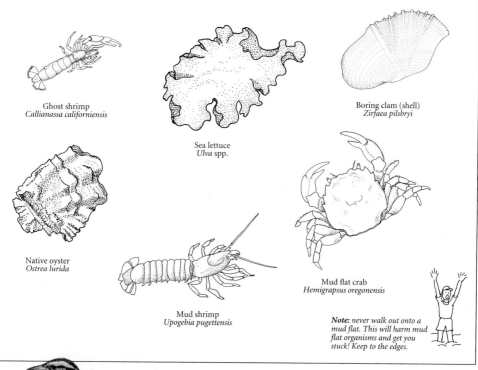

Ghost shrimp
Callianassa californiensis

Sea lettuce
Ulva spp.

Boring clam (shell)
Zirfaea pilsbryi

Native oyster
Ostrea lurida

Mud shrimp
Upogebia pugettensis

Mud flat crab
Hemigrapsus oregonensis

Note: *never walk out onto a mud flat. This will harm mud flat organisms and get you stuck! Keep to the edges.*

WESTERN MEADOW-LARK
Most might associate the flowing melodious song of the meadowlark with grasslands, but it's a common marsh inhabitant also. On warm days these small birds with striking yellow breasts, black collar, and cheery song perch atop fence posts or marsh grasses along the entire bay.

Getting Around
The Bay Trail is paved from the mouth of Marina Lagoon to the San Mateo–Hayward Bridge, then all the way around Foster City. To reach Redwood Shores, use streets to the west (inland side) of Hwy 101, then swing back to Marine Pkwy. Pieces of the trail are completed west of Island Park. At the tip of Redwood Shores the trail is gravel and open from the sewage treatment plant (at end of Radio Rd) along Steinberger Slough to Mariner Park. Park in front of the treatment plant, or at the end of Avocet Dr (off Redwood Shores Pkwy). A bike lane bypasses Redwood Shores and goes directly from Marine Pkwy to Redwood Shores Pkwy via Twin Dolphin Dr.

PORT OF REDWOOD CITY TO RAVENSWOOD SLOUGH

Lessons in history, salt production, and the reclamation of former dump sites are available between the Port of Redwood City and Ravenswood Slough as the nearshore explorer takes in the vast marshland of the San Francisco Bay National Wildlife Refuge.

Redwood City as lumber port in 1850s

Port of Redwood City

 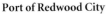

Redwood City grew up around a lumber port. In the 1850s, the shores of Redwood Creek (near today's modern port) were lined with docks stacked with wood products destined for San Francisco and the Sacramento

Pete's Harbor

region. By the mid-1860s, a typical week saw 50,000 board feet of lumber, some 2 million shingles, 100,000 fence posts, and hundreds of cords of firewood loaded onto ships here. Also nearby, the McLeod Co. was busy building oceangoing schooners averaging 100 feet in length with masts 85 feet high.

The port area between Redwood Creek and Seaport Boulevard is

now dominated by Cargill Salt (formerly Leslie Salt) and various cement companies. The main port is a pleasant area to rest, watch boat traffic, and marvel at the gleaming white mountain of salt across the creek. Between Westpoint Slough and Highway 101 to the south, the former marshland is being used as salt ponds by Cargill Salt (see page

71 for more information on salt production). A less formal and quieter waterfront atmosphere can be found at Pete's Harbor, across Redwood Creek at the end of Bair Island Road. The levee system extending north from Pete's is well used by noontime joggers, and the local restaurant and snack stands are popular for lunch.

Port of Redwood City today

Bayfront Park

This former garbage dump is now a neatly contoured park with a 2-mile trail. The entrance is at the bayward end of Marsh Road near Haven Avenue and Bayfront Expressway. Criss-crossing the park is "The Great Spirit Path," a series of rock clusters inspired by Native American pictographs (free guide brochure at parking area). Marsh hawks and meadowlarks work the grasslands here and perch atop the 5-foot white pipes used for checking methane gas leaks.

From the park's top knoll, a 360° view awaits willing hikers. To the north and south are salt ponds. Bayward, Greco Island's marshes are part of the refuge. Between Bayfront Park and Greco Island are a decommissioned sewage treatment plant and the City of Menlo Park Methane Recovery Plant. Methane is extracted from the former dump through an underground network of pipes and used to generate electricity that is then sold to Pacific Gas and Electric Company.

Bayfront Park with Dumbarton Bridge in the background

San Francisco Bay National Wildlife Refuge

San Francisco Bay National Wildlife Refuge encompasses some 19,000 acres of bay sloughs, salt ponds, marshes, mud flats, open water, and upland between Redwood City and Fremont. In southern San Mateo County, the refuge includes Greco Island, the Ravenswood section, and parts of Bair Island. Bair Island is actually three islands: Outer, Middle, and Inner Bair islands. Only 1,000 acres of Bair Island are within the refuge (on segments of the outer and middle islands) so far. Expansion of the refuge, to encompass all three Bair islands, is a high priority for the U.S. Fish and Wildlife Service. Efforts are under way to save the remaining portions from development and include them in the refuge.

On the north side of Dumbarton Bridge is the Ravenswood section of the refuge (no dogs). A levee trail extends beneath high-voltage transmission towers into a barren landscape of earthen banks and muddy holes. A little farther out, however, you'll come upon more pleasant scenery as the trail loops around a salt pond flanked by open bay and marsh.

The Ravenswood section is the only portion of the refuge accessible to waterfowl hunters by foot. Elsewhere they must use boats. During the hunting season, trails are closed here to all visitors except hunters. The hunting season is always in the winter, but it can vary by a few weeks from year to year. Check with the refuge for exact dates of closure.

Bair Island is composed of three islands

Caspian terns at the San Francisco Bay National Wildlife Refuge

TRAINS

In the 1850s, several companies were organized, and reorganized, to connect San Francisco by railway with San Jose, which was then the state capital. Construction of a peninsula railroad line began in May 1861, and two years later the first train steamed south from San Francisco via Daly City to Mayfield (today's Palo Alto). From Mayfield passengers rode stagecoaches to San Jose. The rail line reached San Jose in 1864. In 1907 the Bayshore Cutoff was completed by Point San Bruno, bypassing Daly City and many curves, and shortening travel time.

Getting Around

From Redwood Shores use streets to reach Seaport Blvd and the Port of Redwood City. Just before Seaport Blvd, Bair Island Rd leads to Pete's Harbor. Between the port and Bayfront Park to the south, the use of streets is required. A dirt trail circles Bayfront Park, while the Bay Trail between the park and Dumbarton Bridge and Ravenswood Pier is paved and well signed. One branch of the Bay Trail crosses Dumbarton Bridge on a walking and biking lane all the way to Newark. The other branch (dirt) leads south into Ravenswood Open Space Preserve.

INFORMATION

Bayfront Park
415-366-6609

SamTrans (buses) & CalTrain
1-800-660-4287

San Francisco Bay
National Wildlife Refuge
510-792-0222

Greco
Island

Flood Slough

Bayfront
Park

Independence

Chilco

Bayfront Expwy

Ravenswood Slough

San
Francisco
Bay
National
Wildlife
Refuge

Dumbarton
Pier

Dumbarton
Bridge

Marshlands

Stevens Creek Shoreline Trail

Newark Slough

To Refuge
Headquarters
& Visitor
Center

Salt
Pond

San
Francisco
Bay
National
Wildlife
Refuge

Plummer Creek

Ravenswood
Pier

Ravenswood
Open
Space
Preserve

Dumbarton
Point

SPRR
Bridge

Hwy
84

Hwy
101

New Bridge

Pierce

Willow

University

East
Palo
Alto

Ravenswood
Open
Space
Preserve

Bay

Menlo
Park

E Bayshore

University

Cooley

Clarke

Beech

Pulgas

Weeks

Runymede

Bay

Palo
Alto
Baylands
Nature
Preserve

San Fran Creek

Matadero Creek

Lucy
Evans
Baylands
Nature
Interpretive
Center

SAN
FRANCISCO
BAY

Sal
Po

San
Franc
Bay
Natio
Wildli
Refu

University

Middlefield

Embarcadero

El Camino Real

Alma

Oregon Expressway

Hwy
101

Palo
Alto
Airport

Duck
Pond

Embarcadero

E Bayshore

Sand
Point

Hooks
Point

Byxbee
Park

Calaveras
Point

Palo
Alto
Baylands
Nature
Preserve

Animal
Shelter

Hwy
82

Palo
Alto

Alma

E Charleston Rd

San Antonio

Old Middlefield Wy

Middlefield

Casey

Marine Garcia

Bayshore Pkwy

Shoreline
Lake

Boat
House

Club
House

Mountain View Slough

Shoreline
at
Mountain
View

Stevens
Creek
Shoreline
Nature
Study
Area

San
Francisco
Bay
National
Wildlife
Refuge

Arastradero

Rengstorff

Central Expressway

Shorebird

Amphitheatre

Charleston

Plymouth

Shorebird

Shoreline Blvd

Crittenden

Zook

Zook

Moffett Field Drainage Ditch

Bushnell

Wescoat

Moffett
Field
Naval
Air
Station

Macon

5th Ave

Mathilda

3rd

Cari

Hwy
82

Mountain
View

Castro

Miramonte

Grant

(To be continued)

Evelyn

Mt. View Alviso Fwy

Middlefield

Whisman

Macon

Cody

Maude

Moffett Park Dr

Hwy
101

Hwy
237

Mathilda

Santa
Clara

Borregas

Jav

Sunnyvale

Mary

Evelyn

Central Expressway

Faroaks

Hwy
85

	Bay Trail
	Proposed Bay Trail (now used by public)
	Proposed Bay Trail (not accessible)
	Other Trails
⏦	Boating/Marina
Ⓟ	Parking
⊷	Fishing Pier

0   .5 mile   1 mile

0   1 km

Hwy
280

N

BAY
TRAIL

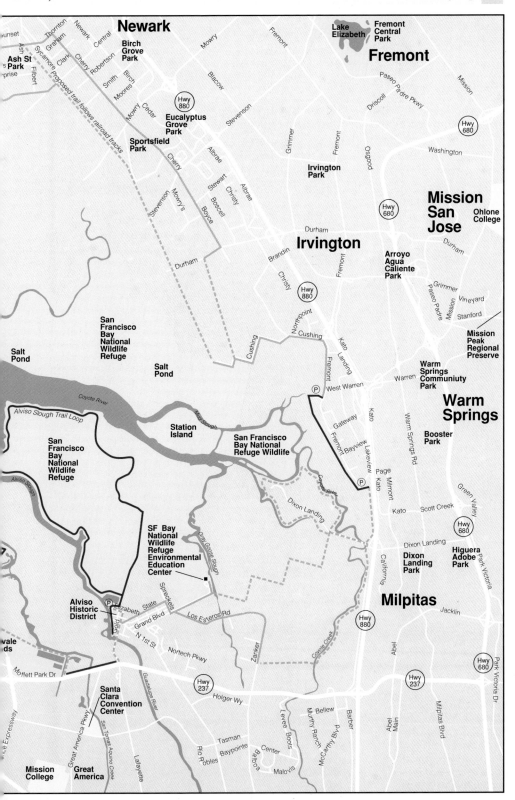

DUMBARTON BRIDGE & PIERS TO MOFFETT FIELD

At the Dumbarton Bridge, between Ravenswood Point on the western shore and Dumbarton Point to the east, the bay constricts to approximately one mile across before widening again to the south. Along this portion of the bay's western shoreline, six creeks and four sloughs enrich the marshes and mud flats, all vital habitat for resident and migratory wildlife. You can hike here, fish from piers, watch the birds. You can also play golf, sail, and attend open-air concerts.

Scientist studying shorebirds in salt ponds, with historic train bridge in background

DUMBARTON CUTOFF

Just south of the Dumbarton Bridge, Southern Pacific's Dumbarton Cutoff train bridge and the Hetch Hetchy aqueduct span the bay. The cutoff was built between 1908 and 1909, the first bridge across the bay. It opened for service in 1910. The structure you see is the original.

This bridge carried six to eight freight trains daily until May 1982, when the Port of San Francisco lost out to the Port of Oakland as the dominant bay port, and the need for the bridge diminished. The swing span was welded open to allow boat passage. In 1993, the San Mateo Transit District bought the bridge, intending to provide new rail service for commuters.

Looking northeast toward Dumbarton Bridge; East Palo Alto and Ravenswood Preserve in foreground

Dumbarton Bridge & Piers

The original Dumbarton Bridge, built in 1927, was the first automobile bridge to span the bay. Today's bridge was built alongside in 1982. In 1985 the original bridge was demolished and its approaches were converted to fishing piers: Ravenswood Pier on the west shore, Dumbarton Pier on the east shore. Ravenswood Pier, .04-mile long and a favorite with fishermen, was closed indefinitely in 1994. Dumbarton Pier is open sunrise to sunset. Cross the bridge, then turn right toward the San Francisco Bay National Wildlife Refuge Visitor Center (see p. 63). From the end of Dumbarton Pier you can see most of the south bay and get a fine view of the Cargill Salt ponds at Newark. But if you're moving south on the west shore of the bay, you can continue from here to the Ravenswood Preserve and Palo Alto Baylands.

Dumbarton Bridge

Ravenswood Open Space Preserve

Channel leading toward salt pond

The Ravenswood Preserve consists of 370 acres of leveed marsh, on both sides of the Dumbarton Cutoff, managed by the Midpeninsula Regional Open Space District. In the preserve's northern portion, accessible from the Ravenswood Pier parking area, a 0.5-mile dirt trail runs on the levee between bay marsh and a brine shrimp pond. The preserve's southern portion is a former salt pond restored to a salt marsh. It has a parking area, 1.5-mile trail, and two observation platforms with views of Palo Alto Baylands Nature Preserve's vast marshland to the south, the East Palo Alto Baylands, as well as of the Dumbarton Cutoff and the southeast bay. Small planes drone overhead as they lift off from the Palo Alto airport to the immediate south. Enormous transmission towers high-step across the preserve north and south after detouring to a substation on Bay Road. The preserve's principal levee is sensitive wildlife habitat and off-limits. Although the preserve's southern part is hemmed in by railroad tracks, housing, and a confusion of junkyards, its vibrant bird-filled marsh is a joy to behold. Park at the end of Bay Road.

COLLECTING BAY BRINE SHRIMP

The bay's tiny brine shrimp, known to many children as the "sea monkeys" in mail order kits, occurs naturally from Saskatchewan, Canada, southward throughout western North America. The minute eggs of the half-inch shrimp are transported by winds and birds and can lie dormant for years until covered with salt water. They hatch within 18 hours to two days, depending on water temperature. About three weeks after hatching, brine larvae quickly grow into adult shrimp, a favorite food of migrating and resident shorebirds and ducks.

About 1 million pounds of brine shrimp are collected commercially in active and former salt ponds around San Francisco Bay where shallow, warm waters and high salt concentrations create optimal conditions for shrimp production. Two south bay companies with specially equipped boats skim the shrimp from the upper layers of salt ponds. Frozen shrimp are sold internationally as aquarium fish food; live shrimp are sold for science research projects and fish food.

Brine shrimp

RAVENSWOOD, A SHORT-LIVED TOWN

During the Gold Rush years of 1849–50, San Francisco was California's unchallenged civic and commercial center, but San Jose was the state's capital. Stagecoach service started between the two cities in 1849, and steam boats maintained regular service. At Ravenswood Point, travelers could switch from coach to steamer, or the other way around, depending upon weather and road conditions. This was one of the few sites along the peninsula where dry land was accessible from deep water. A long wharf was built, a town began to grow; it was named Ravenswood.

In the 1850s, however, after a prominent citizen absconded with the municipal funds, Ravenswood went into sharp decline. Its demise was expedited by the rise of Redwood City and its port to the immediate north. Today not one building, nor even a wharf piling, remains. The old town site is now within the city of East Palo Alto.

State House, San Jose, 1849

Palo Alto Baylands Nature Preserve

In the 1960s, local activists and the city of Palo Alto preserved 1,400 acres of neglected and abused salt marsh. In subsequent years more wetlands were revitalized and restored. By 1993 the Baylands encompassed some 2,100 acres, including a duck pond, miles of scenic trails, and a seasonal freshwater marsh fed by treated wastewater. Plans are under way to breach old levees, dredge silt-filled channels, and revive more marshlands. Countless birds and many other wild creatures thrive here, despite power lines overhead and the airport as neighbor. No dogs are allowed during nesting season, March 15–June 15.

Palo Alto Baylands

The preserve extends inland past Byxbee Landfill Park to East Bayshore and a 15-acre seasonal freshwater marsh dedicated to Emily Renzel, an activist who fought for its revival as a member of the city council and of the San Francisco Bay Conservation and Development Commission. Since 1993, this marsh has been fed daily by some 1 million gallons of treated wastewater from the adjacent Palo Alto sewage treatment plant. The marsh was created with the aid of the California State Coastal Conservancy and is one of several on the bay to use treated wastewater to enhance wildlife habitat. The runoff from the marsh flows into Matadero Creek, which empties into the bay. In summer this wetland is allowed to dry out to minimize mosquito problems, bird diseases such as avian botulism, and excessive vegetative growth.

Lucy Evans Baylands Nature Interpretive Center

Opened in 1969, this unique, many-sided building was the first interpretive center on the bay. It stands on pillars above pickleweed at the end of Embarcadero Road and is a good place to begin a visit to the Baylands. A deck surrounds it, offering close-up views of waterbirds as well as broad vistas across water. A boardwalk leads from the back of the deck out 850 feet to the very

Boardwalk toward open water

edge of the marsh, ending at an observation platform. Waves of green grasses mingle with ripples of blue-gray water where cordgrass meets open water. This would have been a typical bayshore before levees and urban embankments straightened out so much of it. To the south, the tidal salt marshes and sloughs of Palo Alto Baylands merge with a 600-acre city flood control basin, which is also open to visitors. The basin's north side is barren;

Lucy Evans Interpretive Center

its south side is covered with pickleweed. At times, tens of thousands of western sandpipers swarm across the mudflats.

The center's mounted bird exhibits include common marsh species. A self-service Open Ecology workshop provides microscopes, fish and plant specimens, educational leaflets and guide booklets, and other tools to visitors who wish to explore what's around. There are also scheduled natural history programs for children and adults, as well as videos and slide shows. Lucy Evans, for whom the center is named, was a historian, conservationist, and teacher who worked hard to save Palo Alto's Baylands, first as citizen, then as member of the Palo Alto City Council. South of the center, the former marina (now silted-in) and an area of diked-off baylands are being restored to marshland.

WESTERN SANDPIPERS

Close to a million shorebirds have been counted on the bay on a single day during spring migration. Most common are the western sandpipers, who arrive here each autumn from breeding grounds in the Russian and Alaskan tundra. Many winter in Panama, and some 150,000 winter on the bay. Western sandpipers are precision flyers. Flocks lift off together from the mudflats to perform flawless patterns, then settle again to search for food. Biologists are only beginning to learn about these "peeps." In one recent study, 110 were captured in mist nets on the south bay, tagged with tiny radio receivers, and tracked for five weeks as far as the Copper River Delta in Alaska. While in the south bay, these small birds were found to stay within an area as small as 1.4 square miles. In migrating north along the coast, some have been known to fly 1,200 miles in 24 hours.

Western sandpiper

Byxbee Landfill Park

This new park is taking shape atop the eastern portion of Palo Alto's garbage dump, next to a recycling center and the regional water quality control plant. A 34-acre portion of the park opened in 1991, with some interesting site sculptures. The dump's western section is still active, receiving some 100,000 tons of garbage annually, and will not be closed for decades. Eventually, however, it will be capped and Byxbee Park will be expanded to 146 acres.

The park section completed thus far—a cooperative effort by the city, landscape architects George Hargreaves Associates, and artists Peter Richard and Michael Oppenheimer—features artwork designed to emphasize the transition from artificial and controlled environments

Palo Alto Duck Pond

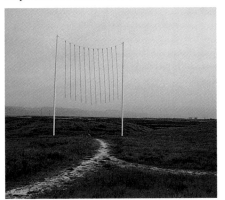

Byxbee Park sculptures

to natural and self-regulating ones. "Chevrons," a sculpture made from concrete highway barriers, is visible to pilots landing at the Palo Alto airport. "Pole Field," a collection of poles of varying heights, symbolizes the transition from park to marshland. Those nearest the park are in rows, those closer to the marsh appear to be more random. "Hillocks" are grassy mounds atop the park's higher points. They are meant to suggest Ohlone Indian shell mounds while adding topography and creating micro-habitats for wildlife. "Keyhole" provides a clue to what lies below: methane from the buried garbage burns off through a vertical pipe set in white gravel.

Duck Pond

Generations of Palo Altans have tossed bread crumbs to the ducks and geese at the Palo Alto Duck Pond since the 1940s. The pond was created from an abandoned swimming pool and is now a refuge for domesticated waterfowl gone feral, injured birds, gulls, ducks, and geese. This is one of the few places on the bay where you may feed birds. Never feed wildlife elsewhere: it impairs their ability to survive in the wild.

Bay Access Ramp

A recently built pier and ramp allow windsurfers and hand-carried boats to launch in the channel to the former yacht harbor.

PALO ALTO REGIONAL WATER QUALITY CONTROL PLANT

This facility provides advanced treatment for wastewater from some 200,000 people and industries between East Palo Alto, Los Altos, and Mountain View. It can process 20 million gallons a day, yielding 1.5 million gallons of reclaimed water for nearby marshes and landscaped areas. The 23 tons of sludge ash produced here each week are trucked to Arizona for removal of gold, silver, and copper (residues from electronics firms). The remaining inert waste is used in construction projects.

DAB OR DIVE

How can you tell one duck species from another, especially from afar, on a marsh or pond full of mallards, gadwalls, teals, wigeons, scaups, and scoters? Markings can be hard to see without binoculars, but you can easily identify many birds from the way they feed and fly.

Dabbling ducks, such as the pintail and mallard, "dabble" for food with their tails in the air and heads underwater. Diving ducks, such as the canvasback, disappear underwater, swimming to the bottom for food with the aid of a paddle-like extra flap in the hind toe.

When dabblers take off, they rise into the air immediately. Divers run and patter along the surface before taking off. You can get a free leaflet describing nine different duck species at the Interpretive Center.

Red-winged blackbird

RED-WINGED BLACKBIRD

The boisterous spring display of male red-winged blackbirds, with their shining red epaulets and throaty "kong-ka-ree" and "o-ka-lee-onk," signals that freshwater is near. On the south side of Byxbee Park, freshwater creeks join in Mayfield Slough. The tule reed and cattail here provide excellent blackbird nesting habitat.

Shoreline at Mountain View Park

"Shoreline," as it is commonly called, is a well-groomed 700-acre waterfront park with an artificial salt lake, a golf course, and the outdoor Shoreline Amphitheater, all beside sloughs and marshes alive with shorebirds and waterfowl. Lawns and open hillsides around the lake are perfect for picnicking, and kite flying is allowed in designated areas. Some 10 miles of trails, both paved and dirt, wind through the park and past Charleston Slough, the historic Rengstorff House, and alongside marshes.

Shoreline at Mountain View Park

Meadowlands

There isn't a clue, not even a whiff, of what lies underfoot when you walk one of the trails at Shoreline's Meadowlands. Believe it or not, the softly undulating hills of this upland area are made of household garbage. In 1968, the city of Mountain View bought a 500-acre shoreline site and prepared a series of landfill cells lined with clay to prevent the leaching of pollutants. San

Francisco then paid for the privilege of dumping its garbage into these cells for the next 13 years. Mountain View also installed a gas recovery system to extract landfill gas, which includes methane, produced from the decay of organic wastes in garbage. The city sells the gas to the Pacific Gas and Electric Company and Laidlaw Gas Recovery, which generates electricity that is sold to PG&E.

By 1983, Mountain View closed the dump, capped the cells, began landscaping, and started restoring nearby wetlands. Today, the only hint of landfill in Shoreline's protective green veneer is a small hidden flare station, which burns off excess gas.

RING-NECKED PHEASANT

This native of Georgia, near the River Colchis, in Asia, was introduced throughout the United States in the 19th century as a game bird. It is now common around farmlands and in the upper zones of bay marshes. The male has brilliant colors and a boisterous "kork-kok" call. The Palo Alto Baylands are home to a healthy population of this exotic species: the flood control ponds north of the Interpretive Center were part of a pheasant farm until the 1960s.

Charleston Slough

Charleston Slough is a ponded habitat dotted with tiny islands, edged with pickleweed, and popular with bird watchers. Over 130 different bird species have been seen in the course of a year along the slough, which snakes north from the foot of San Antonio Road and ends at a levee that cuts it off from the bay. Water from the bay flows in through a tidal gate, is pumped into the lake, then flows out into Permanente Creek and back to the bay. Ducks, terns, and hundreds of white pelicans frequent these shallow waters, as well as Palo Alto's marshy flood

Northern shoveler

control basin to the north. Look for the northern shoveler, a duck with a spoonlike bill, dark head, white belly, and rust-striped wings. When feeding, these ducks often form a tight clump, paddling round and round in a circle, heads underwater. Great flocks of migrating ducks arrive in the fall en route to wintering grounds to the south. In summer, white pelicans and terns feed in open water, while hundreds of avocets breed and raise young along the banks of the slough.

Charleston Slough

Sailing Lake 🎣 🦆 ♿ 🚶 🚲

Shoreline's 50-acre artificial salt lake attracts small-craft sailors and windsurfers (rentals available). A small cafe, sport shop, and sailing club occupy one end of the lake near the parking lot. Lawns planted with pine and willow slope down to the lakefront—good places for a shady picnic. Scores of American coots—black plumage, red eyes, white beaks, and pot bellies—visit the lake in winter months.

Rengstorff House

Sailing Lake with Windy Hill in background

Rengstorff House

The restored Rengstorff House is one of the finest examples of Victorian Italianate architecture remaining on the West Coast. Built by Henry Rengstorff in 1876, the house stood along Stierlin Road (now Shoreline Boulevard) until it was moved to Shoreline Park in 1980. Rengstorff was a poor German immigrant who started out as a farm laborer and eventually acquired six farms. He built this fine home for his wife and seven children. It is made of Douglas fir and shingled with redwood, has 15 rooms, four marble fireplaces, and a staircase railed with hand-turned spindles. The hip roof, widow's walk, and front portico were popular features in the 1800s. Several docent-guided tours are offered weekly. Call for schedule. The house is also sometimes rented for weddings and other events.

COMMON PICKLEWEED

Pickleweed, also known as glasswort, is abundant in the "middle zone" of salt marshes and grows throughout coastal California. Unlike cordgrass and salt-grass, pickleweed does not have special salt-excreting glands. It concentrates salt in its end segments (two modified leaves, fused together around a stem) until they turn red, dry up, and fall off. Its genus name, Salicornia, is derived from Greek and means "salt-horn," referring to its salt-concentrating abilities. Break a green stem open, and you'll find salty juices. Some people gather spring pickleweed and eat it like asparagus. Flower-bearing scales are visible from April through September. In late summer and fall, dodder, a spidery, bright orange parasitic plant, grows atop pickleweed, highlighting sections of the shoreline.

Common pickleweed

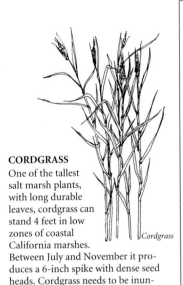

Cordgrass

CORDGRASS

One of the tallest salt marsh plants, with long durable leaves, cordgrass can stand 4 feet in low zones of coastal California marshes. Between July and November it produces a 6-inch spike with dense seed heads. Cordgrass needs to be inundated by salt water daily. It has adapted to the harsh salt marsh habitat: specialized glands eject excess salt from its system and specialized leaves help transport oxygen to its water-logged roots.

LANDFILLS

Ever since towns began springing up around the bay in the 1850s, the seemingly useless muddy zone between them and the water has been visited by an endless stream of vehicles hauling garbage, debris, and soil to be dumped in the bay. Some 85 percent of the bay's wetlands have been filled in, paved over, or planted. Today, countless landfills have left strange hills along the entire bayshore. Some are still active dumps, others sit idle, but some have been capped and converted into parks. Besides Mountain View's Meadowlands, these include Candlestick Point State Recreation Area in San Francisco, Oyster Bay Regional Shoreline in San Leandro, San Mateo's Shoreline Park, Bayfront Park in Menlo Park, Byxbee Park in Palo Alto, and Berkeley's North Waterfront Park.

"Some of our landfills are now richer in resources than some of our mines."

Denis Hayes, 1989

Mountain View & Stevens Creek Tidal Marshes

Two creeks enter the bay at Shoreline at Mountain View Park—Permanente and Stevens creeks. The tide brings salt water into these creeks, and salt marshes line their banks. Since tidal action was restored in 1983 to Mountain View marsh, it has slowly reshaped itself, and pickleweed has begun to grow in its mudflats. Cordgrass, which grows more slowly than pickleweed, has taken hold with the help of planting programs. At Stevens Creek marsh, a culvert system was installed to help increase tidal flow and more cordgrass was planted. Hundreds of birds now feed on the mudflats here. You can watch from numerous benches. Bayward, the large ponds are owned by Cargill Salt. To the southeast are the Stevens Creek Shoreline Nature Study Area, owned by the Mid-peninsula Regional Open Space District, and Moffett Field. The Stevens Creek Trail extends south from the Bay Trail, crossing beneath Highway 101 and linking downtown Mountain View to the bay. Eventually it will connect with the Ridge Trail and extend to the ocean.

Mountain View Marsh

BURROWING OWLS

This is the only owl species that lives underground and is active during the day. About 9 inches tall, brown, and long-legged, it makes its home in the burrows of ground squirrels. To provide burrows in recently covered landfill areas with few squirrels, Shoreline staff built 10 burrow mounds between 1989 and 1991. On the surface, these burrowing owl homes look like big mounds of dirt. Inside, 8-foot-long tunnels lead to nest boxes.

In 1990, park staff counted three pairs of owls raising young in these owl dwellings. The custom homes are still occupied. Look for owls standing at their front doors or atop fence posts along the shoreline trail to Stevens Creek. Listen too. The burrowing owl chatters loudly at intruders, and to scare them further it performs an excellent impersonation of a rattlesnake rattling its tail.

CALIFORNIA GROUND SQUIRRELS

These native squirrels are inordinately common in developed parks around the bayshore. Why? They are masters of disturbed short-grass habitats. No matter how beautiful a park is, in the world of bayshore ecology it is a disturbed habitat. Most important, grasses are kept unnaturally low in many parks, allowing ground squirrels a clear view of approaching trouble. They are colonial nesters and chirp in loud alarm to warn others around active nests.

Stevens Creek Shoreline Nature Study Area

Cross Stevens Creek on one of two bridges and you are in the Stevens Creek Nature Study Area, managed by the Mid-peninsula Regional Open Space District. As you move bayward on the levee trail through this 55-acre holding, huge airplanes may be lifting off from Moffett Field and flying to the coast for maritime surveillance.

Stevens Creek Shoreline Nature Study Area

*"When we try to pick out anything by itself we find
it hitched to everything in the Universe."*

John Muir, 1911

View across Stevens Creek Shoreline toward Moffett Field hangars

Moffett Field Naval Air Station

Moffett Field has been here since 1933. Most nearby residents and visitors recognize its three gigantic hangars. One was built for the airship USS *Macon* in 1933 (now resting on the ocean floor off Monterey Bay); the other two were constructed for blimps in the early 1940s. But Moffett Field also includes expansive marshes and some of the last productive agricultural fields on this part of the bay.

After 60 years of military service, the Navy is turning over the 2,000-acre facility to the National Aeronautics and Space Administration (NASA). But in a sense, the Navy will remain a while: Moffett Field sits atop a toxic plume created by years of leaks from military fuel and oil storage tanks. It will cost the Navy an estimated $150 million over 15 years to clean up this toxic site.

Getting Around

From the Ravenswood Pier parking lot, a dirt levee trail moves south into the Ravenswood Open Space Preserve for 0.5 miles. The Bay Trail route goes west on Bayfront Expressway, then south on University Ave (Highway 109), following a paved trail, then a bike lane. If you want to reach the Ravenswood Open Space Preserve parking lot, continue on streets until the end of Bay St. From here, the Bay Trail runs through the southern portion of the preserve for 1.5 miles on dirt levee trails.

To reach the Palo Alto Baylands to the south, use streets until Embarcadero Rd. Follow Embarcadero Rd to Palo Alto Baylands and Byxbee Park, the Lucy Evans Bayland Nature Interpretive Center, and miles of dirt trails. You can also enter the Baylands from Runnymeade. One dirt levee trail moves south from Byxbee Park, skirting flood control basins, to Charleston Slough and Shoreline at Mountain View Park. The Bay Trail route runs along the shoulder of East Bayshore Rd for about 1.5 miles, then turns bayward on a paved bike path by Adobe Creek and leads to Terminal Blvd and through Shoreline Park on both dirt and paved paths. To reach the Sunnyvale Baylands Park, bypass Moffett Field by using streets.

SUNNYVALE BAYLANDS PARK TO SPORTSFIELD PARK

T his portion of the shoreline is the true southern arm of the bay, and constitutes the heart of the 19,000-acre San Francisco Bay National Wildlife Refuge. Its freshwater creeks and marshes, salt marshes, salt ponds, mud flats, sloughs, and shallow bay water (from the Dumbarton Bridge south, bay waters average 6 feet) support an estimated 250 resident and migratory bird species. Other native wildlife, including the reclusive harbor seal, also flourishes here. Nestled among the region's expansive marshes, the historic sites of Alviso and Drawbridge are visible reminders of the human imprint on the land.

Marshes near Alviso

Sunnyvale Baylands Park

Sunnyvale Baylands includes 105 acres of seasonal wetland and 72 acres of grassy uplands for picnicking, hiking, children's play area, and wildlife habitat. To the north on Caribbean Drive are the Sunnyvale refuse transfer station and recycling center, a landfill (slated for closure after the year 2000), and the Sunnyvale Water Pollution Control Plant. No dogs.

Sunnyvale Baylands Park

Canning local fruit in the 1950s

SUNNYVALE WATER POLLUTION CONTROL PLANT

In 1959, when fruit canneries flourished in this area, this plant was opened to provide primary treatment for 7.5 million gallons of wastewater daily. Since the valley that had been known for its orchards has become Silicon Valley, heartland of the electronics industry, sewage treatment has become more difficult as well as more important. About 30 million gallons a day now undergo a three-step process here. From the north side of the plant, a dirt levee trail ventures along the wastewater ponds toward the bay.

SUBSIDENCE

Some Santa Clara County Water District engineers believe that many wells were dug near the southwestern edge of the bay just before 1900 to accommodate a growing population. By 1915 the first serious drop in the water table was noticed, and well water pressure decreased. The land above the aquifer slowly began to subside across a wide area as increasing amounts of groundwater were extracted to irrigate countless fruit trees and for use in canneries. By the time the district began importing water in 1969, halving its groundwater extraction, the land had sunk an average of 11 feet, a particularly messy problem for flood-plagued towns such as Alviso that were built at or near the level of the bay. The "epicenter" of subsidence is just southeast of downtown San Jose, where the land surface has fallen 13 feet. Since 1969, it is believed the land has stabilized. The district maintains an active groundwater recharge program.

Alviso

Alviso is a historic waterfront town at the bay's southernmost extremity and is now part of the city of San Jose. Offshore are the wetlands of the San Francisco Bay National Wildlife Refuge and the salt ponds of Cargill Salt (formerly Leslie Salt). Onshore, in the 130-year-old town, you can view relics of what was once the busiest port on the bay. You can also enjoy a waterfront stroll and study the consequences of environmental ignorance. Listed in both the National Register of Historic Places and the Environmental Protection Agency's inventory of toxic waste sites, Alviso presents an intriguing cross section of historic and contemporary issues.

Alviso boat landing, 1895

Town and Marina

Alviso's marina silted up years ago. Today only a few derelict boats remain, stuck in the mud.

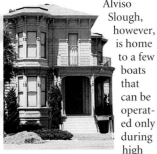

Alviso Slough, however, is home to a few boats that can be operated only during high tides.

Tilden-Laine Residence

Downtown Alviso is not much more than a post office, a library, and a handful of Mexican restaurants, including Rosita's with its ornate bar and filling recipes from south of the border. Weather-beaten shacks roofed with corrugated iron, patched with odd bits of wood and slumped by a 1983 flood, stand amid renovated Victorians, modern split-level homes, and historic landmarks. The Tilden-Laine Residence on Elizabeth Street is the finest remnant of Alviso's heyday. Built by Susan Tilden, a pioneer who rounded Cape Horn and managed her own general store, it was still home to her descendants in the 1990s. Wade Warehouse, the handsome brick building on El Dorado, has been owned by a succession of Wades, beginning with Henry Wade in the mid-

Wade Warehouse

19th century, the first person to bring wagons safely through Death Valley in 1849. Unpaved streets run through neighborhoods that have subsided as much as 4 feet since their founding. Amtrak runs right through town along El Dorado Street. Productive salt ponds and wetland wildlife habitats border nearby garbage dumps.

Downtown Alviso today

WETLANDS

The wetlands around Alviso include some of the southernmost reaches of the national wildlife refuge. Some are seasonal wetlands, flooded by winter rains; others are brackish and freshwater marshes, flushed by both tides and wastewater from the San Jose/Santa Clara sewage treatment plant to the east. There are also salt ponds, leased to Cargill Salt.

HISTORY

Alviso began as Embarcadero de Santa Clara, a small trading post from which beaver skins, tallow, and hides were hauled by boat up to the bay. In 1851, four Yankees bought the ranchlands surrounding the landing from Don Ignacio Alviso, a major domo of nearby Mission Santa Clara, and named their dream of a big new south bay city after him.

Alviso Yacht Club, 1914

Though the dream never materialized, Alviso prospered as steamboats used the docks and warehouses to supply northern California with redwood, flour, grain, fruits, and vegetables. Then, in 1884, the railroad bypassed the town. As cargo began to move by boxcar rather than boat, Alviso declined.

In 1907, Sai Yen Chew began a cannery here. His son, Thomas Foon Chew, became known as the "Asparagus King" for being first to can white rather than green asparagus. By 1920 the Bayside Cannery was the third largest canning operation in the United States. It closed in 1936. Today the building houses the San Francisco Bird Observatory. A mural depicting the evolution of Alviso from Ohlone times to the present is on the side facing Hope Street.

In the 1930s the town became known for tong wars, gambling, and a greyhound racetrack. As groundwater was overdrawn to irrigate the orchards for which Santa Clara County was famous in the 1940s, the soil subsided. Flood after flood plagued the residents. Hoping for help from its better-off neighbor, San Jose, Alviso agreed to be annexed in 1968. Today, this community, now largely Mexican-American, still awaits paved streets and modern flood control.

Meanwhile, other problems developed from decades of landfilling and levee-building with soil and debris containing high levels of asbestos. In 1984, Alviso qualified for federal funds for hazardous waste cleanup. Landfills and levees have been capped, and according to the E.P.A., in 1991 the airborne asbestos levels here were no greater than are found in "other areas of California." However, further cleanup is planned.

A home in Alviso

HERON ROOKERY

Great egrets, great blue herons, and black-crowned night herons nest in alkali marshlands around Alviso. Each pair lays two to five eggs a year. The trail to the heron rookery is open mid-August through March. Though very shy, herons can also be seen from other refuge trails, particularly in the early morning. Flocks of egrets appear at the end of June.

Great blue heron

SAN JOSE WATER TREATMENT PLANT

Nowhere does wastewater disposal have such a crucial impact on the life of the bay as here at its southern extremity, where most fresh water has been diverted, circulation is minimal, and the average depth of the bay is only 6 feet. This is the largest advanced treatment plant in California, sprawling across 1,700 acres and serving more than 1 million people. It processes 167 million gallons daily and recycles more than 4 million gallons a day for landscaping, construction, and dust control throughout Santa Clara County. The sludge-drying operation is the world's largest, yielding 30,000 tons yearly. Because of repeated pollution problems in the south bay associated with this plant's discharge, the outfall pipe may soon be extended to deeper waters north of the Dumbarton Bridge.

San Francisco Bay National Wildlife Refuge

The refuge encompasses some 19,000 acres of bay sloughs, salt ponds, marshes, mud flats, open water, and uplands. It circles the south bay from Redwood City's Bair Island to Coyote Hills in Fremont (with a western gap from Dumbarton Bridge to Moffett Field). Though the refuge is a place specifically preserved as wildlife habitat, visitors are welcome to explore its 30-mile network of trails, and waterfowl hunting is allowed seasonally.

In addition to offering access, the extensive network of refuge trails invites reflection on the south bay environment. Here, it's the natural landscape, rather than the human landmarks, that prevails: still waters, rich mud flats, tide-stirred marshes, distant foothills—a golden blur of water, land, and sky.

Snowy and great egrets at the wildlife refuge, near Dumbarton Bridge

Wetlands

Roughly two-thirds of the refuge consists of reclaimed or working salt ponds. With levees breached and tidal action restored, retired salt ponds make excellent wildlife habitat, rich in the brine shrimp favored by the American avocet, the black-necked stilt, and many other shorebirds. Some ponds are still used to produce salt. Aside from the salt ponds, the refuge incorporates 2,500 acres of freshwater wetlands along riparian corridors, 182 acres of natural tidal salt marsh, and almost 400 acres of mud flats and open water. At low tide, the mud flats can extend bayward for miles. Several wetlands and uplands add to the refuge's diverse habitat.

Alviso Education Center

Alviso Environmental Education Center

The refuge's Environmental Education Center in Alviso is open to the public Saturdays and Sundays, 10 a.m. to 5 p.m., irregularly on weekdays. Call first. The gate is closed when the center is closed.

Coyote Creek

In 1986 tidal action was restored to 260 acres of former marshland along this section of the Bay Trail. An observation platform juts out over the marsh and offers excellent views of feeding shorebirds. On hot days it's good to know that the north parking area of Coyote Creek is shaded by willows (Fremont Boulevard and Clipper Court in the Bayside Business Park).

Coyote Creek

Mowry Slough

Up to 400 harbor seals haul out on the remote shores of Mowry Slough during the March-through-June pupping season. Mowry Slough is the bay's largest harbor seal haul-out. Harbor seals need dry ground to rest, warm up, give birth, and nurse. Mothers sometimes stay out of the water 23 hours a day so their pups can suckle at will. To protect these highly sensitive pinnipeds, Mowry is strictly off-limits to visitors. For the public, a more accessible place to get a distant view of these spotted marine mammals is in Marin County, at the Corte Madera State Ecological Reserve. Other bay haul-out spots include Guadalupe Slough, Greco Island, Yerba Buena Island, and Castro Rocks, under the Richmond Bridge.

DRAWBRIDGE—A GHOST TOWN

Out in the mists and bogs of the refuge stands the ghost of a town where "you wouldn't go if you weren't a different breed of cat," as one old resident put it. Drawbridge got its start on Station Island when the South Pacific Coast Railway built two hand-operated drawbridges and a cabin there in 1876.

Abundant waterfowl attracted trainloads of hunters, some of whom put up cabins on stilts along the railroad tracks. By 1906, Drawbridge had 79 buildings, two hotels, and a house made of a 50-passenger Matson Line lifeboat. Besides stalking mallard and pintail in the marsh, residents and visitors enjoyed swimming, fishing, boating, and "high tide parties" when the water level allowed revelers to dock at one another's back porch.

Drawbridge began to decline in 1936 because of over-hunting, freshwater depletion, and sewage contamination from nearby cities. It wasn't until 1979, however, that the last "different breed of cat" left Drawbridge. Today, access is strictly limited to ranger-led summer tours.

Historic Drawbridge

Newark Slough from south end of Coyote Hills

Newark Slough

Newark Slough curves around hills and meanders through the refuge's reclaimed salt ponds until it reaches the bay. The head of the slough has been an important local access point to the bay since the early 1800s, first as the main embarcadero for Mission San Jose, later as a landing for the growing port community of Newark. Today it serves as a launch ramp for canoes and kayaks near the junction of Marshlands and Thornton roads. Paddling through the refuge is a wonderful way to see marsh animals up close without disturbing them or getting your feet wet.

INFORMATION

Alviso Environmental Education Center
408-262-5513

Mountain View Shoreline Office/Rengstorff
415-903-6392
Amphitheater: 415-967-4004
Golf Course: 415-969-7100
Sailing Lake: 415-965-7474

Newark Recreation Department
510-745-1124

Palo Alto Baylands Interpretive Center
415-329-2506

Ravenswood Open Space Preserve & Midpeninsula Regional Open Space District
415-691-1200

San Francisco Bay National Wildlife Refuge Visitor Center & Headquarters
510-792-0222
The refuge publishes a quarterly calendar of events and newsletter called *Tideline*. A $2 donation will secure a year's subscription.

San Francisco Bird Observatory
408-946-6548

Sunnyvale Baylands Park
408-730-7709

Sportsfield Park

Near the Newark shoreline, adjacent to some salt ponds, Sportsfield now includes one lighted baseball field and three soccer fields. The city of Newark hopes to complete expansion of the park to 27 acres soon, laying in additional baseball and soccer fields, as well as a community center for indoor activities.

Sportsfield Park

Getting Around

At the Sunnyvale Water Pollution Control Plant, a dirt levee trail of about 4 miles extends between the wastewater treatment ponds and wide marshes. No levee connection to Sunnyvale Baylands Park exists, nor is there a pedestrian link to Alviso. Hwy 237 is the only link so far. From Alviso, a dirt levee trail, approximately 8 miles long, leads into the San Francisco Bay National Wildlife Refuge. A similar 3.5-mile trail leaves the refuge's environmental education center off Grand Blvd.

To reach the Bay Trail at Coyote Creek (2 miles of dirt levee) use streets to the parking areas just off Fremont Blvd. Use streets to reach Cherry St to the northwest where the Bay Trail route, paved, continues on Cherry, past Sportsfield Park, to Thornton Ave. Go left on Thornton toward the San Francisco Bay National Wildlife Refuge Headquarters and Visitor Center.

Legend

- **Bay Trail**
- **Proposed Bay Trail** (now used by public)
- **Proposed Bay Trail** (not accessible)
- **Other Trails**
- **BART Line**
- ⚓ **Boating/Marina**
- Ⓟ **Parking**
- 🐟 **Fishing Pier**

Hayward Landing

Hayward Area Rec District

W Winton

Ⓟ

Hayward Municipal Airport

W Winton

Longwood

Winton

Lincoln

Johnson's Landing

Hayward Regional Shoreline

National

Middle Greenwood Park

Santa Clara

Hwy 92

McCone

West

Hayward Shoreline Marsh

Cabot

Depot

Mohr

Chabot College

San Mateo Bridge

Hayward Sewage Disposal Plant

Enterprise

Clawiter

Industrial

Rancho Arroyo Park

Cathy Wy

Eden Greenway

Catalpa

Ⓟ

Breakwater

Whitesell

Eden Landing

Corporate

Sleepy Hollow

Hwy 92

Investment

Tennyson

Mt Eden Park

Hayward Shoreline Interpretive Center

Eden Landing

Arden

Arf Baumberg

Christian Penke Park

Salt Ponds

Hesperian Blvd

Industrial Pkwy

Industrial Pkwy

Mission

Hwy 880

Union City Blvd

Whipple

Whipple

Alameda Creek

Alvarado

Salt Ponds

Alameda Creek

Benson

Alvarado Wastewater Treatment Plant

Smith

Horner

Alvarado

Union City

Whipple

Central

Alameda Creek Regional Trail

Dyer

Alvarado

Hwy 880

Alvarado-Niles

Slough

Union City Blvd

Ⓟ

Northgate Community Park

Milton

Paseo Padre Pkwy

Patterson

Red Hill Top 300ft

Bayview Trail

Alameda Creek

Paseo Padre Pkwy

Fremont

Shoreline Trail

Ideal Marsh Trail

Coyote Hills Regional Park

Ⓟ

DUST Marsh

 Ⓟ Visitor Center

Patterson Ranch

Ardenwood

Ardenwood Historic Farm

Tupelo Ter

Ⓟ

Lakeshore Park

Hwy 880

SAN FRANCISCO BAY

San Francisco Bay National Wildlife Refuge

Apay Way Trail

Kaiser

Paseo Padre Pkwy

Dumbarton Cir

Hwy 84

Newark Community Park & Center

Newark

Salt Pond

Toll Plaza

Marshlands

Quarry Trail

Tidelands Loop Trail

Mirabeau Park

Blacow

Hwy 84

Refuge Headquarters & Visitor Center

Jarvis

Bridgepointe Park

Mayhews Landing

Civic Center Park

Central

Dumbarton Bridge

Dumbarton Pier

Ⓟ

Marshlands

Newark Slough

Salt Pond

Newark Slough Trail

Thornton

Bridgepointe

Spruce

Thornton

Cedar

Birch Grove Park

Enterprise

Wells

Willow

Locust

Enterprise

Sycamore

Ash St Park

Robertson

Cherry

Birch

N

0   .5 mile   1 mile
0   1 km

SAN FRANCISCO BAY NATIONAL WILDLIFE REFUGE TO COYOTE HILLS REGIONAL PARK

This stretch of bayshore offers lessons in human history, natural history, and history in the making. Two centuries ago the Ohlone people maintained large encampments here. You can learn about them, and about the region's plants and wildlife, at the visitor centers of the San Francisco Bay National Wildlife Refuge and Coyote Hills Regional Park. On the northern end of Coyote Hills Park, scientists have designed an artificial marsh fed by stormwater runoff. They are testing its ability to clean this runoff.

Multi-hued Cargill Salt ponds within San Francisco Bay National Wildlife Refuge; Newark and Fremont are to the right.

San Francisco Bay National Wildlife Refuge Visitor Center

The visitor center sits high above the marsh on one of two small hills near Fremont. (To reach Dumbarton Pier, continue on the access road past the center, toward the bay.) The 1.3-mile Tidelands Loop Trail leads from the center to Newark Slough, winding through uplands covered with sweet-smelling sage and fennel, habitat for sparrows, ground squirrels, cottontail rabbits, and gray foxes. The Newark Slough Trail branches off the Tidelands Trail, on the opposite side of the slough, and circles around salt ponds for some 5 miles. Visitor center exhibits describe salt-tolerant plants, endangered species, and bayshore habitats. There is a videotape on local seasons. You are invited to open doors, lift flaps, or push buttons to learn more about your surroundings. Natural history items are for sale. You can reach the slough by boat from a small ramp nearby, at Marshlands and Thornton roads.

Visitor center headquarters, looking north

Birdwatching

Take any trail from the visitor center into the refuge and you'll see many different birds. Don't just watch, however; listen. By tuning into their peeps, cracks, chirps, and warbles, you can tune out the roar of traffic from nearby Dumbarton Bridge. The center publishes checklists of birds, butterflies, mammals, reptiles, and endangered species of the region. A "blind" bench at the edge of the marsh near the center allows you to get most of your body out of the birds' sight. Bring binoculars!

CLAPPER RAIL & RED FOX

In the early morning or evening, you might hear the endangered California clapper rail. Its sound resembles that of hands clapping. Although these rails are very secretive, you can sometimes glimpse one at high tide, when they retreat to higher, more exposed, habitat. Your chances are best during a daytime high tide between November and January.

The California clapper rail walks like a chicken (and kind of looks

California clapper rail

like one), prefers to swim rather than fly across water, and builds its nest in cordgrass. The nest rises and falls with the tide, but the grass keeps it from floating away. This brown bird is one of three endangered bird species living along the bayshore. The others are the peregrine falcon and the California least tern.

Tens of thousands of clapper rails populated the bay's shore in the 19th century. During the Gold Rush era, they were a popular menu item in San Francisco restaurants. By 1975, however, after decades of hunting, loss of habitat, and bay contamination by mercury and selenium, only an estimated 4,000 were counted; by 1991, only some 500. Extinction seemed likely.

Aside from habitat destruction, one of the greatest threats to the rail's survival is the red fox, native of the East Coast, which was introduced to the West to be hunted and raised in captivity for its fur. Some foxes escaped or were released from fox farms in the

Red fox

Sacramento Valley and became established along the coast and San Francisco Bay. Unlike the native gray fox, which prefers uplands and dry regions, the introduced red fox prospers in marshland and can swim. It kills clapper rails, California least terns, and other birds, and eats their eggs. In 1986 the red fox population exploded throughout the marshes of the south bay. Recently, the U.S. Fish and Wildlife Service began to trap foxes in the wildlife refuge and other trouble spots. Where this predator was removed, clapper rail populations rebounded.

SALT MARSH HARVEST MOUSE

The salt marsh harvest mouse, an endangered species, lives only in dense pickleweed on San Francisco Bay. It does not burrow, like other mice, but builds nests of dry grasses and sedge on the marsh surface and sometimes in abandoned swallows' nests. If you part the pickleweed, you may see a network of passages, but you are highly unlikely to see the mice that made them. Only during the highest tides do they emerge from cover, to swim to higher ground and find shelter among Australian salt bushes, fat hens, and other unsubmerged salt-tolerant plants. Biologists make mouse counts at such times.

Its unique physiology allows this little mouse (about three inches long) to survive on plants with a very high salt content. Biologist Howard S. Shellhammer, who has spent more than 30 years studying the salt marsh harvest mouse, says it appears to eat pickleweed. But because it is endangered, it may not be captured for studies that could show what else it eats. It has big brown eyes and fur that ranges from blackish

brown to cinnamon on the back, with a tawny stripe, and a cinnamon-to-white belly. Its scientific name is *Reithrodontomys raviventris.*

COMMON TULE

Common tule, sometimes called bulrush, is an abundant plant in brackish and freshwater marshes. There are nine species of tule in coastal California, 17 in the state. The round stems of common tule can shoot up 15 feet, and produce pale-brown to reddish flower clusters. For the Ohlone, tule had many uses. Now scientists have found yet another: tule removes metals (copper, zinc, lead) from marsh waters and retains them in its root systems, making marsh habitats safer for both wildlife and humans.

Common tule

Ardenwood Historic Farm

More than a hundred years ago, George Patterson turned 3,000 acres of shoreline grasslands and marshes into one of Alameda County's most prosperous farms: Ardenwood. The heart of Patterson's farm remains in operation today as part of a 205-acre historic East Bay Regional Park west of Fremont. Visitors can participate in turn-of-the-century farming activities, take a wagon ride, wander around orchards and wooden barns, and meet chickens, goats, sheep, Belgian draft horses, and other farm animals (fee). The Deer Park picnic area can be reserved by groups. The entire park is closed December through March.

Monarch butterfly

Eucalyptus Forest

Patterson started to plant eucalyptus in the 1880s, when many California farmers were experimenting with growing these Australian natives for lumber, ship masts, and railroad ties. Unfortunately, the wood proved impossible to cut, plane, or work. Patterson's 35-acre grove now provides an excellent windbreak, an overwintering site for Monarch butterflies (November through February), and a forest of fragrant silver-green alleys.

Wagon ride at Ardenwood Farm

House & Grounds

The Park District recently restored the Patterson two-story home, a classic example of Queen Anne architecture with steep roofs, a corner turret, and 15 rooms. Outside, every window, wall, and corner is adorned with carved wood, stained glass, or scalloped shingles. Inside, every piece of furniture, scrap of rug, and strip

Patterson House

of wallpaper harks back to the Victorian era. Formal grounds surround the house with lawns, flowers, a gazebo, and a fountain. Tours available, but limited; first come, first served.

> *"Time was when education moved toward soil, not away from it."*
> Aldo Leopold, 1949

Ardenwood Farm

Farm

Ardenwood uses the farming and food processing methods characteristic of an East Bay farm between 1890 and 1920. Horses draw ploughs over fields, a blacksmith mends tools in a forge, a cook churns butter, cans fruit, and flips corncakes over a wood-burning stove. Park staff—and visitors who sign up—farm 30 acres; other lands are leased to a local organic farmer.

THE PATTERSONS, A FARMING FAMILY

George Patterson went into farming in 1851, after prospecting for gold along the American River. He worked his way up from field hand at Mission San Jose to owner of 6,000 acres in scattered locations around the bay. After his death in 1895, Patterson's wife, Clara, took over. She not only kept the lands productive, she also championed women's rights. Her sons and grandchildren continued farming the land until 1970.

George Patterson

Clara Patterson

Coyote Hills Regional Park

Ohlone legends describe the bay as a giant coyote paw print. The Ohlone lived along the East Bay shore for at least 4,000 years and considered themselves neighbors to coyotes, and all other creatures. In the area of today's 1,064-acre Coyote Hills Regional Park—with salt water on the bay side and tule marshes, creeks, and grasslands on the inland side—lay the bounty that sustained humans and others for some 22 centuries. The reconstructed Ohlone village here provides a tangible link to the bay's past. Trails invite exploration of the park's varied landscape.

Coyote Hills Regional Park

Ohlone Village

Built on the shell mound is an outdoor architectural museum of traditional village structures. The Ohlone cut willows along creeks, bent them into frames, then wove long spongy strands of tule or cattail through the willow branches to build domed dwellings. These kept out wind and rain, and lasted for several years. Reconstructed here are a tule hut, a sweat house, a shaded arbor for cooking and chores, a dance circle, and a pit house.

Reconstructed village

Marshes

West of Coyote Hills lie salt marshes and diked salt ponds swept by bay breezes. Most of this wetland is part of the San Francisco Bay National Wildlife Refuge. To the east, freshwater marshes and seasonal wetlands are sheltered from the wind, and from the rumblings of the Dumbarton Bridge. At the turn of the century, high tide reached far inland, turning the hills into islands and flushing marshes with salt water. The wetland mixture seen today is a result of dike building, duck pond construction, farming, flood control projects, and park development.

In the freshwater marshes the tules and cattails grow tall and thick, turning from green to gold with the seasons. A summer stroll along the boardwalk is like a walk through a sweet-smelling, rustling, fertile wheat field. The boardwalk also traverses quiet ponds where waterfowl and other birds abound, especially during fall and spring migrations. Other wildlife includes muskrats that eat plants and underwater roots, helping keep the marsh clear of debris.

Cattails

> *"I believe a leaf of grass is no less than the journeywork of the stars."*
> Walt Whitman, 1855

Shell Mounds

A 1910 survey found more than 400 mounds of debris from indigenous settlements around the bay. Today, very few remain. Shell mounds contained bones, beads, shells, broken tools, and blackened rock from fire pits. One of the few shell mounds the public can visit in the Bay Area is at Coyote Hills. To do so, you must join a naturalist-led tour. (Call ahead for reservations.)

DUST Marsh

In a 55-acre artificial freshwater marsh in the northeast corner of the park, the natural ability of wetlands to remove waterborne pollutants is being put to the test. Since 1983 this DUST (Demonstration Urban Stormwater Treatment) Marsh, a joint effort of the Association of Bay Area Governments and the East Bay Regional Park District, has been receiving the urban runoff (residential and commercial) from a 4.6-square-mile area of Fremont. Most urban runoff enters the bay without any processing. Such runoff and illegal industrial dumping are the biggest pollution sources on the bay, sending up to 31,000 metric tons of heavy metals, hydrocarbons, PCBs, and other contaminants into the aquatic environment each year. Federal law

DUST Marsh

requires that steps be taken to stop this form of pollution.

Many marsh plants and organisms are highly efficient at removing organic waste and toxins from water, by either storing these substances in their root systems (thereby keeping them out of the food cycle) or transforming them into less toxic components. Heavy metals bond with clay in a marsh and fall to

the bottom. Hydrocarbons tend to float to the water's surface, where they are stirred up by winds and can more readily be broken down by bacteria and absorbed by plants. Therefore, marshes have been used in sewage treatment for some time, in some cases to the benefit of wildlife. The DUST Marsh, however, is California's first experiment with urban stormwater runoff. Studies that have tracked toxins through this marsh indicate that the quality of urban runoff can be vastly improved before it is released into the bay. This project has proved so successful that Alameda County has decided to expand the DUST Marsh by 40 percent. A similar marsh is to be built on the southern edge of the park, and yet another about 5 miles to the north, near Alvarado.

> *"Civilization began around wetlands; today's civilization has every reason to leave them wet and wild."*
>
> Edward Maltby, 1986

Grasslands

Along the park's eastern perimeter, grasslands provide habitat for mule deer, black-tail jackrabbits, snakes, meadowlarks, and other wildlife. These are some of the fallow fields of a former 3,000-acre shoreline ranch owned by the Patterson family, whose home further inland is now a historic park. Willow trees meander across the grassland, marking the paths of streams and underground water.

Coyote's Red Hill

Coyote Hills

The Coyote Hills are stragglers of a well-worn north-south mountain range older than the East Bay hills. Other stragglers appear northward at Albany Point and Point Richmond. After making the steep climb to the summit of Coyote's Red Hill, you will come upon outcrops of chert pushed up from the ocean floor. From these rocky stacks, rusty-red with iron and silver-green with lichen, you can view the shallows of the bay, a tapestry of inland marshes, and the cities of Newark and Fremont to the east.

When California was part of Mexico, this entire area was a large land grant called Potrero de los Cerritos (Pasture of the Little Hills). On the slopes below, fragrant sage and fennel grow among the grasses. Halfway down, in the forested cleft known as Hoot Hollow, great horned owls nest. Glider Hill is a favorite with local remote-control glider enthusiasts.

Mule deer

OHLONE LIFE

Over 2,000 years ago, there were four villages at the foot of today's Coyote Hills. The Tuibun, a community of the Ohlone people, collected mussels and oysters along the shore and fished for salmon in Alameda Creek. They wove dwellings, blankets, and baskets (some, made of sedge, held water and were used for cooking).

A recently built balsa

The men hunted while women collected firewood, seeds, and berries in the fields and hills, and mashed acorns into the mush that was the staple of every meal. The Ohlone were great storytellers and singers, and knew themselves as interdependent with all other creatures and the land. In the late 1700s they welcomed Europeans as guests in their land. The Europeans, however, did not see themselves as guests. They forcibly relocated many of the Ohlone to Mission San Jose.

Ohlone basket

Coyote Hills Visitor Center

The center features exhibits on natural history and the Ohlone way of life, including a balsa (canoe) made of bundled tule. Books and postcards are on sale, and educational videotapes can be checked out and viewed on site. Borrow or buy the Muskrat Trail booklet here for a self-guided tour. Old Way workshops teach how the Ohlone lived. (Call to make reservations.)

Getting Around

The Bay Trail route splits leaving the San Francisco Bay National Wildlife Refuge Visitor Center: one branch goes to Coyote Hills Regional Park; the other (proposed) to Ardenwood Regional Preserve. Before leaving the visitor center, explore the 1.3-mile Tidelands Loop Trail. There are benches and trailside exhibits along the way as the loop moves through upland areas, salt marshes, and salt ponds. Tidelands Trail connects to the Newark Slough Trail, a 5-mile trail that loops around the salt ponds. You will be surrounded by American avocets, black-necked stilts, and Forster's terns. Allow several hours for this walk. If time is a factor, you can visit some restored salt ponds and see an abundance of bird life by taking the 1-mile Avocet Marsh Trail. You can pick this up about 0.25 mile beyond the entrance of the refuge on Marshlands Rd. It starts at the bridge head and goes about

At the Hayward Marsh

a mile before returning to Marshlands Rd.

To reach Ardenwood, use streets. For Coyote Hills, the Bay Trail leaves the refuge visitor center on Quarry Trail (paved and dirt), over Hwy 84 on a bridge, then into the park for approximately 3 miles along the edge of Coyote

Hills' southwest slope, reaching the Alameda Creek Trail (Quarry Trail quickly becomes Apay Way Trail on the north side of Hwy 84, then Bayview Trail after about 1 mile). Several miles later, it continues east on the Alameda Creek Trail for 1.5 miles until Union City Blvd.

ALAMEDA CREEK TO HAYWARD REGIONAL SHORELINE

This 8-mile stretch of shore begins and ends at parks managed by the East Bay Regional Park District. In between, acres of salt ponds and wetlands fringe the southeast bay. If you want to see broad mud flats, this is the place. From the Hayward Regional Shoreline Interpretive Center, about 7.5 miles of well-maintained unpaved trail provide for fine continuous hiking and biking. As you follow the levee trail and view the skylines of San Francisco and Oakland framed by the Hayward Hills to the east and the San Mateo Bridge to the southwest, you can envision what this landscape once looked like, and see what it is becoming.

Hayward shoreline, looking south, with restored marshes at lower right, salt ponds upper left, and Route 92 approaching San Mateo Bridge

Alameda Creek Regional Trail

The 12-mile multi-use Alameda Creek Trail runs from the foothills to the bayshore along Alameda Creek, connecting Vallejo Mill Historic Park with Coyote Hills Regional Park. Along the way you'll find picnic sites and fishing ponds at Niles Community Park and Alameda Creek Quarries Regional Recreation Area.

Alameda Creek once meandered between lush greenery that shaded salmon spawning grounds. In the 1840s, Kit Carson trapped beaver along its banks. A branch of the creek still enters the bay along its historic course, but most of its flow has been diverted to a concrete flood control channel banked by high levees 2 miles to the south. You can hike on either side of the channelized creek. The north levee accommodates horseback riders, the south levee is paved for cyclists. There are numerous access points to this trail.

Between 1910 and 1915 the area around Niles Boulevard and the old train station (end of I Street) was a pre-Hollywood movie production site. It was here that Bronco Billy (Gilbert) Anderson became the first cowboy star of the silver screen. He starred in some 150 pictures shot here, and his movie studio produced a total of 450 pictures in or near Niles. Some Charlie Chaplin films, including *The Tramp*, were also filmed here. The first Saturday in June, Niles celebrates Charlie Chaplin Day with non-stop Chaplin films (and a few of Bronco Billy) and displays of memorabilia.

ALVARADO WASTEWATER TREATMENT PLANT

One of the most advanced—and best smelling—wastewater treatment plants in the Bay Area stands on Alameda Creek, just outside of Alvarado. It has the capacity for tertiary treatment of 35 million gallons of wastewater daily and supplies some 5 million gallons of that treated water to the freshwater and brackish marshes in the southern part of the Hayward Regional Shoreline. The rest is released into a deep-water channel mid-bay off the San Lorenzo shoreline. Alvarado is the only plant in the Bay Area that uses air scrubbers to remove the "rotten egg" smell from the fumes created by the treatment process.

Alameda Creek Regional Trail

Southern Hayward Shoreline

The 1,800-acre Hayward Shoreline Park provides habitat for hundreds of species of birds and other wildlife, including the endangered salt marsh harvest mouse. At first glance, this shoreline looks like many other stretches of marshy waterfront. Wet fields of nubby pickleweed and lush cordgrass extend out to the bay, divided by straight levees and snaky sloughs. Egrets fish the shallow waters, sandpipers forage across mud flats, waves crash on the breakwater, and

Fishing on the Hayward Shoreline

northwesterly breezes build into gales across miles of open water and marsh.

Upon closer inspection of one sector of the freshwater marsh north of the Hayward Regional Shoreline Interpretive Center, however, you'll find that water flows in not from a creek, but from a municipal pipe. The sweeping tides enter the marsh through tiny gates, and the channels look a little too straight to be natural. This wetland has been engineered by humans, first by creators of the early salt ponds, more recently by marsh restoration experts. Between 1980 and 1991, 600 acres were transformed from fallow salt ponds into freshwater, brackish, and saltwater marshes.

Hayward Regional Shoreline Interpretive Center

The wooden building on stilts sitting above the marsh just north of the San Mateo Bridge is the Hayward Regional Shoreline Interpretive Center. It offers an introduction to the local environment and is a good place to begin your visit. You will find interactive exhibits on local wildlife and wetlands, weekend visitor programs, a large map of the area, and a gift shop. There is a Habitat Room where you can examine marsh plants and animals under a microscope.

JOHNSON'S LANDING

Poking out of the water northeast of the interpretive center are the remains of a landing built in the 1850s by John Johnson and once used to ferry passengers, fruit, vegetables, and grain to San Francisco. Johnson was the first commercial salt farmer on the bay. He built levees around 14 acres of salt marsh. The landing was the linchpin of his property, which also included a hotel popular with sportsmen. Many a guest enjoyed a hunt on the marsh, followed by an evening by the hotel fire listening to Johnson's tales of whale hunting, pirates, and his near-fatal tangle with a local grizzly bear.

Johnson's Landing

Northern Shoreline

The northern reaches of the park, between Sulphur and San Lorenzo creeks, include extensive pickleweed marshes, seasonal wetlands, and acres of mud flats teeming with wading birds. Old pilings stand out against the water. Access is easiest from West Winton and Grant avenues. The West Winton trail passes a retired land-fill. The Grant Avenue route skirts the Oro Loma Wastewater Treatment Plant.

Avocets and stilts

ORO LOMA WASTEWATER TREATMENT PLANT

The Oro Loma plant, on the bayshore alongside Bockman Channel, provides secondary treatment for about 11.5 million gallons of sewage daily. A small percentage of the treated water irrigates nearby Skywest Golf Course; the rest is transported into the bay. To the south and inland about a mile is the Hayward Sewage Disposal Plant, providing secondary treatment for some 12 million gallons a day.

MAKING SALT ON THE BAY

Bright pink may seem a strange color for bay water, but the striking hues of salt pond algae are familiar to airline passengers above the south bay. Making salt via solar evaporation requires shallow salty water, lots of sun and wind, little rain, and flat impermeable soil. Since the bay's shore has all these, plus a major market, local entrepreneurs have been harvesting salt on the bayshore since the 1850s. By 1880, dozens of family-owned salt companies were working the shoreline, especially from San Leandro south toward Alvarado (by Union City). Earlier, Native Americans, Spaniards, and Mexicans collected naturally occurring salt deposits along the bay's edge.

For Cargill Co. (formerly Leslie Salt), owner of 32,000 acres of salt ponds (15 percent of the bay's total surface area), today's salt business begins in summer when freshwater flows from north bay rivers are low and the bay is at its saltiest. At

Salt crystals, magnified

this time, Cargill opens the gates to its concentrating ponds (200–800 acres each) to let in bay waters, and depends on the sun to do the rest of the work. In the next five years, the water goes through ten stages of evaporation—moving through different ponds (and changing colors with algae growth) until the concentrated brine turns to "pickle."

In spring of the fifth year, the pickle is pumped into clean, 20- to 60-acre crystallization ponds where tiny crystals of pure salt begin to grow. By fall, the salt is ready for harvest, yielding about a ton of salt for every 10,000 gallons of captured bay water. Free tours of salt facilities and collection methods are available the first or second Saturday of each October. (Cargill Salt is at 7200 Central Avenue, Newark. Call for date.)

Cargill Salt plant, salt mountains, and salt ponds

California horn snail

CALIFORNIA HORN SNAIL

This snail, one of the few native species of invertebrates left in the south bay, lives in salt pans that only fill with water at high tide. It is adapted to withstand high temperatures and strong salinity. When waters retreat, the horn snail draws its foot into its convoluted shell, pulls up its operculum (a kind of shell door), and waits for the next high tide.

Getting Around

From the Alameda Creek Trail, use streets to reach the Hayward Regional Shoreline. You can park at three sites: (1) Hayward Shoreline Interpretive Center on Breakwater Ave; (2) near park office on W. Winton Ave; (3) end of Grant Ave. From the interpretive center the Bay Trail follows a dirt levee for approximately 4.5 miles to the regional shoreline's northern limit at San Lorenzo Creek. From this point an unmaintained trail leads to a paved trail at the San Leandro Marina. The entire stretch from the interpretive center to the marina is about 7 miles.

I N F O R M A T I O N

Ardenwood Regional Park
510-796-0663
    House tours
    510-791-4196
    Deer Park Picnic Reservations
    510-462-1400

Cargill Salt
510-790-8194

Coyote Hills Regional Park
Visitor Center
510-795-9385

East Bay Regional Park District
510-562-7275
The monthly *Log* lists all events at district parks. Call to subscribe.

Hayward Shoreline
Interpretive Center
510-881-6751

San Francisco Bay
National Wildlife Refuge
Visitor Center & Headquarters
510-792-0222

The San Francisco Bay Area has many distinctive native plants that grow nowhere else. You will see many of these, as well as plants that have arrived from elsewhere, as you take trails around the bay. Twelve of the most common are pictured here; ten of them are natives. Plants grow in groups called communities. All the members of a given community can tolerate a particular set of physical conditions. Some thrive in the salt and wet of a salt marsh, others in the salt, wind, and sand of a coastal beach strand or the hot dry windy areas where chaparral occurs. It is easy to learn the most common plants and their communities as you travel around the bay.

Coastal salt marshes occur where tidal waters meet the land. Plants growing here, called *halophytes*, have adapted to wet and salty soils.

Seasonal wetlands, although not tidal, usually have ponded rainwater in winter and spring. The varying degree of saltiness in these ponds limits the plant species that can grow in this habitat.

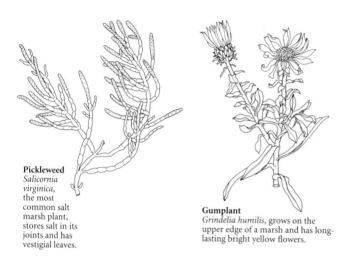

Pickleweed
Salicornia virginica, the most common salt marsh plant, stores salt in its joints and has vestigial leaves.

Gumplant
Grindelia humilis, grows on the upper edge of a marsh and has long-lasting bright yellow flowers.

Saltbush
Atriplex spp., with several representatives growing in wetlands, is in the goosefoot family. This family is also well represented in the desert.

Coastal strand is the first terrestrial plant community above the high tide line. Plants here respond to loose shifting sand, sometimes piled into dunes, by developing deep roots and a sprawling growth form.

Coastal scrub, dominated by a maritime climate, is characterized by low shrubs intermixed with grassy meadows. Coyote brush is the most common plant.

Bush lupine
Lupinus arboreus, a shrubby lupine, blooms profusely in spring with yellow or purple flowers.

Coyote brush
Baccharis pilularis var. consanguinea, blooms in winter on separate male and female plants.

French broom
Cytisus monspessulanis, though pretty in spring with its bright yellow flowers, is a **nonnative weedy species** that eliminates native plants by its aggressive growth.

Oak woodlands are seen by many as the most typical Bay Area landscape. Three species of oak are most common here: coast live, interior, and canyon live oaks. Grassland grows between trees in oak woodlands.

Mixed evergreen forests grow only where coastal fog occurs in summer months. Here, hardwood trees such as tanoak, California bay, and bigleaf maple grow together with redwood, Douglas fir, and other conifers.

Coast live oak
Quercus agrifolia, is a handsome feature on the San Francisco landscape and supports a great deal of wildlife: insects, birds, squirrels, and deer.

California bay
Umbellularia californica, is a common tree in Bay Area forests. Its fragrant leaves are used in cooking.

Madrone
Arbutus menziesii, is a medium-sized tree with smooth, reddish bark, evergreen leaves, and clusters of urn-shaped flowers that mature into orange-red fruit.

Chaparral, one of the most characteristic of California plant communities, occurs mostly on south-facing slopes that are dry in summer. It is made up of hard, thick- and small-leafed evergreen shrubs that are dense and often impenetrable.

Grasslands often occur where the ground has been disturbed or overgrazed, or near outcrops of toxic soil derived from rocks such as the greenish serpentine. Most of the grasses are nonnative annuals that came from Europe with cattle in California's early years.

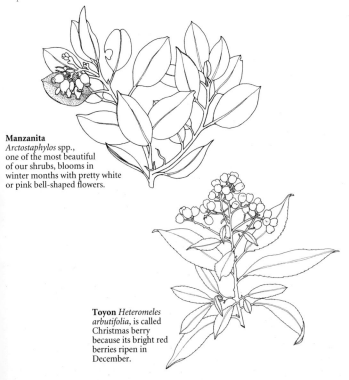

Manzanita
Arctostaphylos spp., one of the most beautiful of our shrubs, blooms in winter months with pretty white or pink bell-shaped flowers.

Toyon *Heteromeles arbutifolia*, is called Christmas berry because its bright red berries ripen in December.

Rattlesnake grass
Briza minor, is a **nonnative weedy species** of grass that has spread rapidly during the past twenty years. Its flower looks like the tail of a rattlesnake. It also rustles when dry.

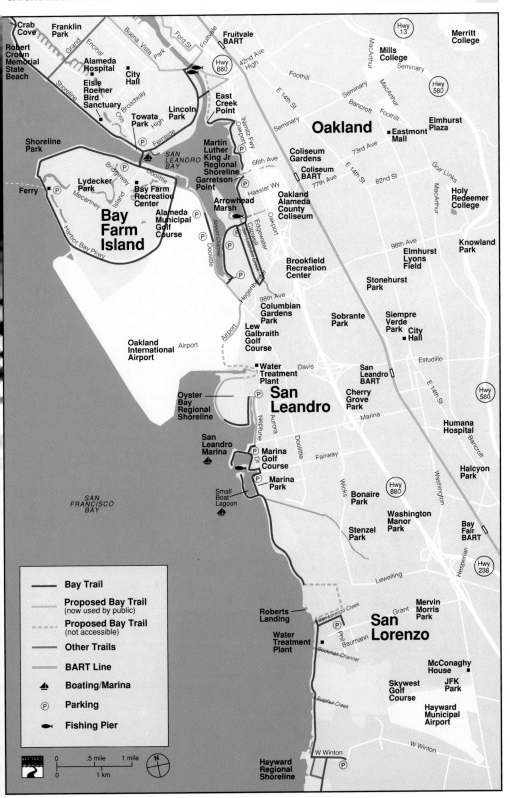

Bay Trail

Proposed Bay Trail
(now used by public)

Proposed Bay Trail
(not accessible)

Other Trails

BART Line

⛵ **Boating/Marina**

Ⓟ **Parking**

🐟 **Fishing Pier**

MARINA PARK TO BAY FARM ISLAND

Moving north from the wildlife refuge and extended parklands of the south bay, the shoreline becomes increasingly sinuous, urbanized, and wonderfully complex. Here, between distinct neighborhoods, restaurants, corner stores, and the Oakland Airport, the bayshore is shaped by parks, piers, and sheltered embayments.

BAY SCOW SCHOONER
During the 19th century, hundreds of two-masted scow schooners plied the bay and delta, hauling food and supplies. These solid working boats, built with heavy timbers, were flat-bottomed, wide, and capable of sailing with 80 tons of cordwood or 1,000 bales of hay onboard, passing through tule grass and marshes. They were called scows after similarly shaped *schouw* boats of the Netherlands, and schooners because of the type of rigging they used. The crew sometimes consisted of families who both owned and operated the vessel.

Marina Park

Marina Park

San Leandro's Marina Park is one of the tidiest and busiest shoreline parks in the East Bay. Here you will find marinas, waterfront restaurants, picnic tables, and a landscaped lawn area. Two playgrounds offer children a chance to swing, whirl, tumble, balance, and climb. Adults can exercise by taking a turn on the grassy point jutting out from the shore. The point (a breakwater, really) features a 1-mile paved loop, a dirt horse trail, and 18 fitness stations coached by gulls and plump ground squirrels. Dogs must be leashed.

Those interested in a more challenging hike or bicycle ride will find few stretches of the Bay Trail more scenic and extensive than the one between Marina Park and the Hayward Shoreline

Interpretive Center to the south. A 7-mile levee-top trail runs briefly alongside a golf course and past a small building in which wastewater is dechlorinated before discharge into the bay. The trail continues past pickleweed marshes and bird-filled mud flats the rest of the way down the Hayward Shoreline (with a break near Roberts Landing).

To the north of Marina Park, two more miles of trails wind along two breakwaters past the

San Leandro Marina and pier (a favorite of windsurfers), the Spinnaker Yacht Club, and bathrooms labeled "Buoys" and "Gulls." From the middle breakwater (South Dike Road) look for the placard describing the 2-mile "boaters' highway" that sailors must navigate to reach deeper offshore waters. At the tip of the northern breakwater look for "Still On Patrol"—a memorial for the 3,515 men who died on the 52 U.S. submarines lost during World War II.

There is something for everyone in Marina Park.

ROBERTS LANDING

In the late 19th century, the slough at Roberts Landing was important to agricultural shipping. Hay, vegetables, fruit, and other products from local farms were loaded aboard scow schooners that sailed into the slough on high tides. On a subsequent high tide, the schooners returned to San Francisco. Unlike Johnson's or Hayward landings to the south, which were constructed on fill, Roberts Landing, owned by Captain William Roberts, was a natural inlet. What remains of the slough today receives tidal action only during exceptionally high tides. A sandy beach fronts the area, and pickleweed gives way to annual grasses as the land rises slightly away from the shore.

Roberts Landing

From 1900 to 1965, the Trojan Powder Works manufactured explosives on this slough. The factory is gone, except for some concrete foundations, but it has left a legacy: the groundwater has been contaminated by toxic levels of beryllium, antimony, and other elements. Decisions about the possible future of this area await the results of studies.

Oyster Bay Regional Shoreline

Less than a mile north of popular Marina Park is the 157-acre Oyster Bay Regional Shoreline, dedicated in 1980 and scheduled for completion in the next few years. It is little known and hard to find but well worth a visit. At its only entrance, at the end of Neptune Drive, a trail moves south, then slowly climbs the hillside through fields of fennel and mustard. In late spring, so many swallowtails, painted ladies, and California sisters frequent these host plants that you feel as though you are walking through a butterfly tunnel.

The trail continues (for a total of 1 mile) over the hill and along the shoreline. Northern harriers, black-shouldered kites, and red-tail hawks patrol the slopes for mice; snowy egrets and ducks fish in the shallows below. You'll

Oyster Bay trails in spring

also see and hear much bigger birds—jets. There's no better spot than atop this park's summit to watch planes approaching Oakland Airport from the south. Beyond the airport, across the water, San Bruno Mountain rises from the bay's western shore. Also at the top of the park is "Rising Wave," a sculpture by Roger Berry, consisting of 17 ten-foot poles set on end. This entire park is being built on top of a former garbage dump.

Rising Wave sculpture

West Coast painted lady

Effluent passes through filters.

SAN LEANDRO WATER POLLUTION CONTROL PLANT

This secondary treatment plant, directly behind Oyster Bay Regional Shoreline, processes some 4.5 million gallons of sewage daily, using 1,000 pounds of chlorine daily for disinfection. Before the effluent is discharged into the bay, chlorine is removed by adding sulfur dioxide. Across Davis Street from the plant are the San Leandro Public Rifle and Pistol Range and the Davis Street Recycling and Transfer Station.

Bay Farm Island's Shoreline Park

Bay Farm Island (formerly known as Asparagus Island) is actually the northern half of the peninsula shared with the Oakland Airport. The island, on which farmers once grew vegetables and fruit, has been expanded considerably by fill and linked to the mainland. The Harbor Bay Island development, which includes luxury homes and a business park, occupies most of the peninsula's northern tip. The northern waterfront is bordered by the nicely landscaped Shoreline Park. Its well-groomed trails (both paved and dirt) extend for about 2 miles from the Bay Farm Island Bridge halfway around the island to the ferry terminal. All along this shoreline you get a clear view (except for occasional fog) to the northwest, beyond gigantic cargo ships anchored mid-bay, to San Francisco and Mt. Tamalpais.

Shoreline Park

OAKLAND INTERNATIONAL AIRPORT

This 3,000-acre airfield, built mostly on tidelands and marshes, is tacked onto the southern end of Bay Farm Island. When it opened in 1927 as the Oakland Municipal Airport, Colonel Charles Lindbergh was present for the ceremonies, flying the *Spirit of St. Louis*. On May 20, 1937, Amelia Earhart and navigator Fred Noonan lifted off from here on their final voyage. Their plane vanished in the South Pacific one month later. Today the site of the original airport, known as North Field, services general aviation and cargo planes, while the modern passenger terminal, built in 1962, serves some 7 million travelers yearly. More than 800 flights depart weekly for domestic and international destinations. The entire airport complex is operated by the Port of Oakland.

Amelia Earhart

I N F O R M A T I O N

AC Transit
1-800-559-4636

BART
510-465-BART

Harbor Bay Maritime Ferry
510-769-5500

Marina Park:
San Leandro Community Services Department
510-577-3462

Oyster Bay Regional Shoreline:
East Bay Regional Park District
510-562-7275

Shoreline Park:
Alameda Recreation & Park Department
510-748-4565

 ### Getting Around

From Marina Park the Bay Trail route follows streets to Oyster Bay Regional Shoreline. At Oyster Bay, the Bay Trail is paved for 1 mile around the park's southwestern edge. An informal dirt path continues around the shoreline but ends after 0.7 mile. Use streets to reach the Bay Trail route by the Oakland Airport. Farther north, at the corner of Doolittle and

Harbor Bay Pkwy, the Bay Trail route circumnavigates Bay Farm Island for 5 miles on sidewalks, and on paved trails through Shoreline Park. At Bay Farm Island's ferry terminal, you can catch a Harbor Bay Maritime ferry to San Francisco, or step aboard an AC Transit bus with connections to the Fruitvale and Coliseum BART stations.

MARTIN LUTHER KING JR. REGIONAL SHORELINE TO ROBERT CROWN MEMORIAL STATE BEACH

Along some 10 miles of bayfront straddling the border between Oakland and Alameda, the shoreline has so many faces it could take days to explore. But even an hour or two is sufficient to bait a hook and drop a fishing line, run along winding shoreline paths, go birding in a sanctuary, or wriggle your toes into the sands of Alameda.

Arrowhead Marsh looking west

Martin Luther King Jr. Regional Shoreline

(Includes Doolittle Area, Arrowhead Marsh, Creek Junction, Garretson Point, Damon Marsh, and East Creek Point.)

San Leandro Bay bears little resemblance to its historic form. Massive filling and development projects have reduced its 2,000 acres of tidal marsh to 70 since 1900, shifted its southward-draining mouth northwest, and surrounded it with an airport, a freeway, cities, and industry.

And yet the bayshore here remains green and open while offering fishing piers, paved trails, picnic areas, and wildlife habitat. Visitors can relax, stretch out on grass, and survey the skylines of Alameda, Oakland, and San Francisco. Egrets hunt in the shallow bay waters, and cinnamon teals find shelter along the edges of inflowing creeks. The endangered California clapper rail nests in the cordgrass. A two-lane launch for nonmotorized boats is at the south parking lot along Doolittle Drive.

Doolittle Area

San Leandro Bay's grassy western shore has three picnic areas (phone to reserve), a boat launch, and a cafe in an A-frame building with floor-to-ceiling windows overlooking Airport Channel. The cafe is open for breakfast and lunch. A pier at the channel's edge incorporates part of an old wharf at which schooners, clipper ships, and speedboats tied up during the bay's century of waterborne commerce.

Arrowhead Marsh

From above, this 50-acre marsh resembles an arrowhead aimed at the heart of San Leandro Bay. Pickleweed and salt grass grow thick here. A short boardwalk extends over the marsh, and a fishing pier is nearby. If you're very lucky, you might see a California clapper rail flushed by high tide onto the joists of the boardwalk. Upslope are a large lawn, picnic sites, a Whale Garden for children (two fiberglass gray whales swimming in sand), and a wooden structure of wheelchair-accessible ramps and decks featuring informational panels and good bay views. On the lawn below this structure, you can't miss Roger Berry's Duplex Cone, a sculpture indicating the sun's path at summer and winter solstices.

Creek Junction

Bridges at the confluence of the Elmhurst and San Leandro creek culverts inspire musings on the sinuous meanders that must have passed below before man so manipulated the course of these waters. Striped bass can be caught here. A well-equipped exercise station invites you to stretch, and waterfowl rest along the shore.

Whale Garden

Garretson Point

A good place to start a bayshore walk is this point dedicated to Skip Garretson, a reporter whose articles in the *Oakland Tribune* played a major part in the struggle to win protection for San Francisco Bay. From the point, you can take the 1-mile Elmhurst Creek Trail down a strip of shore planted with trees and poppies, and scattered with picnic tables and exercise stations, past Creek Junction to Arrowhead Marsh.

Damon Marsh

North of Garretson Point, the shoreline is fringed with salt grass, pickleweed, and the flotsam and jetsam deposited by currents and tides. When the tide is out, shorebirds frequent the mud flats on this 20-acre marsh. When it's in, you may see brown pelicans, cormorants, and other birds drying their wings on a derelict boat marooned in the mud nearby.

East Creek Point

This former 48-acre business lot became part of the Martin Luther King Jr. Regional Shoreline in 1992. A 1-mile trail from here connects Damon Marsh with East Creek Point. This trail will eventually continue northward to the High Street Bridge.

GULLS

Every bit of bayshore has its gulls—the bullies of the bayshore bird world. You can't miss them soaring overhead, resting on old pier pilings, scavenging around garbage cans, or harassing other birds till they drop their food. Unlike other aquatic birds, gulls can eat in any position—whether flying, swimming, swooping, or walking. At San Leandro Bay, they've developed a taste for mollusks, as evidenced by the purplish shells littering trails. The gulls take mollusks high up into the air, then drop them on the hard pavement to crack their shells. To identify gulls, it's best to concentrate on adult birds because young gulls take two to four years to mature while changing plumage, bill, and leg color almost constantly.

ROGUES' GALLERY OF BAY GULLS

Western gull

This year-round resident is one of the largest gulls on the bay, measuring some 27 inches from bill to tail. You'll see it walking up and down beaches, and in great flocks near garbage dumps. The adult has a white head, yellow eyes, a yellow bill with a red dot on the lower mandible, dark wings with white spots at tips, and pink legs and feet. Some 30,000 western gulls nest on the Farallon Islands, 3,000 more on bay islands and bridges. During the winter season (between October and April) more arrive on the bay from outlying nesting sites.

California gull

Another permanent resident, the California gull looks like a slightly smaller version of the western gull, except that it has dark eyes, the wings are lighter gray, and the legs and feet are greenish. This bird has mastered diverse habitats, including schoolyards. It ranges throughout the interior of the western United States and Canada, nesting on islands in salt, alkaline, and freshwater lakes, such as Mono Lake—180 miles (as the gull flies) due east of this bay—where some 65,000 breeding birds have been recorded. In 1981 this gull began to nest in the south bay as Mono Lake's water levels declined, diverted by Los Angeles, allowing coyotes to reach nesting grounds on Negit Island. The population of California gulls in the south bay has since exploded to some 5,000 breeding birds, and this is now the most common gull on our bay.

Herring gull

To distinguish the herring gull from the California gull, look at the eyes, legs, and feet. The herring gull's eyes are white and its legs and feet are pink. This winter visitor is a scavenger, but it also has a taste for mollusks. It is another dump patron and frequent boat follower. You may see it soaring in circles high above the water or shore, calling loudly. It nests in northern Canada and Alaska.

Glaucous-winged gull

This gull is abundant around harbors and occasionally visits dumps. It is one of the lighter-colored gull species, with light gray wings and dark spots on the wing tips. It has dark eyes, and its legs and feet are pink. It nests along the shoreline of the Pacific Northwest and visits the bay in winter.

Ring-billed gull

The most common small gull on the bay (about 18 inches), this winter visitor has a yellow bill with a complete black ring toward its tip, and yellow legs and feet. It nests in the interior of the western United States.

Heermann's gull

Of all the bay gulls, this one is easiest to identify. The adult has a white head, dark gray body, black tail, red bill, black legs and feet, and a white triangle on its wings. It is common here in winter, but unlike all other visiting gulls, the Heermann's gull nests as far south as Baja California and the Sea of Cortez (April to June).

Mew gull

The name comes from the call, a low mewing. The mew gull is small (16 inches), and a winter visitor from nesting grounds in Alaska and northern Canada. The adult has a white head, short and plain yellow bill, white spots on black wing tips, and yellow legs and feet.

Bonaparte's gull

A very small (about 14 inches), almost tern-like bird, the Bonaparte's gull has a black bill and orange legs and feet. Its head is black in summer, but in winter it is white with conspicuous black dots behind each eye. This bird is rare here in summer, but common near salt ponds in winter. It nests in the Alaskan and Canadian interior.

Towata Park

Although this park consists mostly of parking spaces and a few tables, it is strategically placed (off Otis Drive) as a jumping-off point to explore both Bay Farm Island and the island of Alameda.

Robert Crown Memorial State Beach

Speeding through Oakland on Highway 880, few think to take the Alameda exit. On the west side of this 12-square-mile island, however, is the bay's largest and warmest beach. Along the 2.5-mile-long Robert Crown Memorial State Beach you will find sand, shallow warm water, picnic tables, a paved trail, and a visitor center. You can take to the water or head to Crab Cove, where mud flats and rocky shores invite exploration. At the southeastern end of the beach is the Elsie Roemer bird sanctuary and several observation platforms.

Crab Cove Visitor Center

At the Crab Cove Visitor Center, a 240-gallon saltwater aquarium contains various bay organisms.

Black turban snail

Other exhibits include sea shells from around the world and an old black boot encrusted with barnacles. One interactive display invites you to turn wheels to make a bay food chain, and to explore the differences between Pacific, bay, and shoreline wildlife habitats. Another presents traces of life in the mud: golden jelly-like egg cases and spaghetti-like mud piles produced by burrowing lugworms, along with various shells. The center's classroom is designed to resemble an old wharf.

FRUITVALE BRIDGE PIERS

Piers stick out into the dredged shipping channel here at both ends of the Fruitvale Bridge. Fishermen regularly catch perch and striped bass (some close to 50 pounds) here and also land starry flounder, white croaker, various sharks, skates, bat rays, and other fish.

Leopard shark

Crown Beach

Beach

The beach extends south from Crab Cove, beyond banks of man-made dunes. Take your shoes off and stroll around barefoot. You'll find the sand coarse. This is an artificial beach. The sand was carefully chosen for its heavy, large-grained particles to minimize erosion by wind and water. Between 1982 and 1986, some 200,000 cubic yards of sand were dredged from the bay bottom between Alcatraz and Angel islands—enough sand to fill the Oakland Coliseum—barged to Alameda, and hosed onto the beach. This beach replenishment project, called Operation Sandpour, was a joint effort by the California State Department of Boating and Waterways, the City of Alameda, and the East Bay Regional Parks District. Though sand had been imported to Crown Beach for a century, this was the first time large-grained sand was used. The result has been reduced erosion. Do go for a swim. Summer water temperatures tend to hover around the mid-60s °F here. Showers and changing rooms are available at the beach house.

Sandcastle competition

Crab Cove

Forming a small arc between the beach and a rocky promontory to the northwest, Crab Cove shelters grassy fields and a marine reserve with mud flats and shallow waters. Low tides pull the cove's water back like a bed sheet, exposing a wavy bay bottom. Here on the mud flat, you can peek at golden, single-celled diatoms migrating to the surface to catch the light, ghost shrimp sifting nutrients out of the mud, and pea crabs scurrying from one borrowed burrow to another—places where bat rays and flounder will feed with the rising tide. No collecting or digging is allowed in the reserve. (Note: most crabs are found on rocky shores, not in mud flats.)

Borrow an Adventure Pack from the visitor center for a close look at the mud flat. The pack includes a magnifying glass, bug boxes, and laminated cards that describe mud flat organisms and suggest learning games and activities. Please examine organisms carefully (pick crabs up by the back, not the legs), and return them unharmed to the exact place where you found them. Be sure to return rocks to their orig-

Crab Cove

inal position, as overturned rocks strand many animals, leaving them exposed to drying sun and predatory birds. Naturalist-led tours of the shoreline and mud flats are also available.

The promontory, edged with riprap, marks the northwest side of the cove. This artificial rocky shore provides habitat for crabs, mussels, barnacles, and other intertidal organisms equipped with the shells and suckers necessary to survive the daily deluge of sun and salt water. Inland lies a large lawn

area. There was a saltwater swimming pool here at the turn of the century. It has been filled. Scattered over the grass and under trees are seven major picnic areas. A paved trail meanders between beach and lawn, connecting restrooms, parking, showers, changing rooms, and a small inaccessible brackish-water lagoon.

The city of Alameda has been holding its annual Sand Castle and Sculpture Contest at Crown Beach every June since 1967. Hundreds of people participate, sculpting sand into shapes ranging from elaborate cathedrals to fanciful mermaids.

Wheelchair ramp into tidepool

Wheelchair Ramp

At the end of McKay Avenue, a ramp offers wheelchair access to the water. With the help of a guard rail, wheelchair users can move down to the water's edge, or into the water, for a close view of tide pool creatures. During high summer tides, the central 100-foot section of the ramp is sometimes under 2 or 3 feet of water.

Elsie Roemer Bird Sanctuary

At the southeastern end of Crown Beach, sand yields to cordgrass and beach-combing gives way to birdwatching. This small sanctuary, named for dedicated Alameda birder Elsie Roemer, shelters ducks, egrets, gulls, and wading birds, including the American avocet. In spring during breeding season, you may see the gorgeous peachy hues of

Elsie Roemer Bird Sanctuary

the avocet's head from one of the sanctuary's three observation decks. Even more distinctive is the side-to-side sweeping motion the bird makes through the water with its bill as it feeds.

Washington Park

Washington Park 🛇 ♿

Just inland from Crab Cove, Washington Park offers more lawn and picnic facilities, plus two well-groomed baseball fields, courts for basketball, volleyball, and tennis; also a playground with swings, jungle gyms, sand pits, and a real locomotive.

WORLD WAR II DUTY

A modest granite memorial stands on the Crab Cove lawn, "in memory of graduates of this station who gave their lives in service of country 1941–1945." The "station" refers to the U.S. Maritime Service Officers School. During World War II, this was a place where thousands of officers learned how to run the Liberty Ships built by nearby Kaiser Shipyards. The school served the entire western United States. Its eastern counterpart was in New London, Connecticut. Today's visitor center was the school's infirmary.

CONEY ISLAND OF THE WEST

Between 1879 and 1939, the Alameda shoreline was known as one of the finest beach resort areas in the West. Millions visited its beaches, spas, pools, gardens, and amusement park. California's first professional baseball game was held here, and

Neptune Beach ca. 1920

famous local prizefighters gathered to spar on the sand. For 10 cents you could enter Neptune Beach Amusement Park (opened in 1917) and take a dip in a saltwater pool, sample the world's first "Sno cones" for 5 cents, dare a roller coaster ride on the *Whoopee*, or attend gypsy balls, seances, swimming marathons, and beauty contests. The amusement park went bankrupt in 1939 and was closed. During World War II the site was used by the U.S. Maritime Service Officers School. Eventually, it was reshaped into today's park.

Neptune Beach ca. 1920

Granite memorial

🚶 Getting Around

From Bay Farm Island the Bay Trail route splits. One fork returns south to the Doolittle Area of Martin Luther King Jr. Regional Shoreline. It continues on paved trails through the park until East Creek Point. To reach the Bay Trail route at the High Street Bridge and Fruitvale Bridge, use streets. From the High Street Bridge the Bay Trail follows Fernside Blvd onto Alameda Island and continues to Towata Park and the southwestern tip of Crown Memorial State Beach.

The other fork crosses Bay Farm Island Bridge directly to Towata Park and from there to Crown Memorial Beach. A short section of the Bay Trail goes south from Towata Park, under the bridge, past the Aeolian Yacht Club, and along the shore for 1 mile. At Crown Memorial State Beach the Bay Trail is paved.

INFORMATION

AC Transit
1-800-559-4636

Crab Cove Visitor Center
510-521-6887

Martin Luther King Jr. Regional Shoreline & Robert Crown State Beach: East Bay Regional Park District
510-562-7275
The East Bay Regional Park District's *Log*, a monthly newsletter, lists everything going on at Crown Beach and other district parks. Call to subscribe.

Sand Castle Contest
510-748-4565

Washington Park: Alameda Recreation & Park Department
510-748-4565

You can enjoy sweeping views of the bay and surrounding landscape from peaks and elevated sites listed below. At the same time, you can get a sense of local geology. Before visiting any of these "High Spots" (or on the spot) you might read, or reread, "How Rivers, Mountains, and the Ocean Made the Bay," on p. 2. This will provide a context for reading land contours and rocks. Look for the most common rocks of the Franciscan Complex, the mixed bedrock that underlies the sediments of the bay and surrounding hills. It consists mostly of graywacke (sandstone), serpentine, chert, pillow basalt, and metamorphic rocks.

Sandstone

From Edgewood County Park, in south San Mateo County, you can look out over Redwood City and beyond, to the San Mateo Bridge

and the middle of the bay. Look also at the greenish-gray, soapy-textured rock abundant in this park. It is serpentine, an altered rock from the Earth's mantle, squeezed up during subduction. Serpentine is California's official state rock. It is low in nutrients and high in metals toxic to most vegetation. Yet it supports a large variety of native plants, many of which have evolved at individual sites of serpentine.

Serpentine

You will see serpentine many places, including Mt. Diablo, Mt. Tamalpais, and Ring Mountain. (Ring Mountain and Angel Island are also known for unique metamorphic rocks.)

Ancient volcanic pillow basalts (formed on the ocean floor) can be found in the Marin Headlands, while relatively young (non–

Franciscan) volcanic rocks are dramatically displayed here.

Mt. Tamalpais in Marin County has a bit of every Franciscan rock type, but its sandstone and chert formations are particularly impressive, and easily located along numerous trails and fire roads. Bay and ocean views from the mountain's East Peak are fantastic.

After marveling at San Francisco's skyline from Ayala Vista Point, follow the stairs under the Golden Gate Bridge's northern anchor and move downhill. Watch for the contorted layers of chert exposed by road cuts and erosion. Red-brown

Chert

Franciscan chert can be found throughout Marin County, on San Francisco's Twin Peaks, and down the peninsula east of the Hayward Fault.

HIGH SPOTS

San Francisco
- Telegraph Hill/Coit Tower
- Twin Peaks (910')

North San Mateo County
- San Bruno Mountain (1,314')
- Sweeney Ridge Trail*
  (1,200' at highest point)

South San Mateo County
- Hill One (800'),
  Edgewood County Park
- Windy Hill Open Space
  Preserve*(1,900')

Fremont/Hayward
- Mission Peak (2,517'),
  Mission Peak Regional Preserve*
- Red Hill Top (300'),
  Coyote Hills Regional Park
- Vista (934'), Garin (948'), and
  Tolman (900') peaks, Garin/Dry
  Creek Pioneer regional parks
- Dinosaur Ridge (1,000'), East
  Bay Municipal Utility District*

Oakland/Berkeley
- Volmer Peak (1,913'),
  Tilden Regional Park*
- Nimitz Way Trail (approx.
  1,200'), Tilden Regional Park*
- Mt. Diablo (3,849'),
  Mt. Diablo State Park

Richmond
- Nichols Knob (368'),
  Miller/Knox Regional Shoreline

Northeast Bay
- Franklin Ridge Loop Trail (750'),
  Carquinez Strait Regional
  Shoreline

Napa/Sonoma
- Sugarloaf Peak (1,686'),
  Skyline Wilderness Park

North Marin County
- Mt. Burdell (1,558'),
  Olompali State Historic Park*
- Nike Site (1,000'),
  China Camp State Park

South Marin County
- East Peak (2,571'),
  Mt. Tamalpais State Park
- Ring Mountain (602'), Tiburon
- Mt. Caroline S. Livermore (781'),
  Angel Island State Park
- Ayala Vista Point
- Marin Headlands, Golden Gate
  National Recreation Area*

* On the Bay Area Ridge Trail

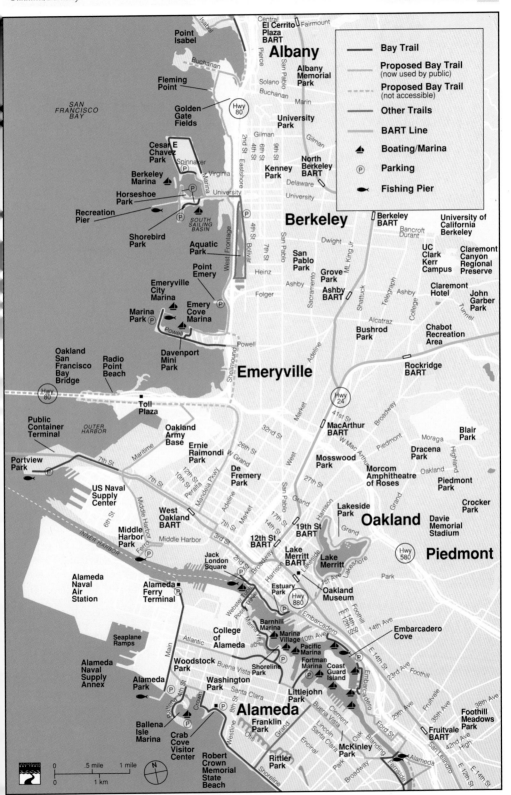

Albany

Berkeley

Emeryville

Oakland

Piedmont

Alameda

| | Bay Trail |
| Proposed Bay Trail (now used by public) |
| Proposed Bay Trail (not accessible) |
| Other Trails |
| BART Line |
⛵	Boating/Marina
Ⓟ	Parking
🐟	Fishing Pier

SAN FRANCISCO BAY

Point Isabel

El Cerrito Plaza BART
Central
Fairmount
Isabel
Pierce
San Pablo
Solano
Buchanan
Buchanan
Marin

Albany Memorial Park

Fleming Point

Hwy 80

Golden Gate Fields

University Park
Gilman
Gilman

2nd St
4th St
9th St

Cesar E Chavez Park
Spinnaker

Kenney Park
North Berkeley BART
Delaware

Berkeley Marina
Virginia
Marina
University

Horseshoe Park

Recreation Pier

SOUTH SAILING BASIN

Shorebird Park

Aquatic Park

Point Emery

Emeryville City Marina

Marina Park
Emery Cove Marina
Powell

Davenport Mini Park

Oakland San Francisco Bay Bridge

Radio Point Beach

Hwy 80

Toll Plaza

OUTER HARBOR

Public Container Terminal

Portview Park

US Naval Supply Center

INNER HARBOR

Oakland Army Base

Ernie Raimondi Park

De Fremery Park

Middle Harbor Park

West Oakland BART
Middle Harbor

Alameda Naval Air Station

Alameda Ferry Terminal

Jack London Square

Seaplane Ramps

College of Alameda

Alameda Naval Supply Annex

Woodstock Park

Alameda Park

Ballena Isle Marina

Crab Cove Visitor Center

Robert Crown Memorial State Beach

Washington Park

Franklin Park

Rittler Park

Shoreline Park

Littlejohn Park

McKinley Park

Barnhill Marina
Marina Village
Pacific Marina
Fortman Marina
Coast Guard Island

Estuary Park
Oakland Museum

Lake Merritt BART
Lake Merritt

12th St BART
19th St BART

Lakeside Park

Davie Memorial Stadium

Crocker Park

Piedmont Park

Morcom Amphitheatre of Roses

Mosswood Park

MacArthur BART
Hwy 24
41st St

Dracena Park

Blair Park

Rockridge BART

Chabot Recreation Area

Bushrod Park

Claremont Hotel
John Garber Park

UC Clark Kerr Campus

Claremont Canyon Regional Preserve

Berkeley BART
University of California Berkeley

San Pablo Park
Grove Park
Ashby BART

Dwight
Ashby
Folger
Alcatraz

Telegraph
Shattuck
College

Embarcadero Cove

Fruitvale BART

Foothill Meadows Park

San Leandro

0   .5 mile   1 mile
0   1 km
N

NORTH ALAMEDA & OAKLAND

Many longtime Bay Area residents know very little of the Alameda and Oakland shorelines, and few visitors explore them. Yet there is much to discover here, including the bay's largest active port, historical sites better known across the world than they are at home, stretches of trail with delightful views, and some of the oldest city homes in the region.

Oakland Estuary, with Alameda to the left, Port of Oakland and downtown Oakland at right, Bay Bridge and the Golden Gate in the background

North Alameda

Alameda Island, known today primarily for Alameda Naval Air Station, is also the site of one of the Bay Area's oldest cities. Alameda was incorporated in 1854, following San Francisco by four years and Oakland by two. The 2-by-6-mile island was a peninsula before the Oakland Estuary was connected to San Leandro Bay in 1901. Ohlone people lived here for at least 4,000 years before Europeans arrived. In the late 19th century, settlers passing through San Francisco built boats on the estuary's shores, and sea captains and sailors retired here in Victorian houses.

Alameda ca. 1910

Parks 🚻 ♿

Aside from Robert Crown Memorial State Beach (see pp. 82–84) and adjacent Washington Park, several neighborhood parks grace the Bay Trail route as it moves north across Alameda. McKinley Park, at Walnut Street and Buena Vista Avenue, has a playground, recreation center, and basketball court shaded by old trees. At Littlejohn Park, between Benton and Sherman streets on Buena Vista Avenue, a large lawn surrounds a baseball diamond. Pine trees shade the children's playground and picnic areas. The park is named after Elector Littlejohn, an activist for social justice, whose children played on the park site when it was only a vacant lot.

Elector Littlejohn

Grand Street Boat Ramp, Fortman Marina, and Shoreline Park

Where Alameda's Grand Street ends at the Oakland Estuary, directly across from Coast Guard Island, there is a public boat ramp and a small fishing pier with cleaning sinks. You don't need a boat or a pole, however, to enjoy the view: the East Bay hills, downtown Oakland, and the working side of the 9th Avenue Marine Terminal are all clearly visible.

Fortman Marina, off Entrance Road, is tucked between the large brick Encinal terminals and an industrial storage tank facility. It has a small public picnic area near the Kensington Yacht Club. To the immediate north is Alaska Basin. Mostly empty and run down today, it was the overwintering site for Alaska Packers Association sailing vessels from the late 1800s until the late 1920s. Dozens of square-rigged fishing boats waited here for the ice to break in the northern Pacific.

Shoreline Park arcs around Marina Village Yacht Harbor

Shoreline Park

and is managed by Marina Village. It is bordered by restaurants, condominiums, and office buildings. To the immediate south is Pacific Marina, home to the Encinal and Oakland yacht clubs. Two public exercise stations just off the Bay Trail invite you to work out while gazing beyond anchored pleasure craft to downtown Oakland.

Grand Street boat ramp

Encinal Boat Ramp & Ballena Bay Point

The concrete-covered breakwater at the Encinal Boat Ramp, at the south end of Main Street, offers a view across the bay to South San Francisco and Hunters Point. In summer and spring you can watch endangered California least terns diving into the bay for small fish just offshore (see sidebar on page 90). You can also put in boats here, fish off the breakwater, or have a picnic. To the north is the Navy's Pier 3, built to accommodate huge aircraft carriers.

Just south of the boat launch is Ballena Bay Point with a unique perspective on Crown Memorial State Beach and Bay Farm Island. You pass a few restaurants, small stores, condominiums, and the Ballena Isle Marina to get to the dirt parking lot at the end of the point.

Gantry cranes at the Port of Oakland can be viewed during a ferry ride.

Alameda Ferry Gateway Terminal

In addition to being a good place to hop a ferry to San Francisco, this terminal, at the northern end of Main Street, is popular with local fishermen and is perhaps the best site for watching the towering gantry cranes load and unload enormous container ships just across the channel at the American President Lines facility. To the northwest, out beyond the channel's opening where small yachts dash between container ships, you can see the Golden Gate Bridge under the deck and between two spans of the San Francisco–Oakland Bay Bridge. AC Transit has regular bus service to this terminal.

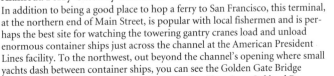

BAY TERNS

Caspian tern
The stocky Caspian tern is the largest North American tern and a common spring nester, and summer visitor, on the bay. It's about the size of a California gull, measuring some 21 inches from head to tail. The adult has a brilliant orange bill, a black cap (which fades in winter), and black legs and feet. The body is light gray above and white below; the tail is moderately forked. This tern nests in small colonies along coasts and inland lakes, rivers, and marshes. It dives for fish in bay waters. Its distinctive and raucous calls—*kowk* and *ca-arr*—are not easily forgotten once heard.

Elegant tern
Small numbers of this tern visit the central and south bay between July and October. It is slightly smaller than the Caspian tern, has a long thin orange bill, its cap, legs, and feet are black, and its tail is much more deeply forked than the Caspian's. When the elegant tern is at rest, a small tuft of feathers can sometimes be seen on the back of its head. This tern nests in the Gulf of California and, to a lesser extent, southern California. Its call is a sharp *kee-rick*.

Forster's tern
The Forster's tern looks like a 14-inch version of the Caspian, except that its bill is thinner and orange-red, its legs and feet are orange-red, and its tail is deeply forked. This is the most common tern on the bay during the spring nesting season and summer. It dives for fish, and also eats insects. The Forster's tern nests in colonies in freshwater and saltwater marshes. Its most common call is a coarse-sounding *kyarr*.

California least tern
The endangered California least tern is the smallest North American tern, measuring only 9 inches from head to tail. It resembles the Forster's tern except that its bill, legs, and feet are orange-yellow instead of orange-red, and its wing beat is quicker. Also, the least tern has black wing tips during breeding season. It once nested farther south on California's coast, but ventured north and began nesting in the Bay Area in the late 1960s as rapid coastal development destroyed traditional southern nesting sites. The California least tern population dropped precipitously during this period. The species was listed as endangered in 1970. Today, it is making a slow comeback. Some 100 pairs have been found nesting in colonies at the Alameda Naval Air Station and the Oakland International Airport, where they are now protected. Smaller colonies have occasionally appeared at several other Bay Area sites. The least tern's calls are a high pitched *kip* note and a harsh *zree-eek*.

Oakland Waterfront

Oakland is the East Bay's largest and most diverse city, yet it is also one of the least discovered. Its 19-mile waterfront is a dynamic mix of world trade and local industry, old warehouses and modern condominiums, yachts and container ships. The Pacific Coast's third largest container port and the transcontinental railroad's western terminus are here.

The working waterfront runs from the San Francisco–Oakland Bay Bridge to Oakland International Airport but is only sporadically accessible to the public between the bridge's toll plaza and Jack London Square, where ship berths and rail yards give way to pedestrian plazas, restaurants, and shopping complexes. Farther south, condominiums with yacht marinas, parks, and occasional restaurants alternate with warehouses and rusty boat repair yards. The estuary narrows before joining San Leandro Bay, where parks and marshlands make up some of the southernmost reaches of the Oakland waterfront.

Looking across the working waterfront toward downtown

AN ALTERED SHORE

Looking out over Oakland's waterfront region 150 years ago, you would have seen the landscape of low hills and oak trees that inspired this city's name. At that time, Alameda was a peninsula, not an island; Lake Merritt a salt marsh, not a lake. Today's tidal channel between the lake and the Oakland Estuary was a meandering tidal slough, and the estuary was a shallow creek. Water covered the 120 acres where the Seventh Street marine terminals stand today. What is now Broadway—Oakland's major street—was a dirt path to the only spot on this marshy shore dry enough for boarding a boat.

Painting of Oakland waterfront in the 1870s

Jack London Square

Jack London Square is the public hub of the Oakland waterfront. Plazas and white-railed boardwalks lead to shops, restaurants, and the ferry that links Oakland with San Francisco. Benches invite you to linger by the water and reflect on views of Oakland, Alameda, and San Francisco.

The Potomac

Sunday farmer's market at Jack London Square

Beneath the square's concrete cobbles lie the pilings of Oakland's first wharf, built in 1852.

At the northwest edge of the main plaza, at the Franklin D. Roosevelt Fishing Pier (with fish cleaning sinks and benches), an elevated platform offers views of Alameda and the gantry cranes at the Howard Marine Terminal. Moored just northeast of the pier are the city's fireboats, as well as President Roosevelt's official yacht, the *Potomac* (for access information, call the Potomac Association at 510-839-7533).

If you follow Water Street into the square, you will pass a bronze bust of Jack London en route to his favorite waterfront haunt—Heinhold's First and Last Chance Saloon—and the tiny sod-roofed cabin in which he lived in Alaska during the Klondike Gold Rush. (The cabin was brought here in 1969.) In the saloon, look on the back wall—you'll see many cards left by visitors from Eastern Europe who came here because they love London's books.

Continuing on, you'll arrive at Jack London Village, a complex built to resemble a North Coast fishing village. You can shop for

Jack London Village

gifts and some unusual items here, and eat outdoors by the water. From the shoreline path, just south of the village, look across the channel to find four enormous concrete ramps, remnants of the Bethlehem Shipways, used for boat building during both world wars.

The Alameda-Oakland ferry runs several times a day between Jack London Square, Alameda, and San Francisco's Ferry Building and Pier 39. It offers a dramatic and exhilarating approach to San Francisco's downtown waterfront and financial district. For some cross-bay commuters the ride is a mini-vacation, a chance to watch the sunset reflected on the water and listen to gulls instead of automobile traffic. For visitors the ferry is an inexpensive alternative to tourist cruise boats. It offers a good offshore view of the Port of Oakland, the Alameda shoreline, Yerba Buena Island, and the underside of the Bay Bridge. If you have binoculars, look for peregrine falcons in the girders in spring. The Oakland ferry terminal is at Clay Street and the Embarcadero.

Jack London's cabin

Jack London

Writer Jack London was born in 1876 in San Francisco, but he grew up in Oakland and Alameda. He began poking around the bay in a small rowboat as a boy and, a few years later, bought a sloop and named it *Razzle Dazzle*. It is said that he used this sloop for midnight raids on private oyster beds in the south bay, sometimes making more money in one night than he could from a week's work in a cannery.

As a young man, London moved with a rough waterfront crowd, drank heavily, and spent hours listening to tales of the sea at Heinhold's First and Last Chance saloon.

Jack London

Here, he met the infamous seal poacher Alexander McLean, captain of a vessel sailors knew as "the Hell Ship" and the inspiration for Wolf Larsen in *The Sea Wolf* (1904). In 1884 London put his first-hand experience as an oyster pirate to work for the other side by joining the bay's Fish Patrol. He later wrote of his experiences in *Tales of the Fish Patrol*, and of the Oakland waterfront in *John Barleycorn* and *The Cruise of the Dazzler*.

Heinhold's saloon

Estuary Park

Estuary Park

Five blocks southeast of Jack London Square is the Oakland water-front's only park with a sizable lawn. To get there from the square use the shoreline path, or the Embarcadero. From the park's parking lot (off Embarcadero), a path bordered by sycamores leads to the shores of the estuary. The path parallels San Antonio Creek, which once drained Lake Merritt. Giant concrete steps provide places to fish and sit. Next to the lawn, checkered daylight filters through a large arbor onto picnic tables. Young struggling palm trees reach skyward along the shoreline path. The city operates a summer boating program that provides canoes, boating equipment, and personnel for wheelchair users and others of limited mobility here, as well as on Lake Merritt. There is also a small boat-launching ramp.

Embarcadero Cove

Beyond Estuary Park the Oakland Estuary widens around Coast Guard Island, headquarters for the captain of the port and the 11th U.S. Coast Guard District. Across the channel's eastern arm is Embarcadero Cove, with the elegant San Antonio Fishing Pier at its north end and picnic tables onshore. Barbecue stands can be found at the end of the path near the entrance to the Embarcadero Cove Marina. Most of the cove's shore is lined with marinas, and the air is full of their sounds— the whip and snap of windblown flags, the clang of bells, the creak of wooden masts. You'll find intermittent access to the shoreline via paved walkways, roads, and marina parking lots.

San Antonio Fishing Pier

Southeast Shoreline

At Alameda's Park Street, the Oakland Estuary narrows and the first of three drawbridges crosses the waterway. Along the Oakland shore are industrial areas and modest neighborhoods. On the Alameda side are more prosperous and picturesque houses and cottages, many with boats docked alongside. Take the steps down to the Fruitvale Pier, and Oakland recedes behind the trees on the bank, leaving you in a green-brown world of leaves and slow-moving water. Farther south, the estuary opens out into San Leandro Bay.

Embarcadero Cove

A large wooden sign, "Embarcadero Cove," announces an odd collection of displaced buildings. Crammed on this patch of waterfront are Victorian gardening sheds and a little red schoolhouse, old train cars converted for use by a yacht club, historic mansions joined to water towers, and Quinn's Lighthouse, built in 1903 at the mouth of the estuary to guide ships into Oakland's harbor. After a new Coast Guard lighthouse replaced it, Quinn's Lighthouse was moved here (1965) and converted into a restaurant. The cove's gardens are delightful, with climbing roses, weeping willows, and miniature white picket fences. Farther south on Embarcadero East, around the Dock Cafe, commercial fishing boats tie up between ocean forays.

Quinn's Lighthouse

Port of Oakland, California's third largest container port

Port of Oakland

The Port of Oakland has planning authority over the city's entire waterfront. West of Clay Street, you'll find a trade and transportation zone of daunting proportions. Steel-limbed gantry cranes loom along the shore like Trojan horses, stretching their necks to hoist containers on and off ships, three football fields long, docked at sprawling truck, rail, and storage yards. Thousands of detached cabs, trailers, and containers clutter the concrete landscape.

In 1962, Oakland berthed one of the world's first container ships—a tanker converted to carry 474 truck trailers. The use of intermodal containers soon reduced loading time from a week to a day, and handling costs from $24 to $4 per ton. Oakland went on to become the Pacific Coast's third largest container port, after Los Angeles and Long Beach. Today the port has 10 terminals equipped with a total of 29 berths, 30 gantry cranes, and 600,000 square feet of covered storage space, all of which serve 40 shipping lines and about 1,400 vessels a year. You can tour the port by car with the help of the *Guide to Marine Facilities,* available from the Port of Oakland.

PORT VOCABULARY

Break bulk:
Cargoes such as coffee, grains, sugar, lumber, and steel that are transported in the ship's hold, rather than in containers.

Ro-ro:
Roll-on, roll-off cargoes, such as large vehicles, are loaded on and off via large ramps.

Gantry cranes:
Rail-mounted cranes on wharves.

Post Panamax:
Ships too big to pass through the locks of the Panama Canal.

Intermodal containers:
Boxes 20 to 40 feet long, in which cargo is moved mechanically between ship and rail or truck.

Stack trains:
Trains equipped to carry two stacked containers per car.

Port Parks 🚻 ♿ 🐟

Two waterfront parks offer close-up views of port activities, fishing, places to rest, and small barbecue stands. Both are hard to find, and rather isolated.

Octagonal fishing pier at Portview Park

Middle Harbor Park is at the end of Ferro Street off Middle Harbor Drive, between high fences topped with barbed wire. It is a tiny oasis of trees and green amid steel and concrete, not recommended for solitary exploration. On one side is the Union Pacific yard; on the other, the American President Lines terminal. From the shore and small fishing pier you can see Alameda across the estuary, and San Francisco in the distance.

Portview Park lies at the tip of an artificial peninsula extending far out into the bay at the foot of Seventh Street. From here, you can survey the port's Seventh Street Marine Container, Trapac and Matson terminals to the north, or scan Bay Area skylines. Beyond the small lawn, fishermen use the park's octagonal pier (which most call the Seventh Street Pier) and riprap shore to haul in striped bass, sharks, and other species. This park was closed after the 1989 Loma Prieta earthquake, and is scheduled to reopen in 1994. Picnic tables and benches have been relocated eastward to Berth 40, but the pier remains in place. A shoreline trail links the old park with the new facilities.

DREDGING

Most San Francisco Bay harbors must be dredged regularly to stay navigable. The U.S. Army Corps of Engineers scoops up millions of cubic yards of sediment from bay channels each year and dumps most of that off Alcatraz. Fishermen have complained that this practice stirs up toxins long buried in mud, smothers bottom-dwelling organisms, and scares fish away. In any event, the site off Alcatraz is filling up, so a search for new sites is under way.

The Port of Oakland, seeking to deepen its main channels, has had an additional problem. Before proceeding, it needs to find sites for the disposal of sediments that would be removed to accommodate ships with a 40-foot draft. A partial solution was recently devised: some of the material may be used to restore tidal marsh habitat in the north bay (see p. 150). Some of the rest may be placed on Galbraith Golf Course, near Oakland Airport.

Dredging keeps the ship channel navigable.

Lake Merritt

Lake Merritt with its surrounding 30-acre Lakeside Park is to Oakland what Central Park is to New York, and the Seine with its banks is to Paris—a beautiful free and open space in the heart of the city, with attractions for everyone. People of all ages stroll along its shores, children enjoy feeding ducks in the

Entrance to Children's Fairyland

duck pond, romping in the playgrounds, or taking rides at Children's Fairyland. Plants from around the world grow in the park, and birds that abound on the lake can be identified at the city-run Rotary Nature Center, which also provides nature walks and other programs. Offerings at the Lake Merritt Sailboat House include varied boat rentals, lessons, wheelchair-accessible boat tours, and an adapted boating program designed for people with disabilities. At night, Lake Merritt glitters with a necklace of lights. Each June, Lakeside Park is the site of the Festival at the Lake, a three-day extravaganza of music and dance, as well as arts, crafts, and food, celebrating the diversity of this city and of California.

Lake Merritt was an estuary, marshy at low tide, a saltwater lake at high tide, until 1869, when Oakland Mayor Samuel Merritt personally funded the building of a dam at 12th Street that turned the estuary into a permanent 150-acre lake. (The mayor owned considerable land on the lake.) A year later, he persuaded the state legislature to declare the lake a game refuge, the first state wildlife refuge in the nation.

Generations later, the avian life on Lake Merritt is extraordinary.

Some 50 waterbird species rest or nest on five "duck islands," built of dredge materials. Many diving ducks stop by during annual migrations, while other waterbirds—including some 500 Canada geese that no longer migrate long distances—can be seen year round.

Lakeside Park is at the northern end of the lake, as are Fairyland, the boathouse, the nature center, wildlife refuge headquarters, and the Junior Center of Arts and Science, which are open to the public. Along the southwestern reach of the heart-shaped

Camron-Stanford House

lake, on Lakeside Drive, the Camron-Stanford home stands alone, one of the last of the elegant Victorian mansions built around the lake in Mayor Merritt's days. Peralta Park and Channel Park follow the lake's former outlet to the bay. Along the pathway are 15 large sculptures. The city hopes to connect these parks with Estuary Park in the future.

Lake Merritt's shores are always delightful.

Getting Around

On Alameda, the Bay Trail route follows streets along the bayside of the island, from Towata Park to the Encinal Boat Ramp. Another portion of the route shadows the Oakland Estuary by following Buena Vista and Atlantic avenues. The Oakland-Alameda Ferry Terminal is at the end of Decatur (off Atlantic). The Bay Trail route leads to Oakland by turning off Atlantic onto Triumph Dr, then follows a paved shoreline path for 0.5 mile. To continue to the Webster Street Tube and Oakland, take streets.

In Oakland the Bay Trail route gets complicated. It joins a branch of the trail moving up from the south along Embarcadero, with paved trail portions running through the Embarcadero Cove Marina and along the waterfront to Estuary Park and Jack London Square. From Jack London Square, use streets to reach Middle Harbor Park and Portview Park. Bikers, be alert throughout the port area: drivers of large trucks may not see you. Railroad tracks can catch a tire.

I N F O R M A T I O N

AC Transit
1-800-559-4636

Alameda-Oakland Ferry
510-522-3300

Alameda Recreation & Park Department
510-748-4565

East Bay Regional Park District
510-562-7275

Junior Center of Arts & Science
510-839-5777

Lake Merritt Sailboat House
510-444-3807

Oakland Parks & Recreation Department
510-238-3866

Port of Oakland
510-272-1100

The *Potomac* Association
510-839-7533

Rotary Nature Center
510-238-3739

EMERYVILLE & BERKELEY TO POINT ISABEL

In 1913 the U.S. Army Corps of Engineers proposed to build parallel seawalls from the Emeryville Crescent area to just north of Point Isabel, creating a 5-mile-long shipping channel to accommodate a shipping boom projected for the entire East Bay. Obviously, the plans came to naught. Today, pockets of beautiful marshes and important wildlife habitat survive

Looking over Oakland's waterfront toward the Emeryville Peninsula and the Berkeley Marina

along this stretch of shore—little jewels of open space that also provide recreation sites for thousands of East Bay residents and visitors.

Emeryville Marina

The artificial 1-mile-long peninsula was one of the last major fill projects permitted on the bay. It shelters marinas and parks at its tip, and provides a foundation for high-rise apartment and office buildings, condominiums, and restaurants near Highway 80. The peninsula is ringed by some 3 miles of paved trails (rough in places). It is serviced by AC Transit.

Emeryville Fishing Pier

Marina Park

🎋 🐦 ♿ 🐟 ⛵ 🚶 🚴

At the tip of the peninsula, small public lawns face the bay, screened on their landward sides by rows of cypress and pines. The sweeping view is superb: Angel Island, the remnants of the Berkeley Ferry Pier, and most of the central bay are before you. On the park's leeward side, the Emeryville Fishing Pier is calmer (and less frequented) on windy afternoons than the Berkeley Pier. Cleaning sinks and benches make it that much easier to haul in the flounder, kingfish, and rubberlip perch this pier is known for.

Emeryville Peninsula

Davenport Mini Park and Beyond

🚻 ♿ 🚶 🚲

Don't blink as you stroll on Powell Street toward Highway 80 or you'll miss Davenport Mini Park—a tiny lawn, with benches, that looks out over the boats in the Emery Cove Marina. The Bay Trail route splits by the mini park. One arm swings north past a restaurant and follows the edge of the peninsula on a wide boardwalk for 0.5 mile. Look for the windproof boardwalk turnout with benches. No bikes or fishing is allowed along the length of this boardwalk, which

ends at a grassy strip near another restaurant and two public piers. Where the route moves next to West Frontage Road, miniature sculptures adorn abandoned pilings in the water.

Davenport Mini Park

The other arm of the route from the mini park continues down Powell Street. On the northern side of Powell Street underpass an old tunnel will be reopened for walkers and bicyclists.

Radio Point Beach, Emeryville Crescent, and Eastshore State Park

As you hustle eastward off the San Francisco–Oakland Bay Bridge, then turn north on Highway 80, the first bay access point seems to be the Emeryville Marina. Look again. Oakland's Radio Point Beach is hidden at the end of a single-lane road near the bridge's toll plaza. This strip of shore is highlighted by three radio transmission towers and graced by a fringe of beautiful marsh. Public access is at the end of the road.

To the northeast is the Emeryville Crescent, a sliver of marsh that has survived decades of sculpture-making, political protests, illegal garbage dumping, and development proposals. Despite the constant roar of cars, thousands of birds stop here in fall and early winter. In spring, nesting avocets prance about and join the killdeers in their plaintive calls. Watch from the observation platform some 300 feet south of West Frontage Road and Powell Street, at the northern end of the crescent.

The stretch of shore beginning at Radio Point Beach that swings around into the Emeryville Crescent has been included in the proposed Eastshore State Park, which is now in the early stages of land acquisition and planning. As envisioned, this park would preserve about 7 miles of shoreline between here and the Marina Bay development in Richmond. Caltrans will dramatically change roadways and interchanges north of Radio Point Beach in the next few years.

Point Emery & West Frontage Road

🚻 🦆 🐟

Point Emery is one of those unexpected pleasures you can discover by patiently poking around the bayshore. In the 1960s the city of Emeryville planned a huge fill project from here to the Emeryville Peninsula. The Bay Conservation and Development Commission refused to permit the filling. Instead the city was required to provide a parking lot, bring in benches, and landscape the point. On the north shore, a small beach is used by windsurfers to

Fishing off West Frontage Road

assemble gear. From its tip, Alcatraz seems to float mid-span against the Golden Gate Bridge.

West Frontage Road, between Point Emery and University Avenue, is well used by locals for fishing, birding, windsurfing, bay watching, lunching, and naps. Caltrans plans changes here.

Radio Point Beach

Shorebird Park

Berkeley Marina 🎏 ♿ ⛵

This 52-acre peninsula at the end of University Avenue is highly popular. Created partly on an old garbage dump, it has some five miles of trails, a pier, parks, restaurants, playgrounds, a berthing basin, small boat launch, and good windsurfing and kite-flying conditions. You might begin your exploration at tiny Horseshoe Park, just south of the marina entrance. AC Transit provides bus service to the Berkeley Marina.

Adventure Playground

Recreation Pier 🐦 ♿ 🐟 🚶

Despite the brisk afternoon breezes that blow across the Berkeley Recreation Pier, this is probably the most visited pier in the Bay Area. Crowds of fisher-

South Sailing Basin & Shorebird Park 🎏 🐦 ♿ ⛵ 🚶

Fourteen exercise stations have been installed along the shoreline path of the South Sailing Basin. If you follow them, they will lead you to a small craft-launching dock (with a nice view of the East Bay hills), California Adventures and the Cal Sailing Club (both offer sailing and windsurfing classes), and eventually to Shorebird Park, where you will find picnic areas, barbecue stands, and a playground.

The Shorebird Park Nature Center is housed in a converted trailer full of educational displays and packed with the bones, shells, skins, and feathers of bay animals. A large saltwater tank contains bay fish, anemones, crabs, and other bay creatures. Classes for children are offered. Behind the center is the Adventure Playground, designed to allow children to experiment with building materials.

South Sailing Basin

men hook striped bass, bullhead, and shiner perch here; non-fishermen enjoy the fresh air while walking out the 3,000-foot length of the pier to take in the view.

When you hike to the end of the pier, you'll see the remnants of an older pier extending out across the water. In 1927 the Berkeley Ferry Pier was extended 3.5 miles out into the bay, to water deeper than 10 feet, so large ferry boats could dock. When the San Francisco–Oakland Bay Bridge was completed in 1936, ferry service stopped, and the pier fell into disrepair. The city of Berkeley acquired it in 1938 and rebuilt the first 3,000 feet in 1958, and again in 1961. Although some complain that the old pilings interfere with small craft navigation, local activists have shown that they serve an important role as micro-habitats for bay life and as perches for birds.

You can walk 3,000 feet out over the bay on this pier.

Berkeley Marina berthing basin

Berthing Basin

The Berkeley marina's 52 acres of water can accommodate some 975 boats. Some nestled in its berthing basin may be houseboats that stay put much of the time. The legality of their presence here is a matter of chronic contention. You will find good lookout points at both sides of the basin entrance, but the northern side seems to be the favorite with shoreline visitors. The Berkeley Yacht Club is at the southern side of the entrance.

Cesar E. Chavez Park

Believe it or not, this popular, attractive park was a garbage dump until 1983. Now, about the only visible evidence of its ugly past is a small metal shed and chimney located mid-park, which vents methane gas. The western shore of this park rivals San Francisco's Wave Organ jetty for the best view of the Golden Gate Bridge. A paved perimeter trail is punctuated by small turnouts with benches. Several dirt trails crisscross the hilly top of the park, leading to picnic areas, kite flying lawns, and great views. You can usually rent a kite at this park, and on breezy weekends you will almost always see people performing dazzling aerial acrobatics. The entire park has been seeded with native grasses. On the hilltop closest to the point, planted with native shrubs and grasses, you can see how attractive a water-saving native garden can be.

Kite flying at Cesar E. Chavez Park

Berkeley's Aquatic Park

This unique park centers on a body of water that is located between Ashby and University avenues on the east side of Highway 80. Construction of Aquatic Park began in the early 1930s when the original shoreline here was filled to create the highway. It was completed in 1935 by the Works Progress Administration. The city of Berkeley acquired the park the following year. The southern basin has been designed for model yacht racing, the middle basin for water skiing, and the north basin for sailing, rowing, and canoeing. The basins are still connected to the bay via tidal gates operated by the city. On the 33 acres of land surrounding the basins, people can jog (numerous exercise stations line the shore), watch birds or engage in disc golfing. By the middle basin, the International Bird Rescue Center tends to injured birds.

Several water sports can be enjoyed here.

THE EAST BAY REGIONAL PARK DISTRICT

In 1934, the East Bay Municipal Utilities District (EBMUD) announced the sale of some 10,000 acres. Citizens in Alameda and Contra Costa counties saw the sale as an opportunity to preserve lands and natural communities and joined in an effort that led to the creation of the East Bay Regional Park District (EBRPD). The park district acquired watershed lands that are now Tilden, Temescal, and Sibley parks and then went on to secure an extensive park system for the East Bay. Today 47 parks (totaling some 75,000 acres) and 11 regional trails are scattered across the district's two-county jurisdiction.

In 1992 the state legislature gave EBRPD the responsibility for acquiring the land, including tidelands, for the 7-mile Eastshore State Park. The district will be responsible for acquisition, cleanup of toxic or hazardous materials, and planning. As this new park is developed, Bay Trail and shoreline facilities will expand and improve.

A beach at Fleming Point

Fleming Point and Buchanan Avenue

This stretch of shore directly behind Golden Gate Fields was home to J. J. Fleming in the late 19th century. Not much is known about him. Remnants of old piers can still be seen in the waters by the rocky point—the only reminders of the original shoreline along this stretch of the bay's edge. Small beaches are tucked up against the base of the bluff, and from on top, the views of the central bay and southern Marin County are spectacular. The former Albany dump on Buchanan Avenue is to become part of Eastshore State Park. Bicycle paths to connect Richmond and Emeryville will be built as Highway 80 is modified.

Getting Around

To reach Radio Point Beach by car, going west, take the last Oakland exit (Watch! If you miss it you may have to take the bridge to San Francisco!) then look for the small one-lane road marked "Radio Stations." (Don't go toward the Oakland Army Base.) This small road dead-ends near Radio Point Beach. From San Francisco take the Oakland Army Base turnoff, go back under the elevated portion of the highway, and follow the signs west, as above. When you leave Radio Beach, take the turnoff to the Oakland Army Base. From

Point Isabel Regional Shoreline & Albany Shoreline

If you are a dog person, you'll love this park, and so will your dog: it is an off-leash area for canines. While dogs are chasing balls, wrestling, and cavorting about, their owners huddle in informal groups discussing their loved ones and telling doggy stories. They keep a sharp eye out for anyone who doesn't pick up a pet's poop and are likely to reprimand such a bad citizen. But even if you're a cat person, Point Isabel is a great place for a walk

there signs guide you onto Hwy 80 north, en route to the Emeryville Marina at Powell St. Between the Emeryville Marina and Fleming Point, the Bay Trail route follows West Frontage Rd, with a branch leading down University Ave to the Berkeley Marina. From Fleming Point use streets (cross under Hwy 80) and move north to Central Ave and Point Isabel Regional Shoreline. Caltrans plans changes here before 1996.

(sans cat), with marvelous bay vistas. AC Transit services Point Isabel.

Leaving the park, at the corner of Rydin Road and Central Avenue, look for the interpretive sign erected by Caltrans. It describes the 270 acres of tidal mud flats and 10 acres of salt marsh between Central Avenue and Golden Gate Fields commonly referred to as the Albany Shoreline. More than 90 species of resident and migratory birds have been seen here. A paved trail extends along the shoreline for 0.5 mile next to Highway 80.

Well-behaved dogs are welcome at Point Isabel Regional Shoreline.

The Bay's Enduring Native People

On November 2, 1769, a group of soldiers from the Portolá expedition climbed a ridge and to their utter amazement looked down upon *un inmenso brazo de mar*—an immense arm of the sea. Beyond it, they reported, lay beautiful plains studded with trees, and from the columns of smoke everywhere they concluded that this land was *bien poblada de ranchería de gentiles*—well populated by the villages of native people.

Indeed, at the time of this first contact scores of villages rimmed the bay, inhabited by an astounding diversity of people. Those who lived on what would be called the San Francisco Peninsula spoke a language called Ramaytush; those in the south bay spoke Tamyen; those

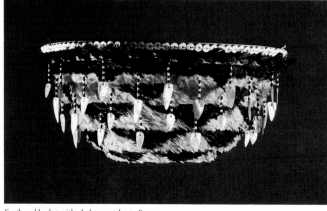

Feathered basket with abalone pendants, Pomo

in the east bay, Chochenyo; those along the southern shores of the Carquinez Strait, Karkin. These four languages, perhaps as different from each other as French is from Italian, were members of the Ohlone group of languages. In what is now Marin County lived those who spoke a dialect of the Coast Miwok language. At the mouth of the Napa River and along the north shores of the Carquinez Strait lived Patwin speakers, while east of the Strait were the villages of the Bay Miwok speakers.

The richness of languages only hints at the diversity and cultural complexity of the peoples who had lived along the shores of the bay for over 10,000 years before the coming of Europeans.

"The Ohlones can provide us with a vision of how a Stone-Age people, a people whom we have so long belittled, had in fact sustained a life of great beauty and wisdom."

Malcolm Margolin
The Ohlone Way, 1978

At the time of contact they lived in dozens of interrelated but politically independent communities. Each community centered on a main village, led (rather than ruled) by a member of a prominent family who would likely be linked to other prominent families in the area by ties of marriage and trade.

While trading was an important part of life—clam shell "money" beads, abalone shells from the ocean, and cinnabar ore (used for paint) from the San Jose area were traded out, while obsidian, pine nuts, and other inland

Chief Huyumbayum and his wife, Merrian Hart, 1905, Coast Miwok

goods flowed in—the peoples of the Bay Area were by and large self-sufficient. Their dwellings were generally constructed of willow frames thatched with tule—readily available, easily gathered materials. Food was likewise plentiful for a people who had the skills and sense of timing needed to take advantage of the great flocks of geese and ducks that darkened the sky each fall, the salmon and steelhead that crowded the creeks at spawning season, the inexhaustible beds of clams and oysters that extended into the clean waters of the bay.

At various times of year people left the shores of the bay to harvest acorns, nuts, berries, roots, seeds, or other goods in the foothills, returning to permanent

Pomo man

villages to winter—to tell wondrous stories of how the world was created and how Coyote conducted himself with such divine foolishness, to celebrate with games, dances, and songs the joy of being human in a land

of ample beauty and great plenty.

It is easy enough to cast a nostalgic look back upon this "lost" world. But in truth many of the languages and stories and much of the knowledge of the people who lived here before us have been recorded. Also, the descendants of the bay's original inhabitants live among us today. Many of them still hold on to parts of their heritage, while some are even relearning languages that have not been spoken for generations, reacquiring and practicing skills that have been too long neglected. The world of the Bay Area's native people is not entirely "lost"; more to the point, it is generally ignored by a different culture that seems to be going too fast to notice it.

Philip Galvan's grandmother and mother were baptized at this font in Mission San Jose, Fremont. His great-grandfather laid the cornerstone for the original church, which was completed in 1809 and destroyed by an earthquake in 1868. In 1982, Philip (far right) laid the cornerstone for the reconstructed church. Sarah, his wife, is on his right. Their son Andrew (center back), who is working toward a master's degree in history, points out that not all Ohlones were forcibly relocated to missions. His family is one of many that chose to join the Catholic Church and remains devout. To Andrew's right is Philip's daughter Eleanor. On the left is Philip and Sarah's granddaughter Desiree Irwin with great-grandchildren Sarah and James Irwin.

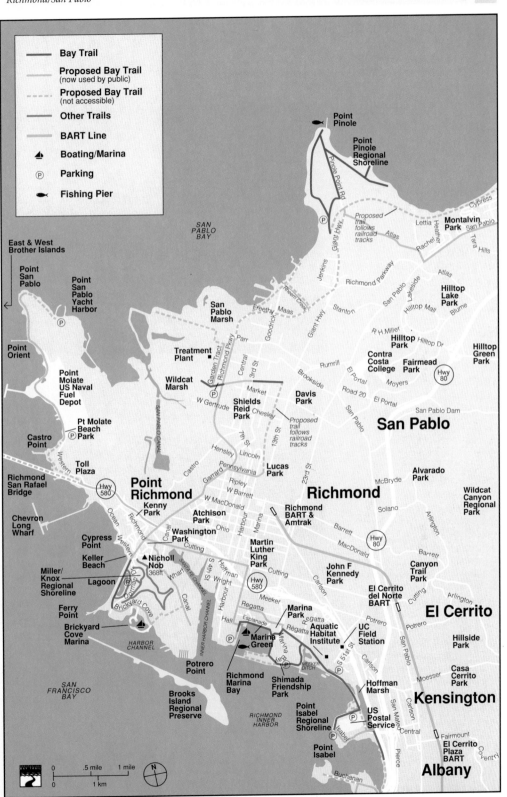

Legend

- Bay Trail
- Proposed Bay Trail (now used by public)
- Proposed Bay Trail (not accessible)
- Other Trails
- BART Line
- Boating/Marina
- ℗ Parking
- Fishing Pier

SAN PABLO BAY

Point Pinole

Point Pinole Regional Shoreline

Pinole Point Rd

Glen Hwy

Cypress

Proposed trail follows railroad tracks

Lettia
Heather
Atlas
Rachel

Montalvin Park

San Pablo
Tara
Hills

East & West Brother Islands

Point San Pablo

Point San Pablo Yacht Harbor

Jenkins

Rheem Creek

Richmond Parkway

San Pablo
Lakeside
Atlas

Hilltop Lake Park

Point Orient

San Pablo Marsh

Freethy
Maas
Goodrick

Giant Hwy

Stanton

R H Miller
Hilltop Mall

Hilltop Park
Hilltop Dr

Hilltop Green Park

Parr

Treatment Plant

Garden Tract
Richmond Pkwy

Central
3rd St

Rumrill

Brookside

El Portal
Road 20

Contra Costa College

Fairmead Park

Hwy 80

Point Molate US Naval Fuel Depot

Wildcat Marsh

W Gertrude

Market

Shields Reid Park
Chesley

Davis Park

Moyers
El Portal

San Pablo Dam

SAN PABLO CANAL

Pt Molate Beach Park

7th St
13th St

Hensley
Lincoln

Proposed trail follows railroad tracks

San Pablo

Castro Point

Toll Plaza

Hwy 580

Castro
Garrard
Pennsylvania
Ripley
W Barrett

Lucas Park

23rd St

McBryde

Alvarado Park

Wildcat Canyon Regional Park

Richmond San Rafael Bridge

Kenny Park

W MacDonald

Atchison Park
Ohio

Harbour
Marina

Richmond BART & Amtrak

Richmond

Solano

Barrett

Hwy 80

Arlington

Chevron Long Wharf

Washington Park

Cutting

Martin Luther King Park

Cutting

MacDonald

Barrett

Canyon Trail Park

Cypress Point

Keller Beach

▲ Nicholl Nob 368ft

Wharf St
4th St
Wright
Hoffman

Hwy 580

John F Kennedy Park

Carlson

El Cerrito del Norte BART

Cutting

Arlington

El Cerrito

Miller/ Knox Regional Shoreline

Lagoon

SANTA FE CHANNEL

Meeker

Regatta

Marina Park
Regatta

Aquatic Habitat Institute

UC Field Station

Potrero

Hillside Park

Ferry Point

Brickyard Cove Marina

HARBOR CHANNEL

Hall
Esplanade

Marina Green

MEEKER DITCH

S 51st St

Casa Cerrito Park

Kensington

SAN FRANCISCO BAY

Potrero Point

INNER HARBOR CHANNEL

Richmond Marina Bay

Shimada Friendship Park

Point Isabel Regional Shoreline

Hoffman Marsh

US Postal Service

San Mateo
Carlson
Central

Moesser

Brooks Island Regional Preserve

RICHMOND INNER HARBOR

Point Isabel

Isabel
Pierce

Fairmount

El Cerrito Plaza BART

Coventry

Buchanan

Albany

0   .5 mile   1 mile

0   1 km

N

RICHMOND INNER HARBOR TO CYPRESS POINT

Highway 580 channels motorists through Richmond's industrial heart while obscuring a segment of bay shoreline rich with history, expansive views, and parklands. Pull off, and slow down. Railroads, the oil industry, the Port of Richmond, and World War II shipbuilding left their legacies on the shore here. Oil, shipping, and some manufacturing remain, but where acrid smoke once drenched the air, trendy

Marshes like this one are precious habitat.

condominiums are now spreading; pleasure boats sail among tankers and cargo ships; and former ferry slips and corporation yards are now public parklands. The departure of heavy industry has, however, left many Richmond residents jobless and has dealt a devastating economic blow to the city.

Point Isabel to Shimada Friendship Park

With the exception of the Cypress Point bluffs to the north, this entire shoreline has been molded and shaped during a century of industrial use. From Point Isabel Regional Shoreline the Bay Trail route moves north 1 mile on an old railroad levee—now owned by the East Bay Regional Park District—to an intersection by Meeker Ditch. A varied pattern of marshes and mud flats extends on both sides of the levee. Inland, the densely vegetated marshes are seasonal—they fill with water after winter storms and exceptionally high tides. Hoffman Marsh, a tidal marsh between the levee and the highway north of Point Isabel, is strictly off-limits to protect wildlife. Bayward, strips of marsh grasses and mud flats

En route toward Richmond Marina

extend from the levee's base. Both areas are important wildlife habitat, particularly for resident and migrating birds.

At the Meeker Ditch trail intersection, one arm of the Bay Trail moves to the northwest and Marina Park. The westward arm hugs the riprap shore for a half mile and leads to Shimada Friendship Park and Marina Bay. This park is named for Shimada, Japan, Richmond's sister city,

and, together with the nearby housing development, exemplifies the shift toward a different use of this waterfront. From Shimada's manicured lawn and large picnic tables you can see Brooks Island stretching across the near horizon only 0.5 mile away. The view to the west is of tankers docked along Potrero Point on Harbor Channel, and the Tiburon Peninsula across the bay. Southward in the distance is Berkeley's North Waterfront Park.

View west from Potrero Point

BROOKS ISLAND

When San Francisco Bay was first mapped in 1775 by José de Cañizares, this sliver of an island was labeled Isla de Carmen. Later it was variously known as Rocky, Bird, and Sheep Island before being named Brooks Island. Ohlone people lived here for perhaps 4,000 years, and two Ohlone shell mounds and burial sites are preserved here in perpetuity. By the 1860s, and into this century, the island was used for fruit growing, oyster cultivation, rock quarrying, yachting, and hunting.

And yet, today, as a 375-acre preserve of the East Bay Regional Park District (75 acres of land and 300 acres of

water), Brooks Island retains much of its native vegetation and wildlife. Although a few guinea fowl and pheasants remain from the days when crooner Bing Crosby and friends used the island as a private hunting reserve, some 100 native species of birds have been recorded here, and many nest here, including Caspian terns and Canada geese. Access to this island preserve is by reservation only.

Brooks Island

Richmond Marina

This relatively new marina (completed in 1982), located on the former site of Kaiser Shipyard No. 2, seems remote from the economic struggle that faces much of Richmond as a result of the departure of industry, which took many blue-collar jobs with it. Here, rows of glistening white sailboats rock gently at berth, orderly clusters of homes flourish from east of Shimada Park to the marina's northern shore, and large parks offer a place to run about or rest.

The sidewalk around the marina, constructed of patterned concrete and sections of boardwalk, connects with the Marina Green and Marina Park. The Marina

Green is a large lawn with benches near the water. Marina Park starts at the marina with a small sandy beach, then moves inland toward a playground and picnic areas. Fishing, with a state permit, is allowed off the marina's riprap shore. Access and conditions are good for intermediate and advanced windsurfing.

It is hard to believe that most of the shoreline between the marina and Potrero Point was occupied by Kaiser Shipyards and heavy industry during World War II, but it was. A few blocks inland from the tidy marina are remnants of the old waterfront: enormous warehouses, industrial facilities, scrap yards, and marine businesses.

HARBOUR WAY & PORT OF RICHMOND

A visit to Harbour Way (via Hall Avenue from the marina, or down from Cutting Boulevard) allows a glimpse of the working side of the Port of Richmond's Santa Fe and Inner Harbor channels, and the former sites of the Kaiser shipyards No. 1 and No. 4. Active gantry cranes loom above ships docked along the channel. Look to the north to catch the action (watch for big trucks on Harbour Way). Chevron's Long

Chevron Long Wharf

Wharf, northward near the Richmond–San Rafael Bridge, is within the boundaries of the Port of Richmond. Even though Richmond's port does not cover as many acres as Oakland's or San Francisco's, it shipped some 26 million metric tons in 1993, mostly oil and oil products—more cargo than all other Bay Area ports combined! Dominating the south side of Harbour Way is the Ford Building, a classic historical example of industrial architecture.

Harbour Way smells like potato chips, thanks to the cooking oil storage tanks nearby. The official entrance to the Port of Richmond is at the southern end of Canal Boulevard, but viewing is better from Harbour Way.

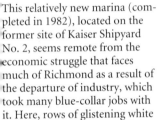

Richmond Marina

AFRICAN AMERICANS

During World War II, Richmond became a major shipbuilding center (as did Sausalito in Marin County and Hunters Point in San Francisco). Workers were recruited throughout the country, especially in the South and the

Midwest, for jobs building Liberty Ships. (You can visit the last unaltered Liberty Ship, the SS *Jeremiah O'Brien*, at Fort Mason in San Francisco.) Richmond's population quadrupled, from 25,000 before the influx began to 100,000 at the end of the war. The number of African American residents jumped from 270 in 1940 to 5,673 in 1943 and to 13,780 by 1947.

Suburban-style homes were built with federal funds for whites only. African American families were either quartered in temporary housing or squeezed into already crowded nonwhite neighborhoods.

When the war ended and the shipyards closed, African Americans, the last to be hired during the Great Depression, were again among the last to be reemployed in peacetime jobs. Poverty and despair took root in Richmond's African American community, as it did in Hunters Point and Marin City.

Richmond workers, 1942–43

Point Richmond   ♿ 🚶 🚲

The community of Point Richmond began as a railroad town in 1897. Santa Fe Railroad purchased the area just north of the small peninsula called Ferry Point, and the town of Santa Fe soon flourished. The town eventually changed its name to Point Richmond, and today it is a distinct neighborhood of the city of Richmond.

Downtown Point Richmond, 1897

Point Richmond's famous indoor swimming pool, the Natatorium (more popularly known as the Richmond Plunge), began in 1911 as an exploratory oil well one block off Richmond Avenue. Instead of an oil geyser, water was discovered. A pool was built, and the community gained a swimming facility that has entertained generations since 1924. After many renovations, the

Natatorium is still in operation, and is a guaranteed lively spot throughout the year. Call ahead for hours and fees. Across Richmond Avenue from the Natatorium is Washington Park, which features a baseball diamond edged by picnic tables and large trees. By moving several blocks northwest on Richmond Avenue you'll locate downtown Point Richmond with its small shops and specialty stores.

Today, Point Richmond's hilly enclave of beautiful old homes, renovated downtown, and small neighborhood parks are a wel-

The Natatorium

come break from the surrounding industrial landscape. The Garrard Boulevard tunnel leads to Miller/Knox Regional Shoreline and bay vistas.

Downtown Point Richmond today

Miller/Knox Regional Shoreline & Keller Beach

🪁 ⛵ ♿ 🐟 🚶🏻 🚴

This open, often windy park is perfect for kite flying, Frisbee tossing, or picnics. There are three parking lots here. The north parking lot is a good take-off point to start the steep hike to the top of Nicholl Nob (370 feet) and its 360° vista. From the picnic grounds (at water level) you can glance beyond the lagoon and active railroad tracks west-ward to the Chevron Long Wharf, Richmond/San Rafael Bridge, Red Rock, Angel Island, and Mt. Tamalpais. The park's lagoon attracts egrets, herons, and resident Canada geese. The 260-acre park is named after Congressman George Miller and former Assemblyman John Knox, longtime supporters of the East Bay Regional Park District.

A fence along the railroad tracks blocks shoreline access except at Keller Beach, at the northern end of the park, where a sandy beach and ample picnic grounds are popular with swimmers on warm summer weekends (no lifeguard). No bikes are allowed into the Keller Beach area. Atop the riprap seawall extending from the beach, anglers haul in starry flounder, cabezon, leopard shark, and other fish as railroad cars rumble by only a few yards beyond a security fence. This area is serviced by AC Transit.

Miller/Knox Regional Shoreline

FERRY POINT FERRIES

The old pump house building and the pier of the Santa Fe Ferry Terminal can still be seen at Ferry Point. This was the western terminus of the Atchison, Topeka, and Santa Fe Railroad. Starting in 1900, ferries, tugs, and barges transported railcars, merchandise, and people from this spit of land to San Francisco's Ferry Building and China Basin terminals. Santa Fe continued barging freight cars from Ferry Point to San Francisco's China Basin until the early 1980s.

Santa Fe Ferry Terminal, 1900s

The Southern Pacific Golden Gate Ferry Terminal was at the foot of Dornan Drive, just west of Richmond Terminal No. 1. These ferries operated in the late 1920s and early 1930s. The East Bay Regional Park District now owns the ferry terminal and adjacent land and plans to renovate the Santa Fe pier. The entire area, some 5 acres, will become part of the Miller/Knox Regional Shoreline.

Brickyard Cove

This development of condominiums, shoreline homes, the Brickyard Cove Marina, and the Richmond Yacht Club is clustered around the former site of the Richmond Pressed Brick Company, which made many of the bricks used in rebuilding San Francisco after the 1906 earthquake and fire. The brick kilns were preserved by the developers of the condominium complex nestled into the hills behind them.

Brickyard Cove

GOLDEN STATE MODEL RAILROAD MUSEUM

This unique museum of working miniature trains (open only on Sundays, May through October, 1–5 p.m.) is in Miller/Knox Park. To make sure it's open before you visit (it's staffed by volunteers), call on Friday or Saturday.

IT'S ART

On Dornan Drive, between the Miller/Knox parking lot and Ferry Point, is an outdoor artists' workshop. "It's Art" occupies a former gasoline distribution terminal. In the bayside yard, separated from Dornan Drive by a cyclone fence, is a scattering of cut stone, scrap metal, and wood. If you want to find out more about this place or anything you notice through the fence, drop a note into the mailbox and someone may respond.

Getting Around

From Point Isabel Regional Shoreline, the Bay Trail route moves north for 1 mile along a former railroad levee, then divides at an intersection: to the left the Bay Trail goes 0.5 mile to Shimada Friendship Park, then continues to the Richmond Marina's southern edge; to the right the Bay Trail route moves 0.5 mile along Meeker Ditch to Marina Park. About halfway between Point Isabel and this intersection, a side trail connects with the Bay Trail from a parking area on South 51st St.

At Marina Park, you can either go directly to the Richmond Marina through the park, or continue on Regatta Blvd and Marina Way to the west end of the marina. A 0.6-mile section of

the Bay Trail follows the shore of the marina. Additional trails and a park are planned for the breakwater that protects the marina.

The Bay Trail route then follows streets to the community of Point Richmond. In Point Richmond the route moves through a residential area on Wine St and Richmond Ave, then continues on Canal Blvd. About 0.5 mile before Canal Blvd ends, the route moves onto a paved road (no cars allowed) to reach Brickyard Cove. From Brickyard Cove, the route follows streets for 1 mile to the western edge of Miller/Knox Park, then continues through the Garrard Blvd tunnel to the community of Point Richmond.

AC Transit
1-800-559-4636

Brooks Island Reservations
510-562-2267

East Bay Regional Park District
510-562-7275

Golden State Model Railroad Museum
510-234-4884

Natatorium
510-620-6820

Richmond Marina Bay
510-236-1013

Richmond Museum of History
510-235-7387

Tides In The Sky

"There is nothing on earth exactly like the fog of San Francisco Bay. None of the thousand evanescent forms of air and water that move across the globe between the equator and the poles is as fantastic in shape and motion yet as tangible and intimate as the thick white vapor that rolls through the Golden Gate in summertime like an airborne flood and spreads to the farthest reaches of the bay and its shores.

"In most parts of the earth, fog traditionally is a dark, disagreeable smudge that comes from nowhere, hides the sun, obscures the vision, afflicts the lungs, and casts a damp pall over the land. In San Francisco the fog is a thing of beauty and wonder, a daily drama of the elements with the wide bay itself as the central stage."

Harold Gilliam, *San Francisco Bay*, 1957

FOG

Summer season fog (typically present between May and August) occurs only in the few regions of the world that enjoy a Mediterranean climate with long dry summers, cold upwelling coastal waters, and steady onshore winds. The beautiful white coolant that pours through the Golden Gate on hot summer days is experienced most directly by those who walk across the Golden Gate Bridge as it comes in. But to gain a macro-perspective, and to understand the geography and mechanics of fog, go to the East Bay shoreline. It is here that you can observe the various moods of fog as it slips through the Golden Gate, eases over bay waters, and gathers against the East Bay hills.

San Francisco Bay's fog forms when summer temperatures soar in the Central Valley. The hot air rises, creating a "vacuum" below. Marine air moves toward the coast to fill that vacuum with the help of northwesterly winds. As this moist marine air passes over the cold (average 55°F) upwelling waters offshore by the continental shelf, it condenses into fog, and is then both pulled and pushed inland. Marine air is dense, and often capped by a warm summer inversion, so it usually stays low, probing coastal valleys for inland routes. The Golden Gate—which acts as a type of "fog funnel"—is the only large breach of the coastal mountains for hundreds of miles in central California, so the fog typically enters the bay and moves toward the East Bay en route to the hot valley. When the ranges of moisture-loving coastal redwoods and fog are mapped and compared, their similarity is striking: fog not only cools, it can also produce measurable quantities of precipitation below trees and shrubs in the form of "fog drip."

Fog has many shapes, depending upon climatic conditions. It can blast into the bay as a wall hundreds of feet tall, creating a regional whiteout in a few hours. It can slither in underneath the Golden Gate Bridge just 30 feet off the water's surface, flick the ramparts of Alcatraz Island, retreat, then inch its way to Berkeley or San Pablo Bay. Or, it can cap the coastal mountains for days, unwilling either to advance or retreat.

RICHMOND–SAN RAFAEL BRIDGE TO POINT PINOLE

ost Bay Area residents view the northward mean-dering shore from the Richmond–San Rafael Bridge to Point Pinole Regional Shoreline as a series of unsightly oil refineries and chemical plants. Certainly there is the sprawling Chevron U.S.A. facility with its acrid smell, as well as some other heavy indus-try, sewage treatment ponds, and a sanitary landfill. But this shoreline also has a patchwork of colorful

Looking toward Point Pinole; Richmond–San Rafael Bridge in foreground

flower nurseries, stables, marshland, preservation areas, historical sites, trails, and open space. This region is accessible, culturally and ecologically diverse, and full of surprises. Take a while to explore the unknown shore of Contra Costa County.

Richmond–San Rafael Bridge from Molate Beach Park

Richmond–San Rafael Bridge

Construction of this double-decker bridge began in 1952, partly encouraged by two major ferry strikes that had seriously disrupted bay transportation. Four years later, the 5.5-mile-long bridge opened to much fan-fare while sealing the fate of the nearby ferry terminal at Castro Point. It is now a vital link between Marin County and East Bay cities. Some 50,000 cars cross it daily.

CORMORANTS UP THERE

A colony of double-crested cormorants has been nesting in the lattice work of girders beneath the lower deck of the Richmond/San Rafael Bridge since at least the early 1970s. Some 300 nests have been counted in recent years. These birds have adapted to urban life. They build nests of sticks, grass, marsh plants, seaweed, feathers, guano, and often also use debris, such as plastic rope and packing tape. To study the birds, biologists dress up like Caltrans workers: they put on helmets, suspension belts, and orange vests.

The cormorants begin to arrive here in mid-March, and most settle beneath the north side of the bridge. To feed their chicks they com-mute to mainland bays and estuaries and forage in fresh and brackish water. Their diet in the bay is not well known, but they may feed on the migrating humming toadfish (see p. 181), which mates noisily and produces young just when the cormorant chicks are most hungry.

Cormorants nesting in bridge girders

RED ROCK, MOLATE, CASTRO ROCKS, RANCHO SAN PABLO, AND CONTRA COSTA

The desolate-looking island rising some 170 feet off the Richmond shoreline immediately south of the Richmond/San Rafael Bridge is Red Rock. An abundance of iron oxides gives it a brick-red hue. To the Spanish it was Moleta, named for the similarly shaped grinding stone. (This name was later misspelled *Molate* and applied to several shoreline sites in the early 19th century.) For a time it was also known as Golden Rock owing to tales of hidden pirate treasure. Red Rock is the exact location where the boundaries of three counties meet: Contra Costa, Marin, and San Francisco. The name Contra Costa is Spanish, meaning "opposite coast"—that is, across the bay from the San Francisco Presidio.

Red Rock

Closer to shore, Castro Rocks are named after Joaquin I. Castro, whose father, Francisco, was granted Rancho San Pablo by the Mexican government in 1823. Rancho San Pablo once encompassed most of the territory from Albany to Point Pinole and inland to the El Sobrante area. If the tide is low, and you drive carefully, you can glance at the harbor seals using this low-lying cluster of rocks as a haul-out.

Chevron U.S.A.

Chevron (formerly Standard Oil of California) is a major physical and economic presence in Richmond. Initial construction of its refinery began here in 1901, and it has since grown to cover 2,900 acres. This refinery's statistics are best understood in a summarized form. (One barrel of oil = 42 U.S. gallons.)

Number of Oil Storage Tanks:	500
Total Oil Storage Capacity:	15 million barrels
Largest Tank:	750,000 barrels
Miles of Pipelines:	Over 5,000
Length of Chevron Long Wharf:	1 mile
Tanker Traffic:	550/year (average)
Barge Traffic:	900/year (average)
Employees in Richmond:	1,500

For group tours of the Chevron facility, you must write in advance. Chevron is the largest oil company facility in Contra Costa County.

Richmond–San Rafael ferries, 1952

Castro Point

This is the site of the former Richmond–San Rafael Ferry Terminal, which operated four ferries between here and Point San Quentin from 1915 until the bridge was opened in September 1956. You could ride the key system trolley to the ferry terminal from much of the East Bay. After the ferry service ended, the pier was converted to the Red Rock Marina and Fishing Resort. This was a productive fishing area until it closed in the late 1970s. Plans call for the pier to be reopened to the public.

Point Molate Beach Park

This shoreline park, off Western Drive, occupies the site of a former Chinese fishing village. The park has barbecue stands, flatbed trains that have been converted to play stations, and a sweeping view of the Richmond/San Rafael Bridge and the San Rafael area across the water.

Point Molate Beach Park

Unfortunately, this city park has seen better days, and the facilities are neglected. The large sign warning "High Explosive Material In Adjacent Area" refers to the Navy's fuel depot.

Point Molate U.S. Naval Fuel Depot

In 1942 the U.S. Navy purchased 400 acres along the Richmond shoreline, including the old Winehaven property, and created a fuel depot. You can visit this depot, which stores fuels for varied military vehicles and ships, and ask to look at the collection of historic photographs of the Winehaven winery. Call ahead for information.

WINE IN RICHMOND?

Between 1908 and 1919, one of the world's largest wineries—Winehaven—stood on the land now occupied by the Navy's fuel depot. It maintained its own school, hotel, post office, and steam-generating plant. The California Wine Association built Winehaven here because of the access to shipping lanes and rail service. California grapes were brought to Winehaven from 40 different growing regions stretch-

Winehaven in 1907

ing from Yolo and Napa counties south to San Bernardino County.

Until 1919, when Prohibition shut it down, Winehaven produced 67 types of wine, brandy, and cham-

pagne. Its annual production averaged 12 million gallons. Some 25,000 tons of grapes could be processed in one crushing; four miles of passages linked 3,000 aging vats; 15 million bottles of wine were kept in storage. About 500,000 gallons of wine were shipped by sea or rail monthly for destinations around the globe; 40 ships sailed annually for New York alone; and Winehaven's bulk tanker ships carried 300 barrels of wine daily to San Francisco.

Winehaven's bottling room, 1920

After the winery was forced to close, alcohol was illegally leaving the facility, so federal authorities knocked the bungs out of the storage vats and some 240,000 gallons of wine flowed into the bay. Legend has it that local fishermen scooped marinat-

Wine label, 1899

ed fish off the surface of nearby waters the next day. The principal winery buildings and employee housing—now national historic buildings—still stand and are used today by the Navy. The brick main building resembles a medieval castle, with turrets and parapets.

ROCK WATCH

Look for road cuts as you wind along Western Drive. What you see are Franciscan Complex rocks, primarily thin layers of graywacke, a type of sandstone. Graywacke is the most common rock in the Franciscan Complex, which also includes chert, pillow basalt, serpentine, and metamorphic rocks. In the East Bay you will

Franciscan rock formation

find Franciscan rocks west of the Hayward Fault. East of the fault, you will see younger sandstone and chert, and more recent volcanic rocks. (For more on bay geology, see pp. 2–3, 85, and 184.)

POINT SAN PABLO & SARDINES

The tip of Point San Pablo is now the site of Richmond Municipal Terminal No. 4. The cove to the northeast was home port for some 100 sardine boats during the 1940s, until the fishery collapsed. During the height of the season, purse seiners often delivered over 10,000 tons of sardines here in a 24-hour period. The fish were processed onshore for the production of fish meal and fish oil.

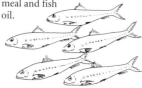

EAST & WEST BROTHER ISLANDS

East and West Brother Islands are near the tip of Point San Pablo, and directly southeast of The Sisters, islands off Point San Pedro in Marin County. These two points, and their sibling islands, mark the entrance to San Pablo Bay.

The lighthouse on East Brother was built in 1873–74, and is one of the 17 lighthouses erected in the region. Only three remain: East Brother's, the South Hampton Lighthouse on Tinsley Island in the Delta, and the Carquinez Lighthouse (see page 131). East Brother's is the oldest lighthouse still working. The station was staffed until 1969, when

East and West Brother Islands

the light and fog signals were automated and the buildings were boarded up. That same year, the station was adopted into the National Register of Historic Places. In 1979, a non-profit organization was formed

to preserve the station. It eventually obtained a lease to the island and began a restoration program. Today, the buildings have been completely restored and the organization operates an expensive bed and breakfast getaway here (proceeds help pay for maintenance costs).

As Bay Area explorer and writer Margot Patterson Doss notes, East Brother's ugly relative, West Brother Island, is as "bare as a basking whale," even though it once supported enough grass to provide pasture for the lightkeeper's goat. Today its guano-covered crown is frequented by gulls, cormorants, and other seabirds.

Point San Pablo Yacht Harbor

Point San Pablo Yacht Harbor

Roaming the western breakwater of this isolated harbor, you may feel transported back in time, and far from the heavily urbanized Bay Area. Behind you are grassy hills; bayward the entire San Pablo Bay lies still and blue. Marking the end of the winding 4-mile Western Drive, this sleepy harbor is home to a few houseboats, some two dozen pleasure boats, a scattering of commercial and sportfishing boats, and a wealth of human characters, including former whalers.

The harbor's principal buildings are the San Pablo Bay Sportsmen Club, the Galley Cafe, and the harbor master's office. The western breakwater was built by sinking an abandoned fleet of steam schooners, then filling the boats with dirt. Look offshore and you can see the ribs of one ship that was spared but eventually burned to the waterline.

WHALING

Whalers sailed into San Francisco Bay as early as the 1820s, seeking supplies and rest. By the mid-19th century, whale hunters called frequently on San Francisco while following gray whales migrating to the Bering Sea and Arctic Ocean for the summer, and to Baja California for the winter. Many whaling stations sprang up along the California shoreline. After the transcontinental railroad reached the Bay Area in 1869, many whalers chose San Francisco as a home port to speed the transport of their products—principally whale oil and bone—to East Coast markets. By the late 19th century San Francisco was the world's largest whaling port.

The whaling industry collapsed just before World War I as petroleum replaced whale oil and spring steel replaced whale bone. The whaling station at Point San Pablo, now reduced to a burned-out building west of Point San Pablo Yacht Harbor, was active until 1971, when it was closed by federal order after the United States banned whaling. It was the last active whaling station in the United States.

Wildcat Marsh

At Wildcat Marsh you can see a living marsh, rescued in the midst of a heavily industrialized landscape.

Contra Costa County and the U.S. Army Corps of Engineers had plans to control floods by building a concrete-lined channel on the creek that feeds into the marsh—Wildcat Creek—where it flowed through the communities of San Pablo and Richmond. This channel would have dumped sediment into the marsh, turning it into an upland. Activists and resource agencies had a different vision: a natural, sinuous, tree-lined waterway through the heart of a low-income urban area. Both visions would guard against flooding; the latter was far more appealing, and eventually won favor. With the help of the Corps, riparian growth along the creek will be restored. Chevron voluntarily restored Wildcat Marsh, following a plan prepared by the State Coastal Conservancy. A berm was constructed where the creek enters the marsh to keep out stormwater and direct most of the sediment into the bay, where it disperses.

Today, Wildcat Creek is just beginning to develop into the envisioned verdant passageway through an otherwise bleak urban landscape, and the East

Wildcat Marsh in spring

Bay Regional Park District has completed the first phase of a creekside trail and has plans to extend the trail from the observation platform atop the berm overlooking vibrant Wildcat

Approach to observation platform

Marsh all the way up to Wildcat Canyon in the East Bay hills. Parking for the marsh and creek trail is located off the west side of Richmond Parkway at Wildcat Creek between Gertrude and Pittsburg avenues. As you walk

the trail westward from Richmond Parkway to the observation platform, look to the left. That's the modified creek channel. From the platform, you will notice the Chevron refinery to the southwest and a junkyard to the immediate south. To the north is the West Contra Costa County Sanitary District's sewage treatment plant. To the northwest is a sanitary landfill, separating San Pablo Marsh from Wildcat Marsh. Two ponds may be seen in the marsh near the platform. Canada geese often rest nearby. The pickleweed here is habitat for the endangered salt marsh harvest mouse. The endangered California clapper rail forages in the cordgrass along marsh channels. A plaque in the floor of the observation platform will help you orient yourself and make other discoveries.

GIANT POWDER COMPANY

After several deadly explosions at its San Francisco and Berkeley factories in the late 19th century, the United State's first producer of dynamite—the Giant Powder Company—moved to Point Pinole's isolated peninsula in 1892. The company town of Giant grew rapidly, drawing on the large Croatian community of nearby Sobrante. Giant's products were used internationally for mining, dam building, and other large construction jobs. Although it's hard to detect evidence of Giant's plant in the park today, the company produced explosives here until 1960.

Point Pinole
Regional Shoreline

The sweeping grasslands and stately eucalyptus groves of Point Pinole Regional Shoreline would be spectacular anywhere in the Bay Area, but here, along this stretch of industrial bayshore (which some locals call the oil coast), the tranquillity and recreation opportunities of this park are especially welcome. This is one of the largest waterfront parks in the entire Bay Area, taking in some 2,150 acres on the Point Pinole peninsula and adjacent marshlands. It is also one of the biggest holdings of the East Bay Regional Park District.

From the parking lot (fee, weekends and holidays) visitors must cross the Paul J. Badger Bridge to enter the main park. Stop on the overpass for a few minutes and you might see a Southern Pacific or Amtrak train rumble by directly beneath you. Moving into the park, beyond a playground and picnic area, 11 miles of trails crisscross the peninsula, weaving through meadows and stands of eucalyptus that shelter monarch butterflies and varied birds. Although most of the grasses here are introduced

Point Pinole Pier

species, as are the eucalyptus, you can also find native bunchgrass.

A paved trail, just under 1.5 miles long, leads across Point Pinole to the park's sturdy fishing pier. A shuttle runs between the parking area and the popular 1,260-foot-long pier. (Call ahead for the shuttle schedule.) The pier was built next to the remains of a wharf that transported explosives from the turn of the century until 1960. Now anglers catch flounder, perch, striped bass, sturgeon, jacksmelt, and kingfish, to name but a few species. The view from the pier is spectacular. Bayward the vista takes in five counties; inland, the bluffs of Point Pinole rise above the rocky beach and the bay to your right, and to your left the Whittell Marsh covers the park's shoreline.

Point Pinole

Getting Around

To reach Western Dr and Point Molate Beach Park from Point Richmond, use streets. Bicycle lanes on both sides of Hwy 580 from Point Richmond's Castro St lead to Western Dr (experienced bikers only, no pedestrians). Western Dr is the last exit off Hwy 580, heading west, before the Richmond–San Rafael Bridge. From the south side of Hwy 580, the bike lane leads to a bench that overlooks the Chevron Long Wharf and Red Rock. This paved trail continues under the bridge to Western Dr. Just beyond the spot where the trail meets Western Dr, the road splits. Follow the "Point Molate" sign to the left. Western Dr continues for 4 miles, ending at Point San Pablo Yacht Harbor. To reach Wildcat Marsh from Hwy 580, take Castro St and proceed to Richmond Pkwy. To Point Pinole Regional Shoreline, use streets. Because some of Richmond's inland districts have had problems with street crime, be sensible when venturing away from the shoreline.

INFORMATION

AC Transit
1-800-559-4636

Chevron Public Information
510-242-5403
For Group Tours, write
Chevron USA
P.O. Box 1272
Richmond, CA 94802-0272

East Bay Regional Park District
510-562-7275

East Brother Light Station
510-820-9133

Point Molate US Naval Fuel Depot
510-231-7900

Point San Pablo Yacht Harbor
510-233-3224

Richmond Parks
510-231-3004

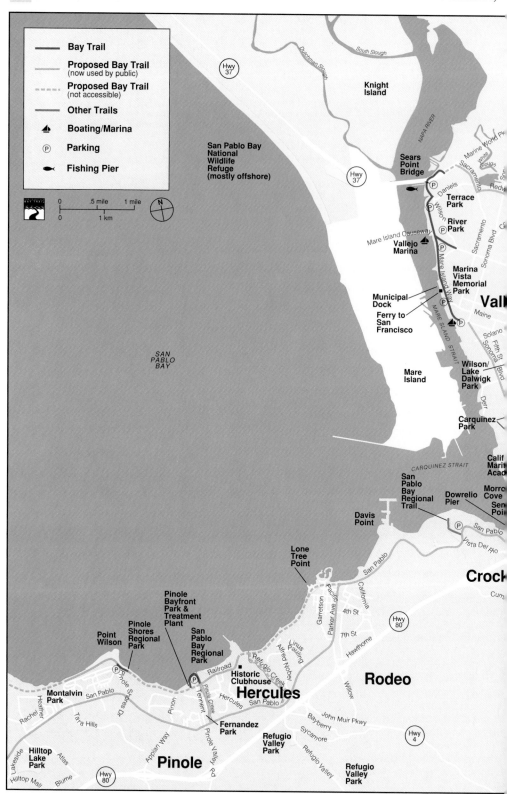

Legend:
- Bay Trail
- Proposed Bay Trail (now used by public)
- Proposed Bay Trail (not accessible)
- Other Trails
- Boating/Marina
- ⓅParking
- Fishing Pier

0   .5 mile   1 mile
0   1 km

N

San Pablo Bay National Wildlife Refuge (mostly offshore)

Hwy 37

Hwy 37

South Slough

Dutchman Slough

Knight Island

NAPA RIVER

Marine World Pky

White Slough

Sacramento

Sears Point Bridge

Daniels

Terrace Park

Redw

Mare Island Causeway

Vallejo Marina

River Park

Sonoma Blvd

SAN PABLO BAY

Marina Vista Memorial Park

Municipal Dock

Ferry to San Francisco

Vall

Maine

MARE ISLAND STRAIT

Mare Island

Wilson/ Lake Dalwigk Park

Solano

Fifth St

Sonoma Blvd

Derr

Carquinez Park

CARQUINEZ STRAIT

Calif Marit Acad

San Pablo Bay Regional Trail

Dowrelio Pier

Morro Cove

Sen Poi

Davis Point

San Pablo

Vista Del Rio

Ⓟ

Lone Tree Point

San Pablo

Crock

Pinole Bayfront Park & Treatment Plant

Pinole Shores Regional Park

San Pablo Bay Regional Park

Garretson

Pacific

Parker Ave

California

4th St

Cum

7th St

Hawthorne

Hwy 80

Point Wilson

Ⓟ

Railroad

Historic Clubhouse

Refugio Creek

Linus Pauling

Alfred Nobel

Rodeo

Willow

Montalvin Park

Pinole Shores Dr

San Pablo

Heather

Rachel

Tara Hills

Pinon

Terment

Hercules

San Pablo

Hercules

John Muir Pkwy

Bayberry

Sycamore

Hwy 4

Fernandez Park

Pinole Creek

Pinole Valley Rd

Refugio Valley Park

Refugio Valley

Hilltop Lake Park

Lakeside

Atlas

Appian Way

Blume

Hilltop Mall

Hwy 80

Pinole

Refugio Valley Park

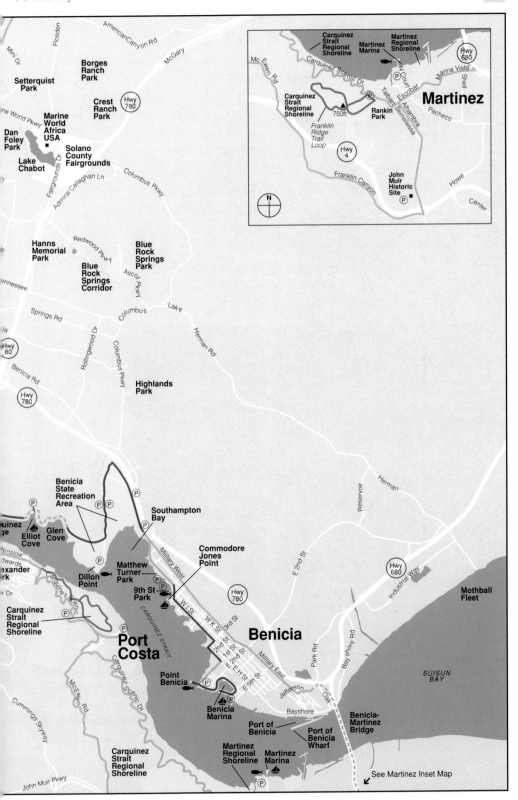

Fresh water meets salt water along the Carquinez Strait, which links the Sacramento/San Joaquin Delta and Suisun Bay with San Francisco Bay. The shoreline is known for its industry, quaint historical towns, and extensive shoreline parks. Before the Europeans' arrival, the rich salt/freshwater environment supported many Karkin Indian villages. When Spain and then Mexico took over, new settlers put cattle out to graze in the hills and planted orchards in the valleys. Soon marshes were diked and towns appeared. The strait became a major transportation nexus as grain, fruit, and cattle were shipped from here to ports in Europe and Asia. Shipbuilding became established and the oil industry took hold. Oil is still processed here at some half-dozen facilities that are conspicuous both on the landscape and in the local economy. But there is much attractive green space as well. Numerous city and county parks grace the shoreline. The East Bay Regional Park District manages more than 2,000 acres between Pinole and Martinez. Some areas along this shoreline are not yet accessible.

Working on the Bay Trail near Vallejo

People in all nine counties on San Francisco Bay are working to realize the vision of the Bay Trail.

PINOLE SHORES REGIONAL PARK TO SAN PABLO BAY REGIONAL TRAIL

Most people who pass this stretch of shoreline while traveling on Highway 80 see it as one continuous oil refinery zone. There is the vast UNOCAL complex in Rodeo, and a few smaller refineries to the immediate north. If you get off the freeway, however, you can visit five shoreline parks, large stretches of preserved marshland, and shoreline bluffs overlooking the entire San Pablo Bay.

Pinole Shores Regional Park

Pinole Shores Regional Park

At the end of Pinole Shores Drive (disregard the "Private Drive, No Trespassing" sign; this is public), a small parking lot marks the entrance to Pinole Shores Regional Park. A paved trail leaves the parking area and leads some 100 yards to the northeast. Several turnouts with benches are good perches for gazing out across San Pablo Bay (which the Spanish called "Circular Bay") and looking down the cliff face at trains rumbling by on the shoreline tracks.

To the southwest, a rough dirt path slices across grassy slopes for a mile, past Point Wilson. It runs between the shoreline railroad tracks and a neighborhood just upslope. Pinole Shores Regional Park eventually will be linked with Point Pinole Regional Shoreline to the southwest, and with San Pablo Bay Regional Park to the northeast.

Pinole Bayfront Park & San Pablo Bay Regional Park

The beautiful picnic area of Pinole Bayfront Park overlooks extensive mud flats and patches of fine marsh grasses visited by shorebirds. A trail (paved, then gravel) follows the shoreline for several hundred yards, and works around the front of the city of Pinole's sewage treatment plant. A small boat ramp (for hand-launched craft only) is to the northeast of the plant, on the shore of Pinole Creek.

You can cross Pinole Creek on a footbridge (alongside the railroad tracks) and follow a dirt path into San Pablo Bay Regional Park, which is undeveloped except for a small segment of paved trail near the intersection of Santa Fe and Railroad, opposite the small neighborhood park. Eventually, shoreline explorers will be able to wander unimpeded between San Pablo Bay Regional Park and Point Pinole Regional Shoreline— a stretch of some 5 miles.

Pinole Bayfront Park

PINOLE

The name Pinole originates from *pinolli*, the Aztec word for toasted and ground seeds. As the Spanish moved north through Mexico and then California they changed the word to *pinole*, and used it to describe a variety of flours and seed cakes. In 1775 some local inhabitants offered *pinole* to José de Cañizares (first sailing master of the frigate *San Carlos* under Lieutenant Juan Manuel de Ayala) near today's city of Pinole, and the name has become permanently linked with the location.

Old company buildings–Historic Clubhouse

HERCULES AND THE HISTORIC CLUBHOUSE

In the 1890s the Hercules Explosives Company (formerly California Powder Works) relocated from San Francisco to this remote spot because its city property became part of Golden Gate Park. In 1900 the town of Hercules was incorporated, centered around the company's headquarters, employee housing, and manufacturing plant. The concrete walls of the 1913 headquarters building are a foot thick and faced with brick to withstand any accidental factory explosion. In 1964 the company switched from explosives to fertilizer production. The plant closed in 1974. Many of the old buildings still stand, and several are occupied by small businesses. The entire old Hercules complex is known as the Historic Clubhouse. Tenants in the old headquarters building maintain that during recent earthquakes they never felt a tremor.

Pinole Creek and Fernandez Park

A tram once ran along Pinole Creek, bringing produce and livestock from creekside farms and ranches to the wharf that jutted out into the bay where Pinole Bayfront Park is today. A paved path follows the old tram route for half a mile along the tree-lined creek, ending near Pinole Valley Road. As the path nears San Pablo Avenue (about a quarter mile from bay shoreline), it passes Fernandez Park, with playgrounds, picnic areas, baseball and basketball areas, and a large lawn with shade trees.

Fernandez Park

Rodeo and Lone Tree Point

During California's Spanish era, cattle were rounded up from nearby hills and led to the shoreline at the point where the town of Rodeo is today. They were herded onto boats and taken to Vallejo for further fattening. Raucous rodeos are said to have taken place here during roundups. After California became a state, and the railroad arrived, roundups and cattle shipment ceased.

Lone Tree Point

Today, a couple of aged marinas provide a place to stroll, and evoke a time when a lucky fisherman could reel in hundreds of fish in a single day here. This area provides a quiet break, and a bit of isolation, in this mostly industrial landscape on the border of one of the Bay Area's few remaining working-class towns. From the edge of the marinas you can survey San Pablo Bay and the immense UNOCAL refinery to the northeast. A few restaurants provide hearty meals.

To the immediate southwest of the marinas, a lone eucalyptus stands on a grassy bluff overlooking a small beach. This is Lone Tree Point, a small regional park. In the near future the East Bay Regional Park District will develop parking, access points, and trails here.

Rodeo Marina

San Pablo Bay Regional Trail

Some 3 miles northeast of Rodeo, on the bay side of San Pablo Avenue, is the San Pablo Bay Regional Trail. It consists of several miles of dirt paths winding through some 25 hilly acres, offering sweeping views of San Pablo Bay; turkey vultures and red-tailed hawks search the grassy slopes for meals. The sole access point to this trail is difficult to find. It's on the turn of San Pablo Avenue, at the top of a hill, across from Vista Del Rio Road. Parking here is scheduled to be improved, but until it is, only two cars can park off-road at the access point. There is no other parking nearby.

On San Pablo Bay Regional Trail

THE OIL COAST

UNOCAL facility

Oil has had a strong presence along this Contra Costa County shoreline since 1896, when Union Oil built the Bay Area's first oil refinery in Rodeo. Six petroleum refining and storage facilities now occupy over 8,000 shoreline acres in the northeast bay (one is in Solano County), constituting the Bay Area's largest waterfront industry. Some 1,100 oil tankers pass through the Golden Gate each year en route to the northeast bay's Oil Coast. An additional 2,600 cargo ships call at other ports on the bay. On shore here, the UNOCAL facility alone covers more than 1,000 acres in Rodeo. Its refinery operates around the clock, employs 500 people, processes some 100,000 barrels of crude a day, and makes products ranging from jet fuel to food-grade waxes. Half of its output is gasoline. In Martinez, the Shell Oil refinery produces some 320,000 barrels of petroleum products daily (1 barrel=42 U.S. gallons).

For better or for worse, our society depends on oil and its byproducts. Oil also continues to be a major polluter of Contra Costa County's shoreline and the entire San Francisco Bay. Petroleum and chemicals used in its processing enter the water and air through routine refinery waste discharges and some accidental spills. Selenium from refineries processing lower-grade crude oil between Richmond and Benicia threatens bay ecosystems and the health of people who eat fish. This may be the most serious preventable toxics problem in the bay today, according to some scientists. In addition, motorists who dump used automotive oil in the gutter or on the ground contribute a significant amount of pollution. When it rains, this oil washes down storm drains and creeks into the bay. (See p. 156 on how you can help to prevent this.)

THE SALT WEDGE

Bay waters are a mix of Pacific Ocean salt water and fresh water from numerous rivers—principally the Sacramento, San Joaquin, and Napa rivers. The salt-to-fresh transition is gradual between the Golden Gate and the Sacramento/San Joaquin Delta.

Salt water is denser than fresh water, so it "wedges" underneath incoming fresh water, forming a mixing zone that moves up and down the bay's estuary several miles daily, depending on the tides and freshwater flow. This migrating mixing zone is highly productive. The shallow waters of the

Zooplankton Nauplius

Suisun and San Pablo bays nourish phytoplankton (small plants that float in the water) and zooplankton (small floating animals), which in turn feed numerous aquatic species.

Phytoplankton Coscinodiscus

Because of freshwater diversions by federal and state water projects, the salt wedge has shifted upstream. Around 1900, so much freshwater flowed down through the Carquinez Strait that residents of Crockett drew their drinking water directly from the strait. Today, fresh water has retreated to the confines of Suisun Bay, some 6 to 8 miles to the east. Not only has

this damaged phytoplankton and zooplankton—and therefore fish populations—but also such freshwater marsh plants as tule and bulrush have retreated upstream, while salt-tolerant cordgrass has moved in. A range of species adapted to fresh water has been displaced from historic habitats.

To say that water issues are complicated could qualify as the understatement of the century. Industry, agriculture, fish and wildlife protection agencies, municipalities, and environmental groups have claims on the fresh water that naturally flows into the delta and bay. While they compete, the salt wedge continues to migrate upstream, spreading damage to the bay/delta's farms, as well as to its fish, wildlife, and plants.

THE CARQUINEZ STRAIT— CROCKETT TO MARTINEZ

Thousands of years ago, during a much wetter climatic period, water carved through the mountains here at the confluence of the Sacramento and San Joaquin rivers. These two great rivers drain almost the entire western Sierra Nevada and the interior slopes of the coastal mountains. Much of their flow is now diverted and captured for various uses, but they continue to feed fresh water to San Francisco Bay through the maze of rivers, creeks, and sloughs of the Sacramento/San Joaquin Delta. This fresh water is essential to the health of the bay. It mixes with salt water as it passes through the Carquinez Strait into San Francisco Bay. The strait is six miles long, no more than half a mile wide at several points and as deep as 122 feet near Dillon Point. It is a transition zone and a meeting place, ecologically, sociologically, and economically.

The Karkin who lived along the shoreline, harvesting its natural bounty, greeted some of the first European explorers here in the 18th century. Later, industry and commerce flourished as transportation via water, cart, and rail converged here. Now the old towns along the strait are attractive to people and businesses seeking to get away from congestion and other problems faced by metropolitan centers on the bay. This is a great shoreline area to explore, and it's surprisingly little known by Bay Area residents.

Carquinez Strait

FIRST ENCOUNTERS

In 1775 Father Vicente Santa María (chaplain of the frigate *San Carlos* under the command of Lieutenant Juan Manuel de Ayala) and several sailors approached a Karkin village in the *San Carlos*'s longboat. The priest's report provides a glimpse into the past and a feeling for the distant meeting of two cultures that profoundly influenced the Bay Area's history and environment:

"Our men made a landing, and when they had done so the Indian chief addressed a long speech to them. He would not permit them to sit on the bare earth; some Indians were at once sent by the chief to bring some mats cleanly and carefully woven from rushes, simple ground coverings on which the Spaniards might lie at ease. Meanwhile a supper was brought them; right away came atoles [porridge], pinoles [seed cakes], and cooked fishes, refreshments that quieted their pangs of hunger and tickled their palates too. The pinoles were made from a seed that left me with a taste like that of toasted hazelnuts. Two kinds of atole were supplied at this meal, one lead-colored and the other very white, which one might think to have been made from acorns. Both were well flavored and in no way disagreeable to a palate little accustomed to atoles. The fishes were of a kind so special that besides having not one bone they were most deliciously tasty, of very considerable size, and ornamented all the way round them by six strips of little shells [sturgeon have shell-like dorsal plates]. The Indians did not content themselves with feasting our men, on that day when they met together but, when the longboat left, gave more of those fishes and we had the enjoyment of them for several days."

CARQUINEZ ETYMOLOGY

Carquinez Strait and Suisun Bay were first described by Europeans during the Lieutenant Pedro Fages overland expedition of 1772. The Spanish named the strait Boca del Puerto Dulce—Mouth of the Freshwater Port. The present name is derived from the earlier local inhabitants, the Karkin. The spelling *Karquines* was commonly used on documents until the early 19th century.

Crockett 🪑 🐟 ⛰️ 🚶

Crockett is a great walking town, and a stroll in its downtown neighborhoods will bring you past historic buildings, antique shops, parks, and restaurants. In the Crockett Historic Museum (open 10 a.m. to 3 p.m., Wednesdays and Saturdays) on Loring Avenue, items from the town's past are on display, and friendly volunteers answer questions. One of the more unusual exhibits is a mounted sturgeon, largest recorded in California. It weighed 468 pounds when caught in San Pablo Bay in 1992. (In the Black Sea, a related species of sturgeon can weigh up to 2,500 pounds!)

Under the southwestern foot of the Carquinez Bridge is the Crockett Marina and Dowrelio Pier (off Dowrelio Drive). Here you might land a flounder, sturgeon, shad, salmon, steelhead, or striped bass. (This is a private pier, so a fishing license is required.) The marina offers boating, a seafood restaurant, and great views of the bridge, the opening of the strait, and—across the water—the California Maritime Academy.

Carquinez Bridge

The town of Crockett is named after Joseph B. Crockett, who owned 1,800 acres here in the 1860s, jointly with his partner, Thomas Edwards. Edwards' first house, built in 1867, stands on Loring Avenue, across the street from the Crockett Historic Museum, and is now referred to as The Old Homestead.

It can be argued that when the Carquinez Bridge was completed in 1927, Crockett was bypassed by both traffic and time. In 1958, another three-lane bridge was erected alongside the original structure (Carquinez Bridge is really the Carquinez Bridges). Today, some 100,000 drivers skirt Crockett daily via this bridge. Free limited shuttle service for bicyclists is offered by Caltrans maintenance vehicles. Call Caltrans for further information.

The Old Homestead in Crockett

Advertisement from the 1930s

Grain and Sugar

When the Central Pacific Railroad (later known as the Southern Pacific) arrived at the strait via Martinez in 1879, this shoreline became a major shipping center for California agricultural products. Large sailing vessels, river steamboats, scow schooners, and rail cars met here to transfer grains, particularly wheat.

By 1884, grain wharves extended almost continuously along some 4 miles of the strait, from Crockett to Port Costa, as California's prized wheat fetched top prices on England's Grain Exchange. Many of the old wharf pilings can still be seen.

During the 1880s the grain facilities at Port Costa—which could service over a dozen transport ships at once—stored some 70,000 tons of grain in specially equipped warehouses. It wasn't unusual for dozens of ships to be anchored here waiting to load up with hardy California wheat before heading around Cape Horn en route to European markets. As transcontinental rail service improved, grain was more frequently sent to Eastern ports via rail cars to shorten the delivery time to Europe.

In 1893 the international wheat market collapsed and during the ensuing decade the grain wharves were gradually abandoned. Port Costa continued as an important railcar ferry terminal, but the great warehouses and associated businesses fell into disrepair. Crockett's Starr Flour Mill converted to a beet sugar refinery, and in 1906 C&H Sugar (short for California & Hawaii) bought out the beet refinery and opened its own operation, using sugar cane. It is now the world's largest sugar cane refinery.

Carquinez Strait Regional Shoreline

The 1,294-acre Carquinez Strait Regional Shoreline is composed of several pieces of land stretching from eastern Crockett to Martinez. Nearly 14 miles of dirt trails wind through coastal scrub and grasslands, past bay laurels, buckeyes, and through oak woodlands. Common resident wildlife species include the western meadowlark, western bluebird, American goldfinch, golden eagle, gray fox, mule deer, and raccoons (listen for their songs; look for their tracks).

Western bluebird

The shoreline's bluffs rise 750 feet to summits and ridges with sweeping views. Look for tugboats pushing barges up the strait, directing large ships, or moving from one job to another. From Franklin Ridge (in the eastern part of this shoreline

park) you can see Mt. Tamalpais to the west, Mt. Diablo to the east. To reach the western part of the park, use the Bull Valley Staging Area; for the eastern part, use the Carquinez Strait East Staging Area.

Martinez Regional Shoreline

Port Costa

This quiet small town was a focus of the world grain trade a century ago (see p. 125). The original downtown—a large block of multistory buildings fronting the Carquinez Strait—now offers a variety of shops and restaurants. Typical of the buildings here is the McNeer warehouse, which once stored wheat, hay, and potatoes and now hous-

McNeer Warehouse

es several different businesses. Built in 1886 as "the first fireproof building in Contra Costa County," this structure survived devastating fires in 1889, 1909, 1924, and 1941, and earthquakes in 1892 and 1906.

The town is now separated from its waterfront by fencing and railroad tracks. In the last century, however, Port Costa was a major ferry terminal and a critical rail link to Benicia and all points eastward. Among the ferries stopping here was the *Solano*, built in 1879 and touted as a

The Solano

"wonder of the age." It was longer than a football field and had four sets of tracks on deck, to carry two complete passenger trains at once. It plied the waters of the strait until 1930 when the Southern Pacific Company completed the steel span connecting Martinez and Benicia.

> **THE MOTHBALL FLEET**
>
> After World War II, more than 300 military ships were anchored in neat rows just east of Benicia. In the ensuing decades, the Mothball Fleet (as most folks call it) has shrunk in size to a few dozen ships. A few are being maintained in case of military emergencies; the rest are gradually being scrapped.
>
>
>
> *Mothball Fleet*

Martinez Regional Shoreline

In 1974 the city of Martinez teamed up with the East Bay Regional Park District to transform a seldom used 350-acre waterfront property into a park that has become wildly popular. The marshland was protected, and what was once industrial fill became picnic grounds and athletic facilities for soccer, bocce ball, and baseball. The baseball complex is named for Joe DiMaggio, a Martinez native.

Martinez Pier

Three miles of dirt and paved trails wind through the park; they also lead toward the Martinez Marina and public pier. The pier was built from the remains of the bay's last automobile ferry slip, which closed in 1962 when the Benicia-Martinez Bridge opened. Anglers here hook striped bass, flounder, and sturgeon. Pier visitors can look east toward the Shell Oil refinery, and west down the strait toward the Carquinez Strait Regional Shoreline. In the town of Martinez, Rankin Park (off Talbart Street) maintains a large playground and picnic area.

STRIPED BASS—TROUBLED "NEW NATIVES"

One of the first railcars to arrive in Martinez from the East Coast, in 1879, carried 132 live young striped bass. They were released into the Carquinez Strait. Three years later, 300 more were shipped in and released. The West Coast's entire striped bass population evolved from these introductions. That's right, this popular game fish is not a true native, but what some biologists call a "new native"—an introduced species that has been here long enough to become established. Of California's 30 or so freshwater game fish, less than a fourth are native or endemic species!

Stripers (as aficionados call them) can grow to four feet in length, weigh 90 pounds, and live for over 20 years. Most pier catches, however, weigh less than five pounds. These bass are anadromous—they spend part of their lives in fresh water, and part in salt water. Each winter they migrate from the open ocean near the Golden Gate, and from salty bay waters, into the brackish delta. They spawn the following April or May, then return to salt water.

Stripers are in trouble in the bay. State biologists believe legal stripers (over 18 inches) numbered just under 2 million in the early 1970s. Today, because of pollution and freshwater diversions in the delta by federal and state water projects, the population of legal stripers hovers around 800,000. Present efforts to save the striped bass include complicated diversion pump screens (which critics say don't work), costly hatchery programs, and high-stakes water politics.

Striped bass

John Muir and the Martinez Adobe

The most famous structure in Martinez is the home of John Muir, the visionary explorer and naturalist who is revered in the West, both for his wilderness conservation work and for his writing. Muir was the chief advocate for the establishment of Yosemite National Park in 1890 and played a key role in the creation of several other national parks. From 1890 until his death in 1914, he lived and worked here when he was not climbing

"I only went out for a walk and finally concluded to stay out till sundown, for going out, I found, was really going in."
John Muir, 1913

mountains, crossing glaciers, and exploring great forests. The John Muir Home is now an 8.8-acre National Historic Site (by intersection of Alhambra Avenue and Highway 4). Both the mansion and the Vicente Martinez Adobe, a two-story adobe ranch house built in 1849, are open to the public.

John Muir Home today

CHINOOK SALMON, THE ROYAL NATIVE

Before streams and rivers were dammed and their flows diverted for varied human uses, hundreds of thousands of chinook salmon would arrive through the Golden Gate annually and pass through the Carquinez Strait en route to their spawning grounds. As recently as 1969, some 117,000 winter run chinook made the journey. By the mid-1980s, however, only 2,000 returned from the ocean, and in 1991 a mere 191 were counted. The Sacramento River winter run chinook salmon is now listed as a federal threatened and state endangered species.

Chinook salmon

The only salmon species to enter San Francisco Bay, the adult chinook averages 20 pounds and a length of 2 feet. The salmon's life cycle takes it from fresh water to salt and back again to the same stream to spawn. Four times a year—in fall, late fall, winter, and spring—different races of chinook enter the bay and try to reach their ancient spawning grounds in the Sacramento and San Joaquin river systems. But this has been ever more difficult because of freshwater diversion, destruction of spawning sites, dams that block passage, and pumps and fish screens. The winter run salmon, unable to pass Shasta and Keswick dams, have been forced to spawn south of them, where high water temperatures in early summer often kill eggs and young.

Though the winter run salmon have suffered most disastrously, other runs have also declined precipitously. Diversion pumps for the Central Valley Project and the State Water Project, located in the delta, combine with some 1,800 agricultural diversion pumps to capture and kill millions of eggs, larvae, juveniles, and some adults. Fish screens installed to keep fish out of the pumps become barriers that kill or damage many juveniles making their way downstream. Survivors are trucked downstream past the pumps, but this transport also takes a toll. The California Department of Fish and Game is trying to mitigate the losses by various means, including improved fish screens and release of hatchery fish. But these amazing salmon migrations can only be expected to survive if adequate freshwater inflow into the bay and delta is secured, and the spawning habitat is protected.

Getting Around

To reach Pinole Shores Regional Park from Point Pinole Regional Shoreline, follow San Pablo Ave northeast to Pinole Shores Dr. Pinole Shores Dr winds through a housing complex to the park. To continue on to Pinole Bayfront Park and San Pablo Bay Regional Park, return to San Pablo Ave and continue northeast to Tennent Ave, then turn bayward to the end of Tennent. The half-mile trail up Pinole Creek starts on Railroad, a quarter mile northeast of Pinole Bayfront Park. The proposed Bay Trail route then follows San Pablo Ave all the way to Rodeo, then eastward to Crockett. In Rodeo, take Pacific Ave to reach the marinas and Lone Tree Point.

Through Crockett the route follows city streets—Dowrelio, Loring, Rolph, Winslow—to Carquinez Scenic Dr. It then continues on Carquinez Scenic Dr, through the Carquinez Strait Regional Shoreline, to Port Costa. Just above Port Costa the route divides. The first branch continues on Scenic Dr to Martinez, but don't try to drive: The middle portion of Scenic Dr is indefinitely closed to motor vehicles but accessible to bikers and hikers. This first branch continues through Martinez on Talbart and Escobar streets, then goes northeast on Marina Vista to Hwy 680 and the Benicia-Martinez Bridge. The second branch—popular with bicyclists—follows the rural inland route from Carquinez Scenic Dr to McEwen Rd, crosses under Hwy 4, then joins Franklin Canyon Rd, moving east and parallel to Hwy 4. It then connects with Alhambra Ave and moves north toward the strait and Martinez, to connect with Marina Vista, and the first route.

INFORMATION

AC Transit
1-800-559-4636

Benicia–Martinez Bridge Caltrans Shuttle Service
510-286-0589

Carquinez Bridge Caltrans Shuttle Service
510-286-0589

City of Pinole Parks
510-724-9010

Crockett Historic Museum
510-787-2178

East Bay Regional Park District
510-562-7275

Hercules Parks & Historic Clubhouse
510-799-8291

John Muir National Historic Site
510-228-8860

Martinez Leisure Services
510-313-0930

BENICIA TO VALLEJO

"On crossing from Martinez a great change comes over the landscape. There are open groves, beautiful trees, and cool shade; here, not a tree to break the wind or to invite rest in its shade. Yet the land is fertile, and rich fields of grain lie on every side."
William H. Brewer, 1862

Benicia waterfront with pilings, facing southern shores

The northern expanse of the Carquinez Strait, the mouth of the Napa River, is an open landscape including facing steep wooded hills on the strait's southern shores. Rolling grasslands ease down to shoreline parks and public areas that offer a variety of recreational activities. The Bay Trail route briefly dovetails with the Bay Area Ridge Trail here, and together they traverse an area enduring both rapid population growth and industrial and military cutbacks. This area also has significance in California history.

Benicia

Benicia was established in 1846 by Mexican General Mariano Vallejo (see p. 144) and a young U.S. lieutenant, Robert Semple. They named it for the general's wife and hoped to see it grow into a port city to rival San Francisco, 27 miles to the southwest. At first Benicia's prospects looked good. It became an important transshipment point, the center of wooden shipbuilding for the Pacific Coast, home to the Pacific Mail Steamship Company, and the site of the Benicia Arsenal. In 1853 it became the state capital. But San Francisco kept growing; the capital was moved to Sacramento; some key industries shut down; and history bypassed Benicia.

Ironically, much of Benicia's charm today exists only because its grand expectations

Old Union Hotel on First Street

came to nought. It offers tranquillity amid historic and scenic charm within easy driving distance from dense urban areas. The old State House (corner of 1st and West G streets), is a state historic park. The Benicia Arsenal (end of Military East) has been successfully converted to civilian use. Many of the arsenal's 19th century buildings house artists' studios and businesses. (The Exxon refinery is also on arsenal property.) On First Street, along the waterfront, old brothels and taverns have been refurbished as restaurants and antique shops. Where ships were built and launched, people now picnic, fly kites, and exercise by the water.

Shoreline Parks

West of Point Benicia are waterfront homes, several street end parks, and two large waterfront parks. The Bay Trail route is well marked between the point and the Benicia State Recreation Area, some three miles.

Popular 9th Street Park, at the shoreward end of West 9th Street, in an old neighborhood, has a small pier and a shoreline known by anglers for striped bass, salmon, and flounder. It also has a lawn, playground, and picnic areas. Matthew Turner Shipyard Park, at the end of West 12th Street, is a California Registered Historic Landmark. This six-acre waterfront park has picnic areas, a lawn, and a great view of Carquinez Strait Regional Shoreline.

Ninth Street Park

Benicia State Capitol

Matthew Turner Shipyard, 1898–1900

SHIPYARDS

Benicia's shipbuilding history dates from 1849 when independent craftsmen labored on the shores here. In 1850 the Bay Area's first major ship repair plant, the Pacific Mail Steamship Company, started operations in town. In 1882, Matthew Turner relocated his San Francisco shipyard to Benicia. Turner became known as North America's most productive shipbuilder. He and his workmen constructed 228 vessels, and 169 of them were launched in Benicia. The shipyard closed in 1903 and a park was built on its site and named in Turner's honor. At low tide, some old pilings and platforms protrude offshore.

Benicia Marina & Pier

From the Benicia Marina's eastern end at 5th Street, a 1-mile trail (paved, fine gravel, dirt) swoops around berths and the Benicia Yacht Club, then continues to the tip of Point Benicia and the public pier at the foot of 1st Street. From the pier (known for its catches of sturgeon, salmon, flounder, and striped bass) you have a panorama of the Carquinez Bridge to the west, Carquinez Strait Regional Shoreline across the water, and Mt. Diablo rising from the distant landscape to the east. The sprawling Shell Oil refinery in Martinez occupies the foreground.

In earlier years, travelers en route from the East Coast to San Francisco arrived at the Southern Pacific Railroad Station that still stands at the foot of 1st Street, next to a wooden building that housed the Jorgenson Saloon. The train ferry carried the travelers from here to Port Costa, where they transferred to another train, and then yet another ferry, which delivered them to their destination.

Benicia Marina

Benicia State Recreation Area

A walk across the 438 acres of the Benicia State Recreation Area offers a sense of the shoreline as it was in the time of the Karkin people. Grassy hills slope down to Southampton Bay, giving way to stands of willows and cattails along freshwater channels; farther out, a rich variety of marsh plants thrives. Large numbers of resident and migratory shore-birds frequent this embayment, along with mockingbirds, red-winged blackbirds, and several species of sparrows and finches, as well as the ubiquitous European starling. The ridgelines behind the recreation area may soon be developed, but open space and natural rhythms are likely to prevail here.

A paved trail, with a parcourse, leaves the eastern parking lot (off Military West) then turns into a paved trail/road at the main entrance (state park road, fee). From the main entrance you can hike, or drive, out to the Dillon Point parking lot, passing two wooded picnic areas en route. The distance between the eastern parking lot and the Dillon Point parking lot is nearly 1.5 miles. (Dogs on leash.) To reach the point—an especially good fishing area for sturgeon, striped bass, king salmon, and flounder—walk down to the shoreline from the parking lot and follow the gravel trail for a quarter-mile.

About half a mile before you arrive at the Dillon Point parking lot, the Bay Trail route veers west off the paved trail/road and leads to Regatta Drive and the Glen Cove neighborhood on a dirt path. Look carefully—tall grass and shrubs may obscure the trailhead.

Benicia State Recreation Area

Benicia–Martinez Bridge

BENICIA–MARTINEZ BRIDGE

This bridge is 6,215 feet long, hangs nearly 140 feet above the water, and carries 75,000 vehicles a day. For bicyclists and hikers there is a regularly scheduled shuttle service on Caltrans maintenance vehicles. Call Caltrans for information. The opening of this bridge, 6 miles east of the Carquinez Bridge, on September 16, 1962, marked the end of automobile ferry service on the bay; the car ferry between Martinez and Benicia ceased to run.

Glen Cove Marina

To the immediate west of Southhampton Bay, beyond Dillon Point and within Vallejo's city limits, is Glen Cove. The Glen Cove waterfront is presently inaccessible, but the city plans to develop a 15-acre waterfront park here soon. It will include the renovated Stremmel Mansion, built in the 1930s and now boarded up. The isolated mansion is surrounded by eucalyptus, palms, and pines, and will be used for activities ranging from environmental education to weddings.

The Glen Cove Marina is actually located in Elliot Cove, due west

Carquinez Lighthouse

at the end of Glen Cove Marina Road; from here you can take in the view from a bench atop a small breakwater. Across the strait, the C&H factory and the town of Crockett dominate the foreground. On the ridgeline above town, rows of brightly colored new homes stand in contrast to the muted tones of Crockett's older homes below.

Another big draw to the Glen Cove Marina is the Carquinez Lighthouse. It stood just off the mouth of the Napa River, guiding ships from 1910 to 1957, when it was decommissioned. Shortly thereafter it was sold and barged to its present location. It now houses the Glen Cove Marina harbor master's office.

Glen Cove Marina

Bay Area Ridge Trail

From the eastern end of Benicia to the vicinity of the Carquinez Bridge, the Bay Trail route is joined by the Bay Area Ridge Trail, a 400-mile, multiple-use trail on the ridgetops surrounding the bay being coordinated by the Bay Area Ridge Trail Council. When completed, this trail will connect over 75 parks and open spaces in nine counties and will be linked with the Bay Trail in numerous places. The two concentric trails will eventually allow hardy souls to circumambulate the bay on two routes: along the shore, and over the peaks. Over 168 miles of the Ridge Trail are already in use. You can call the Ridge Trail Council for information on this trail, and to find out about trail-related events (see page 133).

California Maritime Academy

The California Maritime Academy, founded in 1929 as the California State Nautical School, wraps around Morrow Cove to the west of Semple Point. All U.S. merchant ships are required to have aboard a licensed officer trained in maritime regulations. This training is provided here.

California Maritime Academy's shoreline

The academy's shoreline—highlighted by a row of stately palm trees—has a section of public shore, about a quarter-mile long, with a grassy picnic area. Expansive views of San Pablo Bay and the Carquinez Bridge are unavoidable. The academy's 7,000-ton training ship, the *Golden Bear*, is open for group tours. Contact the academy for further information.

Vallejo

This city, another founded by Mariano Guadalupe Vallejo, in 1850, served as the state capital from 1851 to 1852. Today Vallejo is a city of some 116,000 people, and home to commuters to Oakland, San Francisco, other Bay Area cities, and Sacramento.

Vallejo's Shoreline Parks

The city has extensive water-frontage along Carquinez Strait. Several city parks offer sites for relaxation or exercise as you move toward Vallejo's true waterfront, on the Napa River. Carquinez Park, off Sonoma Boulevard, is split in two by a city block. It has large lawns and playing fields. Wilson/Lake Dalwigk Park (between 5th Street and Curtola Parkway) has several miles of hard-surface trails, as

Georgia Street, Vallejo, 1886

Vallejo Marina

well as playgrounds, and a body of water that would be more appropriately named Marsh Dalwigk than Lake Dalwigk.

Between the small boat-launching ramp at Maryland Street and the Vallejo Pier—a stretch of some 3 miles—you will find a promenade, parkland, and marina. Moving up the path en route to the Vallejo/San Francisco Ferry terminal, you will pass sculptures that incorporate maritime paraphernalia such as anchors and warped propellers. Anglers can drop a hook and line over the railing along the promenade. The train ferry to San Francisco ran from this waterfront from the 1890s to the 1920s, carrying passengers, cattle,

and merchandise. Opposite today's ferry terminal, across Mare Island Way, is Marina Vista Memorial Park. A winding parcourse follows a paved path past a playground, picnic areas, lawns, and a mounted torpedo. Vallejo Transit serves this entire area, with connections to BART.

Moving farther upstream brings you past the Vallejo Municipal Dock, the Vallejo Yacht Club, and spacious Vallejo Marina. From the northern corner of the marina, you can follow a path underneath the Mare Island Causeway to River Park with its 55 acres of grassland, brush, and shoreline marshes. The park is crisscrossed by gravel trails and dotted with comfortable benches.

Vallejo Fishing Pier

Directly upstream from River Park, tucked against Sears Point Bridge, is the Vallejo Fishing Pier. It has seen many uses. From 1892 until the 1920s, the Union Brick and Tile Company loaded bricks here on boats destined for San Francisco. Later, it was incorporated into a drawbridge that linked Mare Island with the mainland. When the Sears Point Bridge was built, the drawbridge was demolished, except for this 1,000-foot portion, left for anglers and walkers to enjoy.

A little snack stand greets you at the pier's entrance, and the parking area under the bridge has a most spectacular view. To the north, the entire Napa River, with its marsh-fringed shoreline, opens up in front of your car. Rugged summits rise in the distance overlooking the Napa Valley—Elkhorn Peak and Arrowhead Mountain. But most people come here to fish, not for the view: This pier is best known for huge sturgeons—some weighing up to 200 lbs—that have been caught here. Bring a strong pole (and enjoy the view).

Vallejo Fishing Pier

MARE ISLAND

When José de Cañizares first saw this island in 1775, he named it Isla Plana, or Flat Island. Some 150 years later, as General Vallejo was crossing the Napa River, he lost some horses to the swift current and apparently thought that one of his favorite mares was among them. Later he learned that the mare had swum to the island. He allowed it to live out its natural life here, the story goes, and the island became known as Mare Island.

Mare Island, however, is best known for its military history, which began in 1854 with the establishment of the

Mare Island waterfront, 1940

Navy Yard here. During the 1860s the Russian government arranged for its North Pacific fleet to be serviced at Mare Island because Russia lacked dry docks at its own bases. During World War II, 100,000 workers labored around the clock to launch over 400 ships here. More recently, Mare Island Naval Shipyards serviced several nuclear submarines. In 1993, this base was designated for closure in 1996. Access is severely restricted, so if you want to find out more, visit the Vallejo Naval and Historical Museum (corner of Marin and Capital streets in Vallejo). It offers group tours to Mare Island, and can occasionally accommodate individuals.

Welders, Mare Island Naval Shipyard, 1943

Getting Around

Through most of Benicia, the Bay Trail route follows two paths. One begins at the Benicia-Martinez Bridge toll area and follows surface streets to the Benicia State Recreation Area. The second route begins at the Benicia Marina and follows a well-signed Bay Trail route for some 3 miles through neighborhoods to the recreation area. This latter route parallels the shore, passing the Point Benicia Public Pier, historic 1st St, the old State Capitol, the 9th St Park, and Matthew Turner Shipyard Park.

These two routes converge in the east parking lot of the Benicia State Recreation Area. The route then moves through the recreation area for just under 1.5 miles, then follows a hard-surface path to a Glen Cove neighborhood on Regatta Dr. Follow Regatta westward to Glen Cove

Pkwy, continue on the parkway to Glen Cove Marina Rd en route to the Glen Cove Marina (located in Elliot Cove). At the marina another hard-surface path begins, leading up a steep hill to the vicinity of the Carquinez Bridge and into another neighborhood, on Waterview, overlooking the bay. Eventually a trail will take you under the bridge to the California Maritime Academy. Meanwhile, use streets.

From the California Maritime Academy, use streets to reach Carquinez Park, Wilson/Lake Dalwigk Park, and Vallejo's waterfront promenade. A paved trail continues along the waterfront to River Park. For the short distance between River Park and the Vallejo Fishing Pier, use streets. From the pier, the Bay Trail route is not yet developed. The proposed route moves east to Hwy 29 and Broadway en route to Napa.

INFORMATION

Bay Area Ridge Trail Council
415-391-0697

Benicia Bus Service
707-422-6378

Benicia Capitol State Historic Park & Benicia State Recreation Area
707-745-3385

Benicia City Parks
707-746-4285

Benicia-Martinez Bridge Caltrans Shuttle Service
510-286-0589

California Maritime Academy
707-648-4200

East Bay Regional Park District
510-562-7275

Glen Cove Marina
707-552-3236

Mare Island Public Information
707-646-3537

Vallejo Parks & Recreation
707-648-4600

Vallejo Naval & Historical Museum 707-643-0077

Vallejo Transit
707-648-4666

Like people who live in the Bay Area, many of the aquatic species in San Francisco Bay have come from elsewhere within the past 150 years. Almost none of the 6.5 million human beings who live in the nine Bay Area counties today have roots in this land that go back more than 200 years, and, according to the 1990 Census, only 47.4 percent are native Californians. Likewise with the bay's water species. An estimated 150 to 200 marine and brackish water invertebrates, fish, and algae are nonnatives: they have been brought here, either deliberately or accidentally, and have adapted to local conditions. Though nobody will hazard even an educated guess as to how many plants and animals live in the bay—ranging from sturgeon and striped bass to microscopic plankton—in some parts of the bay all the species are nonnative, according to James Carlton, a specialist in aquatic animal invasions. The presence of these aliens (also known as exotic or introduced species) has increased the bay's biodiversity, but often at the expense of natives.

James Carlton with Atlantic green crab

Throughout the world, people are moving across time zones and crumbling borders at an ever-accelerating rate, and they are taking other life forms with

them, either accidentally or deliberately. Myriad organisms are spreading into new environments, vastly changing plant and animal communities. "This worldwide process, gathering momentum every year, is gradually breaking down the distribution that species had even a hundred years ago," the eminent British ecologist Charles S. Elton wrote in his pioneering work, *The Ecology of Invasions by Animals and Plants*, published in 1958. Perhaps nowhere is this mingling of species from different regions—and the frequent conflict among them—more visible than in California, particularly in San Francisco Bay.

Alien organisms began arriving in large numbers in 1848, when thousands of ships brought men from many ports in search of gold in the Sierra foothills. The hulls of the Gold Rush ships carried stowaways: barnacles, worms, and other aquatic animals and plants. In addition, Eastern oysters and at least 29 species of fish have been imported and released into rivers and the bay for sport and commerce. With each crate of oysters, many other alien species arrived.

Lately, it has become evident that it is hazardous to move organisms around as though they were pieces on a game board, without regard to life's interconnections. Now wildlife management agencies are expending enormous effort trying to preserve what is left of some natives. (See p. 64 for the story of the alien red fox and the California clapper rail.) But the mixing continues. New species keep arriving, in the ballast water of ships, in people's luggage, in many other ways that are hard to control.

An alien species that succeeds in adapting to a new habitat can

wreak havoc on a native ecosystem. Typically, these are species that tolerate greater environmental fluctuations than do natives. Many flourish around natural and human-caused disturbances, and these abound in the bay. Leaving behind the predators that kept their populations in balance in the native habitat, some of these species become invasive and undergo population explosions.

The Asian clam *Potamocorbula amuresis* is native to Asia's east coast and one of San Francisco Bay's most recent alien invaders. It was first detected in 1986 and within a short time was seen in concentrations of up to 1,500 per square meter in Suisun Bay, consuming amazing amounts of food and dominating habitat that would otherwise serve native species. Before long it was the most abundant invertebrate species in Suisun and San Pablo bays and had changed the food chain in the upper estuary.

Asian clams

To keep aquatic alien species out of the bay is extremely difficult. Boats offer them many travel opportunities. In spring 1994, no regulations had been adopted in California or elsewhere in the United States governing the disposal of ballast water, except along the Saint Lawrence Seaway. One way you can help native species is by never releasing live bait fish or other aquatic species—pet fish, turtles, salamanders, frogs—into the bay or nearby streams, ponds, and reservoirs.

Many animals and plants released into the bay do not survive, and some find their niche within the ecosystem without causing trouble. Some are benign, or even outstandingly valuable. A prime example is the striped bass, which was introduced into the bay and delta in 1879 and is now a prized sport fish and a focus of conservation programs (see p. 127).

As scientists struggle to understand the species that have already invaded the bay, they worry about what might be coming next. They worry especially about the European zebra mussel, *Dreissena polymorpha*, which is causing untold damage in the Great Lakes. It was first seen in Lake Erie in 1983, probably having arrived through the Saint Lawrence Seaway in the ballast water of a ship, and now clogs freshwater pipes, obstructs boat plumbing, and invades piers not only in Lake Erie but also in Lake Michigan and Lake Huron. One study estimates that this single species will cause billions of dollars' worth of damage in eastern waterways before the year 2000. It may be only a matter of time before it reaches the bay. Already, dead zebra mussels have turned up on boats being transported overland to California.

The effects of transferring aquatic organisms is often not understood until it is too late to control. Therefore, it is wise to be as careful as possible to slow down the "great historical convulsion in the world's fauna and flora" that Elton began to describe forty years ago.

> *"All things considered, man, whether by intent or inadvertence, is the principal agent responsible for introducing organisms of all sorts to North America and elsewhere."*
>
> Joel W. Hedgpeth, 1993

Here's a sampler of undesirable aliens in the bay— species that have not found a comfortable niche within the ecosystem but, rather, have overwhelmed and displaced native species' populations:

Atlantic cordgrass

◆ The Atlantic green crab, which arrived on this continent from Europe some decades ago, is a small species that eats just about anything—including the invasive Asian clam. It is also very prolific, and more tolerant of environmental fluctuations than native crab species. This crab apparently made its way here from the East Coast.

Atlantic green crab

◆ The shipworm *Teredo navalis* uses its shell to tunnel into wood. It appeared here early this century and was soon causing serious damage to ships and wooden structures, even causing ferry slips and pier warehouses to collapse into the bay. Its destructive abilities were so great, and its spread so rapid, that efforts to control it led to one of the earliest studies of a bay species. Today, shipworms are kept in check by chemical treatment of lumber and hulls.

◆ Atlantic cordgrass was introduced to the bay in the early 1970s as part of a salt-marsh restoration project in Hayward because it grows vigorously. It adapted extremely well—too well. Soon it was outcompeting native cordgrass and spreading quickly to mudflats, where native cordgrass does not grow, and converting these ecologically rich areas into relatively barren cordgrass islands.

Shipworm Teredo navalis

Oil tanker

Tankers bring crude oil to refineries along the Carquinez Strait, in Hercules, Martinez, and Richmond. Sometimes several are anchored south of the Bay Bridge, near the Alameda Naval Air Station. After the oil is refined, petroleum products are transported to further destinations by barge, ship, or truck.

Container ship

These cargo ships carry intermodal containers designed to be transferred mechanically between ships and trucks or trains. The containers are 8 feet wide, 9.5 feet high, and either 20 or 40 feet long. They are moved by huge gantry cranes that stand on the shore. The largest (Post-Panamax class) container ships are more than three football fields long (almost 1,000 feet) and 16 containers wide—too big for the Panama Canal.

Break bulk and container combination

This ship has its own gantry cranes aboard to move cargo between the shore and the ship's hold. The containers it also carries are moved by shore cranes.

Roll on/Roll off ship

These "Ro/Ro" ships are built to transport large vehicles. On the bay they look like giant boxes. In this ground-level view the stern ramp is down, ready for vehicles to be driven aboard or ashore.

U.S. Coast Guard cutter

The primary mission of the high-endurance, high-speed cutters is maritime law enforcement. They patrol to ensure that U.S. fishing rights are protected and to interdict illegal drug shipments. They also undertake search and rescue missions.

Ocean tug

Tugs such as this one pull barges up and down the coast and in the bay. They also assist larger container ships and tankers in docking in the bay.

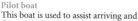

Whale boat

You may notice these sturdy 26-foot-long boats, with eight rowers each, practicing along the San Francisco waterfront and in the Oakland Estuary. The modern era of whale boat racing as a sport began in 1934, but it goes back to the last century, when there were always seamen around and they had access to boats. Whale boats were used by whalers but also on many other ships and at shoreline life saving stations. The whale boats today are built to historical specifications. They weigh more than 2,000 pounds.

Pilot boat

This boat is used to assist arriving and departing ships. It carries the pilot, who is familiar with local waters, to and from cargo ships entering and leaving the bay.

Four-person shell

Crew teams often practice and race lightweight shells on the Oakland Estuary and other calm bay waters.

This northern reach of San Francisco Bay—San Pablo Bay—comprises some of the region's most critical wildlife habitat. Much of the land across San Pablo Bay's northern shore has been set aside for wildlife or military use. Yet its intricate network of freshwater tentacles offers varied opportunities for exploration. You move inland here, into a landscape that is intimately connected to the entire bay by its many waterways. The Napa River, numerous sloughs, Sonoma and Tolay creeks, and the Petaluma River to the west are interwoven with grasslands, marshes, oak woodlands, and fertile agricultural fields. The waterways are ecological transition zones, joining aquatic and terrestrial habitats that are vital to many species.

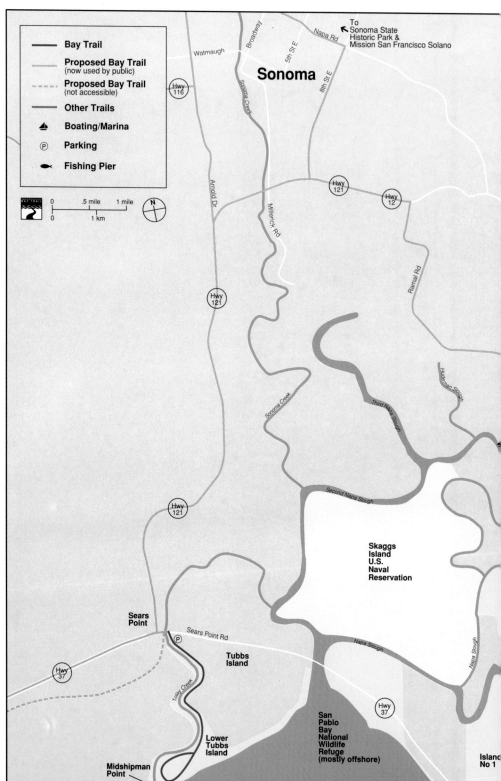

Bay Trail

Proposed Bay Trail
(now used by public)

Proposed Bay Trail
(not accessible)

Other Trails

⛵ Boating/Marina

Ⓟ Parking

🐟 Fishing Pier

0   .5 mile   1 mile
0   1 km

N

Sonoma

Watmaugh

Broadway

5th St E

Napa Rd

8th St E

To
Sonoma State
Historic Park &
Mission San Francisco Solano

Hwy 116

Sonoma Creek

Arnold Dr

Millerick Rd

Hwy 121

Hwy 12

Ramal Rd

Hwy 121

Sonoma Creek

Huseman Slough

Third Napa Slough

Second Napa Slough

Hwy 121

Skaggs
Island
U.S.
Naval
Reservation

Sears
Point

Sears Point Rd

Ⓟ

Tubbs
Island

Napa Slough

Hwy 37

Today Creek

Napa Slough

Hwy 37

Lower
Tubbs
Island

San
Pablo
Bay
National
Wildlife
Refuge
(mostly offshore)

Island
No 1

Midshipman
Point

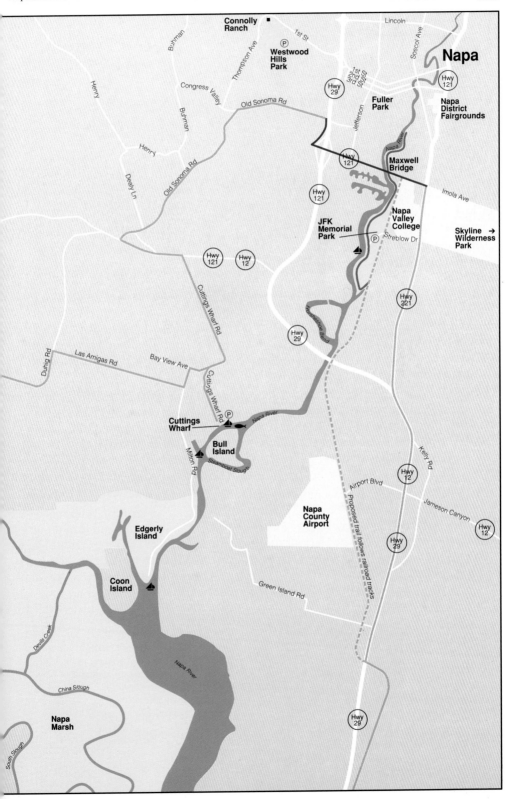

NAPA

Mention Napa and most people think of California wine. This is the most famous of California's wine-producing regions, and it attracts roughly 4 million visitors a year. Most come to sample the fruits of viticulture in their many varieties, and to enjoy the manicured landscape, chateau-style wineries, fine restaurants, and the area's Old World feel. But

Napa Valley vineyards

there is far more to discover along this northern reach of bayshore. Bountiful populations of birds and other wildlife find sanctuary here. Tranquil hills and shaded waterways invite exploration by bike and on foot. You can also fish, soak in a mudbath (in Calistoga), or ride in a hot air balloon.

Rolling hills rise to the east of Napa Valley, while to the west the Mayacamas Mountains separate it from neighboring Sonoma Valley. Napa Valley is about 30 miles long, and widens from slightly over a mile in the north to about six miles south of the city of Napa. The Napa River flows off the slopes of Mt. Saint Helena, through the city, and into the bay. In the last century, scow schooners and steamboats navigated all the way to the Third Street Bridge in downtown Napa. The best way to see the old waterfront now is by boat. In the future, Napa hopes to open its downtown riverfront to public access, as Petaluma, Sacramento, and some other riverfront cities have done.

Most towns in the Napa Valley sprang up in the late 1840s to house and feed miners en route to the gold fields in the Sierra foothills or the quicksilver (mercury) mines on Mt. Saint Helena and in Lake County. Early agriculture was mainly fruit, grain, and cattle. Since the 1850s, however, wine has ruled the landscape and the economy. More than 36,000 acres of vineyards produce about 9 percent of California's wine grapes.

HOT AIR BALLOON RIDES

Just after sunrise on clear mornings, up to 20 colorful balloons launch from several locations between Yountville and Saint Helena and ascend over the vineyards. Flights last about an hour, and the view of the valley is magnificent. Call the Napa Visitors Bureau for more information.

NORTH BAY SALT PONDS

At the edge of the Napa River and San Pablo Bay, 9,850 acres of a former salt farm were acquired by the state in 1994, to be managed as a wildlife preserve by the Department of Fish and Game. Many species of shorebirds, waterfowl, and other waterbirds feed in the interconnected salt ponds and tidal marsh.

Mew gull

RIVER BOATS

California's numerous rivers were an early, and natural, transportation network. Steamboats began running on the Sacramento and San Joaquin rivers during the Gold Rush in 1849, linking foreign ports and San Francisco with California's vast interior. Trips up the shallow Napa and Petaluma rivers—and far up the Sacramento River to Red Bluff, and the San Joaquin River into Fresno County—were accomplished with smaller steamboats with as little as 15 inches of draft.

The first steamboats came from the East Coast via the Strait of Magellan under their own power, or were dismantled and transported on sailing ships! By 1851 there were 28 steamboats plying the Sacramento and San Joaquin rivers, ushering in the "glory years" for California steamboats. Luxurious boats such as the *New World*,

Chrysopolis, and *Capital* (277 feet long) offered fast and comfortable passage between San Francisco and Sacramento. However, by the late 1920s most of the steamboats were gone, casualties of the more competitive railroad and automobile. The last working survivor of the more than 300 California steamboats was the *Petaluma*, which transported goods for the ranches of Sonoma County until 1950.

Steamboat Capital, *built in 1866*

North on Highway 29

North of Vallejo, the Bay Trail route follows Highway 29 in slicing through agricultural land en route to Napa Valley proper. You pass a scattering of houses, roadside businesses, and clusters of developments, but the landscape is more rural than suburban. This is especially true to the east: rolling grazing lands ease into a variety of agricultural patterns as the route moves north, and soon the characteristic clean rows of vines define the land. Thanks to strong agricultural zoning, the value of vineyards, and shared interests between growers and conservationists, the valley has not succumbed to the urban pressures that have destroyed many other agricultural areas near large cities.

John F. Kennedy Memorial Park

John F. Kennedy Memorial Park

🌲 🦆 ♿ 🐟 ⛴ 🚶‍♂️ 🚴

Just south of downtown Napa, along the Napa River off Highway 121, is John F. Kennedy Memorial Park. As you wander the park's 340 acres, over grasslands and beneath magnificent oaks, you may sense you're far from the bay or a river. This is especially true during the dry summer months. But just climb to the top of the levee trail on the park's western edge, and the Napa River will be rushing past your feet en route to the bay.

Along rural Highway 29

INTREPID FISHERMEN

If you ever drive on Highway 37 in autumn, you may see crowds of fishermen along the highway's northern shoulder between the Napa Slough and the Napa River. These determined anglers often endure chilling fog and blasting winds in their quest for the striped bass that congregate in the shallow waters of the former salt farm's "Island No. 1" (inundated year-round). To stop and start along the highway is extremely dangerous, so don't. To find out more about striped bass, and about fishing in this area, contact the California Department of Fish and Game (office in Yountville).

The park's picnic area, playground, soccer and baseball fields, boat launch, and adjacent Napa Municipal Golf Course are guarded by raucous bands of acorn woodpeckers. Egrets and herons work the river's edge. Dogs may be off leash, but they must be under voice command.

Napa

When Padre José Altimira entered the Napa Valley in 1823, he came across several thousand Indians living in villages scattered along the valley floor. Pioneers soon followed, the indigenous peoples were displaced, and by 1848 the city of Napa was founded. During the next decade the city flourished as cattle ranches, sawmills, orchards, grain fields, and small wine growers shared the fertile valley. The Napa riverfront was a busy place throughout the rest of the century, and San Franciscans frequently took the three-hour steamboat trip up the Napa River for business and pleasure. Hot springs in the area were a major tourist attraction.

It's peaceful on the Napa River, in town.

Calistoga continues as a popular resort, featuring mudbaths.

The city of Napa is bypassed by major highways, and therefore often missed by visitors. Slow down and pull over. Not only do some 64,000 people live here (more than half the county's population), the town is also rich in history, packed with excellent restaurants, and graced with shady parks and quiet side streets. Historic walking tours of Napa and other cities in the valley are offered by the nonprofit Napa County Landmarks.

Skyline Wilderness Park

To the east of Kennedy Park are the 850 rugged acres of Skyline Wilderness Park. Most of the topography here is steep (Sugarloaf Mountain tops out at 1,630 feet), but a comfortable picnic area and a gradual 2.5-mile trail to Lake Marie ensure fun for the entire family. A segment of the Ridge Trail moves through this park on the 4.4-mile Skyline Trail. No dogs. (Fee.)

Public dock at Cuttings Wharf

Westwood Hills Park

Due west of downtown Napa is Westwood Hills Park, 110 acres of oak and eucalyptus groves and meadows. Some 3 miles of dirt trails wind through the park, leading to numerous benches and a scattering of picnic spots. The Napa Valley Naturalists maintain the Carolyn Parr Nature Museum near the parking lot (off Brown's Valley Road). No dogs and no bicycles.

Adjacent to the park's western border is the Napa County Land Trust's Connolly Ranch. It maintains a feeding area off Brown's Valley Road where visitors can feed geese, goats, chickens, ducks, pigs, turkeys, sheep, and horses. Bring some vegetables, fruit, or dried bread to offer. If you want to tour the ranch, call the land trust.

Westwood Hills Park

Cuttings Wharf

As you stand on the small public dock at Cuttings Wharf, cattails and tule reed texture the shores of the Napa River; the scent off the fresh water conjures up images of glistening trout, leisurely canoe rides through crystalline waters, and long cool drinks. Yet you're only about 10 miles from the bayshore as the crow flies.

Cormorant nesting colony on tree snags on the Napa River

It was the abundant fresh water of the Napa River that attracted Francis Cutting to this very spot in 1893 to expand his San Francisco–based fruit packing business into fruit growing. From the original wharf here, steamboats hauled fruit from Cutting's orchards, and neighboring orchards, to Bay Area canneries. Cutting's operations ended in 1909, and the wharf was acquired by Napa County and eventually opened to the public.

Northern California Wine Country

The Napa and Sonoma valleys, and much of the land to the north and west, are internationally famous for their wine. Because this region's cool, wet winters, fog-influenced summers, and fertile soils uniquely favor wine grape production, wineries have been here for over a century. California has more than 326,000 acres in vineyards, and produces some 400 million gallons of wine annually at more than 770 wineries. More than 36,000 acres of the vineyards and almost one-half of those wineries are in Napa and Sonoma valleys. Vineyards have also been expanding in Mendocino County, to the north, where many pear, prune, and walnut orchards have been cut down to make room for grapes. The state's biggest wine-producing county is Fresno, in the Central Valley, but connoisseurs favor northern California wines.

The first vineyard was planted in Napa County in 1838. By the 1870s many more were established. Meanwhile, near the Russian River in Sonoma and Mendocino counties, Italian immigrants were developing another region. Wine grapes were introduced in the Sonoma Valley at Mission San Francisco Solano, founded in 1823 by Franciscan monks. Agoston Haraszthy, a Hungarian immigrant who founded Buena Vista

Buena Vista Winery cellar door

Winery in 1857, is credited with the amazing expansion of wine varieties in northern California. In 1861 he brought from Europe some 100,000 cuttings from 300 different varieties of wine grapes!

A Napa vineyard in spring

Getting Around

With the exception of a trail in Kennedy Park, the Bay Trail route has not been developed in this area. Its route follows roadways, moving north on two branches that follow Hwy 29 and Broadway. These parallel trails join at American Canyon Rd. At the junction of Hwys 29, 12, and 221, the route moves north on Hwy 221—past John F. Kennedy Memorial Park—to Imola Ave and the city of Napa. As the route moves west on Imola Ave to Old Sonoma Rd you pass over the Napa River on the Maxwell Bridge. Old Sonoma Rd winds through a rolling landscape of vineyards to Cuttings Wharf Rd and on to the Napa River. Watch for the huge eucalyptus windbreaks in this area—a sure sign that the winds can be strong in the north bay. From Cuttings Wharf the route goes back up to Las Amigas Rd to Ramal Rd en route to the Hudeman Slough boat ramp (see p. 146) and eventually Sonoma.

INFORMATION

Carolyn Parr Nature Museum
707-255-6465

City of Napa Parks
707-257-9529

Department of Fish and Game
707-944-5500

Napa Chamber of Commerce
707-226-7455

Napa County Landmarks
707-255-1836

Napa County Land Trust
707-252-3270

Napa Valley Transit
707-255-7631

Napa Valley Wine Train
1-800-427-4124

Napa Visitors Bureau
707-226-7459

SONOMA

I f you want wine country charm with a pinch more history, and a dash less crowds, then Sonoma rather than Napa might be the place to go. There are probably more state historic parks in a 20-mile radius from downtown Sonoma than anywhere else in California. You can ride in a balloon here as well as in Napa. Call the Sonoma Visitors Center for information.

The Sonoma Valley is some 17 miles long and 7 miles wide, and the town of Sonoma is situated about mid-valley. The Mayacamas Mountains separate the valley from Napa to the east, and to the west the Sonoma Mountains help temper the cool winds off the Pacific. About 6,000 acres of the valley floor are dedicated to wine grapes.

A typical rural Sonoma County road

GENERAL MARIANO GUADALUPE VALLEJO

General Mariano Guadalupe Vallejo

Mariano Guadalupe Vallejo was one of California's most important, and durable, citizens of the 19th century. Born in Monterey in 1807, when Spain still controlled the region, he rose quickly through the Spanish military ranks and survived the 1822 transition to Mexican rule to become *Comandante General* of Alta California for Mexico in 1835. Despite a minor setback during the 1846 Bear Flag Revolt (p. 146), he continued his political career as a U.S. citizen after California became one of the United States in 1850.

Although Vallejo played a key role in the founding of Benicia and Vallejo (he owned the land), he lived most of his life in Sonoma, where he helped to raise his 13 children. In 1834 he was deeded the Rancho Petaluma, one of the earliest and largest land grants in northen California, encompassing some 45,000 acres. As commander general he was in charge of the settlement and of protecting Mexico's northern frontier. But he found ample time to pursue personal interests and amass a fortune in land and livestock. His troops "gathered" laborers by raiding Indian settlements, and tracked down "infidels" who fled the missions.

Sonoma State Historic Park

This state park doubles as a functioning downtown area bustling with residents and visitors. On every corner, at every turn, history is before you. Historic buildings including the Jacob Leese residence (1846), the El Dorado Hotel (1843), and the Swiss Hotel (1850) ring Sonoma Plaza (a national historic site itself). State park buildings line the plaza's north side.

The dozen or so buildings of the state historic park include Mission San Francisco Solano (1823), the Barracks (1840), and La Casa Grande—home to General Mariano Vallejo for some 20 years starting in the late

Sonoma Plaza

1830s. To begin a visit in downtown Sonoma, go by the visitors bureau in the plaza for free information and suggestions offered by friendly volunteers.

To the north of downtown (off Highway 12 and Arnold Drive) is the 803-acre Jack London State Historic Park. The writer spent his final days at his residence here. You can tour the grounds, the ruins of Wolf House, the House of Happy Walls (built as a

Swiss Hotel, built in 1850

museum by his wife, Charmian Kittredge, after London's death in 1916), his cottage, some outbuildings, and his grave.

Mission San Francisco Solano

Mission San Francisco Solano

This was the northernmost of 21 missions established by Franciscan monks in California between 1769 and 1823. It was founded on July 4, 1823, and was at the peak of its prosperity in the early 1830s, when about a thousand Miwoks, Pomos, Wintuns, and other indigenous people were rounded up in their villages and brought here to work. In 1837, smallpox killed almost the entire Indian population of Sonoma. The state acquired the mission and its grounds in 1906. There are two excellent museums here, one in the old military barracks and one in the mission. (One fee for all state historic park buildings.)

Ruins of Wolf House, which burned down in 1913, a month before Jack London was to move in

Hudeman Slough Boat Ramp

To get a true feel for the wide open, windswept expanses of the north bay, venture down Skaggs Island Road, through the hay fields, to Hudeman Slough boat ramp. Winds blasting off San Pablo Bay race across this country with no more than grass-covered levees to slow them down. They even toss about the turkey vultures and black-shouldered kites soaring over the fields, as well as the terns and egrets working the sloughs and watery byways.

Hudeman Slough Boat Ramp

SEARS POINT RACEWAY

This race track—one of the largest in the western United States—was first opened in 1968 on some 800 acres of former grazing land just north of Highway 37 on Highway 121. Since its opening, scores of local and national racing, drag car, and motorcycle events have taken place here, and the raceway's popularity has soared. In 1993 more than 145,000 people came to watch the Save Mart Supermarkets 300 Race. Not all people who drive north on Highway 121 have wine on their minds!

VALLEY OF THE MOON VINTAGE FESTIVAL

This lively event has been held in downtown Sonoma every fall (September, usually) since 1897, and is advertised as "the oldest wine festival in California." It celebrates the grape harvest, and the region's history and lore (p. 143). Wine tastings, music, and historical presentations run throughout the weekend. Call ahead for specific dates.

Blessing the grapes at the festival

THE BEAR FLAG REVOLT

Sonoma's central plaza is the birthplace of the California Republic. On June 14, 1846, a small group of pioneers (also called "brigands" and "American highwaymen") rode into the town, "captured" Mexican *Comandante General* Mariano Vallejo, and declared independence from Mexico. Vallejo, ever the astute tactician and politician—and known to favor U.S. annexation, despite his official position—surrendered cordially after serving brandy to his captors. Later, the "revolutionaries" moved to the central plaza and replaced the Mexican flag with a handmade "Bear Flag," a version of which remains the state flag today. (When the handmade flag was first hoisted, it is reported that a perplexed crowd of *Californianos* thought the bear was a pig!) After Vallejo returned from a two-month detention at Fort Sutter in Sacramento, he was one of the few *Californianos* who went on to become an important California politician. He is buried in the cemetery overlooking the town.

San Pablo Bay National Wildlife Refuge

Open bay waters, tidal wetlands, and mud flats between northern Mare Island and the vicinity of the Petaluma River mouth have been preserved as the 13,000-acre San Pablo Bay National Wildlife Refuge. It is mostly off-shore. The few accessible parts of the refuge are difficult to reach, but they offer a dramatic feel for the bayshore primeval.

Hundreds of acres of tidelands and marsh along the shore here provide habitat for the endangered salt marsh harvest mouse and many other species. More canvasback ducks and scaup feed on the tidal areas here during the winter than anywhere else on the Pacific Coast. Hundreds of thousands of migrating shorebirds rest and feed on mud flats throughout the refuge, and harbor seals find shelter on countless muddy shoals.

The most accessible portion of the refuge is Lower Tubbs Island (off Highway 37 near Tolay Creek, east of Sears Point and Highway 121). It is some 3 miles

Lower Tubbs Island seen across farmlands; Highway 37 is in the foreground.

to the island, and another 1.5 miles to Midshipman Point, all on a levee-top dirt trail. Jack rabbits and pheasants dash across the trail as you move from hay fields to marshland. San Pablo Bay and the entire north bay command the horizon. The terrain is flat, exposed, and windblown.

This is a landscape of extremes, and somehow nature seems intensified here. Winds are not cool, they're freezing; the sun does not warm, it pinkens your brow in an instant; and yet, you can be chilled in summer, and overheated in winter. Shorebirds don't trickle through your view here, they explode across the sky

in gray-brown clouds united by the communal energy unique to migrants.

Waterfowl and pheasant hunting is permitted in designated areas of the refuge. Hunters and hikers should contact the refuge for current information (refuge headquarters in Newark). No dogs.

Elegant terns

 Getting Around
With the exception of the trail in San Pablo Bay National Wildlife Refuge, the Bay Trail route follows roadways throughout this entire area. The route moves into Sonoma via Ramal Rd, Hwy 121, and 8th St. It then follows streets to the junction of Hwys 121 and 116, where it splits, following each of those highways southward to Hwy 37. The route then follows Hwy 37 to the southwest and Hwy 101.

San Pablo Bay National Wildlife Refuge

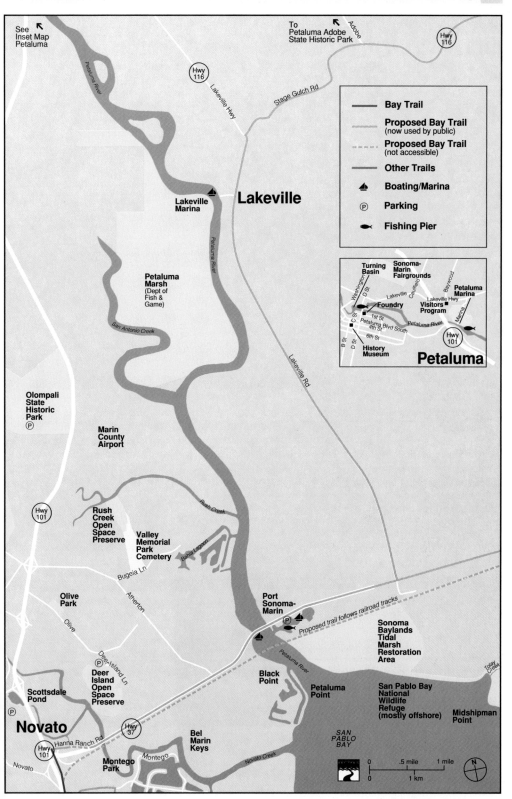

See
Inset Map
Petaluma

To
Petaluma Adobe
State Historic Park

Adobe

Hwy
116

Petaluma River

Hwy
116

Lakeville Hwy

Stage Gulch Rd

Lakeville

Lakeville
Marina

Petaluma River

Petaluma
Marsh
(Dept of
Fish &
Game)

San Antonio Creek

Olompali
State
Historic
Park
P

Marin
County
Airport

Lakeville Rd

Rush Creek

Hwy
101

Rush
Creek
Open
Space
Preserve

Valley
Memorial
Park
Cemetery

Bahia Lagoon

Bugeia Ln

Olive
Park

Atherton

Olive

Deer Island Ln

P

Deer
Island
Open
Space
Preserve

Scottsdale
Pond

P

Novato

Hwy
101

Hanna Ranch Rd

Novato

Hwy
37

Montego

Montego
Park

Bel
Marin
Keys

Novato Creek

Port
Sonoma-
Marin

P

Proposed trail follows railroad tracks

Petaluma River

Black
Point

Petaluma
Point

Sonoma
Baylands
Tidal
Marsh
Restoration
Area

Tolay Creek

San Pablo Bay
National
Wildlife
Refuge
(mostly offshore)

SAN
PABLO
BAY

Midshipman
Point

	Bay Trail
	Proposed Bay Trail (now used by public)
	Proposed Bay Trail (not accessible)
	Other Trails
⚓	Boating/Marina
Ⓟ	Parking
🐟	Fishing Pier

Turning
Basin

Sonoma-
Marin
Fairgrounds

Baywood

Washington St

D St

Lakeville

Caulfield

Foundry

Petaluma
Marina

Lakeville Hwy

Marina

Visitors
Program

1st St

Petaluma Blvd South

4th St

Petaluma River

B St

C St

D St

6th St

History
Museum

Hwy
101

Petaluma

0   .5 mile   1 mile

0   1 km

N

PETALUMA/NOVATO

Stretching along this shoreline and northward along the Petaluma River is a flat and fertile region of marshes and diked haylands that sustains some dairy and poultry farms, related industry, and a growing human population in Petaluma, Novato, and along the Highway 101 corridor. This is a gentle, welcoming landscape, perfect for leisurely bicycle rides and hikes. You can also sail, row, or paddle on the Petaluma River and its countless sloughs.

Looking toward the mouth of the Petaluma River

Sonoma Baylands

On the north shore of San Pablo Bay, near the mouth of the Petaluma River, you can study a pioneering attempt to resolve an environmental dilemma. A tidal marsh will be reconstructed here, with the use of clean dredged material from the Port of Oakland, if a 1994 plan is carried out. The port has been losing Pacific container trade to other ports partly because it was not able to dredge its channels to accommodate large container ships. Its problem: lack of a suitable site to put the dredged material. Fishermen and environmental groups protested plans for dumping into the bay or the ocean. No suitable sites on land were available. Here, however, nearly 3 million cubic yards of clean silt can be put to beneficial use in a project to restore 322 acres of diked baylands to salt marsh, for the endangered salt marsh harvest mouse, the endangered California clapper rail, migratory shorebirds, and other wildlife. The dredged material would be used to raise the elevation of a hayfield, a former marsh that subsided after it was diked off. This would jumpstart the natural restoration process. After the elevation is raised, the tide would sculpt new channels and recreate the marsh. This is the largest single marsh restoration effort so far in California. It shows how economic growth and jobs can be created by a cost-effective project that provides environmental benefits. The State Coastal Conservancy and the Sonoma Land Trust launched this project, which has broad public and government support.

Some hayfields are being restored as marsh habitat for wildlife.

Petaluma:
The River and the City

Petaluma is at the head of the Petaluma River, which is actually not a river but a 14-mile-long tidal slough. It was once surrounded by a large saltwater marsh teeming with birds, a breeding ground for crab, sturgeon, shellfish, and other marine life. Herds of elk and deer roamed the valley and wooded hills beyond. After the disovery of gold in the Sierra foothills in 1848, hunters flocked here for game to feed Gold Rush crowds. They set up camps by the river, where Petaluma later developed. Later, disillusioned miners came here to settle as farmers and ranchers.

Petaluma's Washington Street ca. 1900

Downtown Petaluma today

By the 1850s, the Petaluma River was one of the busiest waterways in California. On a typical day, scow schooners and sailboats would crowd the turning basin. They were met here by overland stage and freight lines—first horse-drawn wagons, then trains—that linked Petaluma with Santa Rosa, Healdsburg, Tomales, and Sonoma. Lumber, grains, hay, and milk products would be taken on board; other goods were unloaded for distribution throughout the region. The first steamboat came up the river in 1852; the last made the journey in 1950. Some ship captains who came to know the beautiful valley returned to live here in retirement.

Later, Petaluma became "the egg capital of the world," with families raising chickens, as well as food for them, on ranches as

small as six acres. Jewish immigrants arrived from Europe and from eastern cities to seek a life on the land that also allowed them to pursue art and literature. In the 1960s, these family farmers were driven out of business by large-scale egg producers in the south, who raised their birds in cages in huge barns that were lit 24 hours a day. Many local farmers sold land to developers and retired. A Yiddish reading circle continued to meet weekly to discuss radical literature as late as the mid-1970s. Petaluma continues to attract independent and creative souls. Many artists and musicians have settled in the area. Twice a year, you can see some of their work during an Art Trails tour. (Call the city's Visitors Program.)

The west side of downtown Petaluma is a pleasant place to stroll past buildings dating from the 1870s. You can pick up a free map and walking guide at the Visitors Program. A feed mill at B Street and Petaluma Boulevard (west side of river at the Turning Basin) has been converted to a retail and restaurant complex. Public docks are also located here (to reserve a berth, contact the Visitors Program). A small fishing pier is at the end of C Street. One block downriver at D Street, old warehouses have been reconstructed as the Foundry, a complex of galleries, offices, riverside shops and cafes, and private docks (open to pedestri-

ans). The North Bay Rowing Club maintains a dock here. (The river offers excellent rowing conditions, as it is slow and calm and has little boat traffic.)

This is still a working waterfront. Commercial fishing boats dock at the downtown Turning Basin. Several industrial firms still barge goods from South San Francisco and San Pablo Bay. But people also come here to relax on shoreline benches, dine *al fresco*, shop, or take a boat ride. You can cruise down the river while eating lunch or dining to live music aboard the *Petaluma Queen*, a triple-tier stern-wheeler built and operated

Petaluma Queen

by the Barker family, who used to build fishing boats. (Compare it with relics of old paddlewheelers at the Petaluma Historical Museum.) Or you can take a historical or nature tour (limited to six people) on Captain Larry's Electric Ferry. Call for schedules and charter information.

Port Sonoma-Marin

Port Sonoma-Marin and Black Point Public Boat Ramp

Many drivers don't realize Port Sonoma-Marin exists as they zip over the mouth of the Petaluma River on Highway 37. If you slow down and turn toward the bay on the east side of the bridge, however, you will find a popular marina and windsurfing site. A half-mile trail (rough pavement) will take you around the marina, and a quiet fishing spot can be found at the river's mouth (end of the frontage road). From the tables by the river, you can look upstream as well as across the river toward houses with long catwalk-like piers at Black Point. On the river's west side, below the Highway 37 bridge, the Black Point Public Boat Ramp offers good access to the water, as well as picnic areas and fishing opportunities. Road access is by Harbor Drive off Highway 37.

Petaluma and Lakeville Marinas

Petaluma River Turning Basin

One mile downriver from the Turning Basin is the Petaluma Marina (east of Highway 101, off Lakeville Highway). It has 190 berths, ample parking, a launch ramp (overnight fee), and riverbank fishing for striped bass, sturgeon, and the occasional salmon. Immediately south of the marina, on the river's eastern bank, is the 150-acre Schollenberger Marsh. The city of Petaluma, with the help of the California State Coastal Conservancy, hopes to open a park here soon with trails, a fishing pier, and a marsh restoration project. Several more miles downriver is the small Lakeville Marina (Lakeville Road access due south of intersection of Lakeville Highway and Stage Gulch Road).

GREENING THE HILLS WITH RECYCLED WATER

After seasonal rains have ended and the rolling hills of Sonoma have turned to gold, you will notice that some southeast of Petaluma stay green. They are being irrigated with treated wastewater. Petaluma pioneered in this form of recycling and today reclaims about half the wastewater that enters its treatment system, using it to irrigate about 700 acres of farmland, a 100-acre golf course, and 15 acres of trees throughout the city. An additional 160 acres of storage ponds created as part of the reclamation program now also provide wildlife habitat. (To watch birds there, call the City of Petaluma Wastewater Facility to make an appointment.)

Recycled water keeps fields green.

Wastewater reuse is just one of Petaluma's creative efforts to preserve local agriculture. Another is the Sonoma County Farm Trails program. Pick up a map at the Petaluma Visitors Program, at the entrance to the Petaluma Marina, just off the Highway 101 exit to Highway 116 East (look for blue-and-white signs), and visit farmers who sell fruit, vegetables, poultry, and dairy products directly to you.

Black Point Boat Ramp

Petaluma Marsh

About midway downriver, between downtown Petaluma and Port Sonoma-Marin, the Department of Fish and Game's 2,000-acre Petaluma Marsh Wildlife Area encompasses the river's western shore. Although it is only accessible by water, it is well worth exploring. If you can manage to sail or paddle into the small sloughs here you'll get a duck's water-level perspective. Seasonal hunting is permitted throughout the marsh, so call the Department of Fish and Game office in Yountville for season dates. This office monitors San Francisco Bay's wildlife and game resources and administers large tracts of state-owned wildlife habitat.

Petaluma Marsh

PETALUMA ADOBE STATE HISTORIC PARK

East of downtown Petaluma, off Adobe Road, is the Petaluma Adobe State Historic Park (fee), the restored *rancho* of General Mariano Vallejo. It is open to the public and available to school groups for overnight stays. A festival takes place here annually.

General Vallejo's Adobe

Olompali State Historic Park

When Juan Manuel de Ayala was searching for a water route into present-day Sonoma County in 1775 he was the first European to visit the Olompali Indians. Numerous artifacts have been found in the park, and it is now believed that these Miwok people lived around this site since at least 2,000 B.C. Camilo Ynita, the only Native American ever to receive a Spanish land grant (1843), ran cattle and grew grain across some 8,800 acres here, trading with the Russians at Fort Ross, until an Anglo family, the Burdells, purchased the land in the mid-19th century and built most of the buildings now at the state park. The remains of Ynita's 1840s adobe are still visible inside a special display building. Today Olompali is a 700-acre state historic park (fee) with excellent interpretive displays and 3 miles of trails winding under gnarled oaks and across lush meadows. The park is accessible from southbound Highway 101 only. It connects to an additional 1,600 acres of Mount Burdell Open Space held by the Marin County Open Space District.

Olompali State Historic Park

Rush Creek Open Space Preserve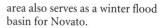

This 36-acre preserve, north of Valley Memorial Park Cemetery, is a valuable marshland habitat in the Petaluma River floodplain.

Together with the 194 adjoining acres held by the Department of Fish and Game, the Rush Creek Preserve helps ensure that resident and migratory waterfowl can find shelter and food. The

Rush Creek Open Space Preserve

area also serves as a winter flood basin for Novato.

The Rush Creek Preserve is surrounded by private oak woodlands, but you can reach it by parking on Bugeia Lane (off Atherton) and walking alongside the cemetery's western boundary. Look for a metal livestock gate and entrance (no sign) by a prominent row of eucalyptus trees. Follow the eucalyptus for a half mile to the preserve. A 1-mile section of fire road cuts across this preserve. Dogs permitted off leash, but must be under voice command. No bikes.

Deer Island Open Space Preserve

The 135 acres of oak savanna in the Novato Creek floodplain, known as Deer Island, are also held by the Marin County Open Space

Deer Island Open Space Preserve

District. The preserve is immediately north of Highway 37 and open all year. (Park on Deer Island Lane off Olive and look for green preserve sign by old homestead.) A dirt trail, some 2 miles long, ambles across this preserve and affords visitors 360° views. Hikers may be serenaded by the ratcheting of acorn woodpeckers while gazing out over inundated marshland and flocks of waterfowl. Dogs permitted off leash, but must be under voice command. No bikes.

Acorn woodpecker

Scottsdale Pond

Immediately off Highway 101 and Rowland Avenue is a favorite spot for birdwatchers, dog owners, and walkers: Scottsdale Pond. Although a *de facto* undeveloped park, it is technically a flood control basin that drains to Novato Creek. The pond itself covers some 7 acres and is ringed with cattails and brush. It is surrounded by an equal amount of open space crisscrossed by informal paths and dog runs. Both resident and migrant birds feed along the pond's edge and bathe in its fresh water. The city hopes to expand this "park" by acquiring some adjacent marshland soon.

Scottsdale Pond

The Marin Museum of the American Indian

Excellent exhibits of Miwok crafts and domestic items—including rabbit skin clothing, arrowheads, and tools—make up this museum. The collection of Indian baskets from around the state is small but exquisite. A small store sells books and Native American crafts. Outside, some native plants grow in a small garden. They include canyon sage and matilja poppy. The museum is in Novato's Miwok Park (off Novato Boulevard) and admission is free, but donations are gladly accepted.

Antique doll

Indian basket

Novato History Museum

Housed in a restored 1850s Victorian (off DeLong Avenue at Reichert Avenue), the Novato History Museum is a quaint collection of antique dolls, miniature trains, and a variety of everyday 19th century items. It also features an exhibit on nearby Hamilton Air Force Base. Admission free, but donations accepted.

> ### MARIN COUNTY OPEN SPACE DISTRICT
> Since 1972 this public agency has helped preserve and protect over 12,000 acres in Marin County. The district itself manages some 9,000 acres of open space across 25 preserves. Call its office for a listing of preserves and the schedule of free field trips.

INFORMATION

Captain Larry's Electric Ferry
707-874-1000
(Bay Area: 1-800-974-0974)

City of Novato Parks
415-897-4323

Department of Fish & Game
707-944-5500

Golden Gate Transit
415-453-2100

Marin County Open Space District
415-499-6387

Marin Museum of the American Indian
415-897-4064

North Bay Rowing Club
707-769-2003

Novato History Museum
415-897-4320

Olompali State Historic Park
415-892-3383

Petaluma Adobe State Historic Park
707-762-4871

Petaluma Historical Museum
707-778-4398

Petaluma Parks & Recreation
707-778-4380

Petaluma Queen
707-762-2100

Petaluma Visitors Program
707-769-0429

Petaluma Wastewater Facility
707-762-5892

Port Sonoma-Marin
707-778-8055

Sonoma County Farm Trails
707-996-2154

Sonoma County Transit
707-576-7433

CLO, THE UDDERLY AMAZING COW

Highway travelers throughout the north bay enjoy billboards featuring Clo the cow, cartoon mascot and official spokescow for Clover-Stornetta Farms. This Petaluma-based dairy business buys milk from 20 local dairy ranchers who belong to the 80-year-old California Cooperative Creamery. (Some 500 dairy producers in the north bay, Central Valley, and Nevada belong to this cooperative.) Clover-Stornetta markets some 1,500 dairy-related products, including ice creams and 300 varieties of cheese. Clo has adorned milk cartons since the 1950s and has been seen on billboards for decades, dishing up puns and one-liners, attired to match her words. She grew so popular that when Clover-Stornetta held a contest for Clo jokes and puns in 1988, more than 8,000 entries poured in. Among Clo zingers:

> *Tip Clo Through Your Two Lips*
> *Clo's Encounters of the Curd Kind*
> *Splendor in the Glass*
> *Clo's Line*
> *Moooey Bueno*

Getting Around

From Sonoma, the Bay Trail route follows roads through this area. Almost none of this trail has been developed for hiking or biking so far. The route moves south along Hwys 121 and 116 to Hwy 37. The Hwy 116 portion of the route goes past Lakeville, and parallels a section of the Petaluma River before joining Hwy 37. From Hwy 37, the route moves west—past Port Sonoma-Marin—to Hwy 101 and the Bay Trail route as it winds south along Marin County's shoreline.

There are many simple but important ways you can help to protect the bay and its shoreline for your own and future generations' enjoyment.

Storm Drain Pollution

During storms, rainwater moves over the surface of the ground and soaks into the soil. In most places, the soil is a natural filter that cleans water before it reaches creeks and bays. But in much of the San Francisco Bay Area, there are so many buildings, parking lots, and streets that rainwater can't soak into the ground. Instead, it flows downhill across pavement and concrete until it enters a storm drain and pours into your local waterway *without* being cleaned. Along the way the water picks up oil and pollution from the streets. (See p. 67 about the DUST Marsh.) This runoff also carries wastes that people pour directly into their gutters and local storm drains. Did you know that just one can of motor oil can contaminate up to 250,000 gallons of water?

In San Francisco Bay, and across the United States, it is estimated that half of all water pollution comes from storm drains. *It is pollution that is preventable.*

Team applying storm drain stencil

What Can You Do?

Neighborhood storm drain projects and recycling programs abound in the Bay Area. By participating in these programs you will not only be helping to improve the nearest stretch of shoreline, you will help the entire bay. To find out how to

prevent storm drain pollution, contact the San Francisco Estuary Project's Paint the Drain Campaign at 510-286-0460, or your city's Public Works Department. Ask what you can do in your neighborhood to prevent this form of pollution.

Finished storm drain stencil

What to Do with Wastes

Used motor oil, antifreeze, pesticides, herbicides, oil-based paints, gasoline, paint thinner, and turpentine should be poured into separate, sturdy, sealed containers. Do not mix such wastes. Tape the caps on, label with a permanent ink marker, and ask your city's recycling program where you can drop them off, or have someone pick them up. Call the California Integrated Waste Management Board Recycling Hotline—1-800-553-2962—for the recycling center or program closest to you, and for information on less toxic alternatives to common household cleansers and pesticides.

Chlorinated water from swimming pools and hot tubs should be allowed to stand for two weeks before draining, without adding additional chlorine. Chlorine will completely evaporate from pool and tub water within two weeks.

Excess or old latex paint should be air dried in its can, then discarded in trash. Pour clean-up water (followed by a good rinse of tap water) down sinks that lead to wastewater plants. Don't pour clean-up water down storm drains.

If you see what you think is harmful waste going down a storm drain, entering a creek, or being dumped along a shoreline, report it to one of the agencies or organizations listed on p. 186.

How can you recognize such waste?

- Oil leaves sheen on water, as does gasoline.
- Antifreeze produces milky or bright green water.
- Excessive silt muddies the water. Its presence may indicate illegal shoreline activity.
- Most soaps and detergents create suds.

Loss of Wetlands and Shoreline Wildlife Habitat

Since 1850, 85 percent of the bay's wetlands have been destroyed, either buried under landfill or diked off and dried out. The destruction of shoreline habitats threatens the health of the bay and the survival of resident and migratory wildlife.

What Can You Do?

- Join one of the organizations fighting to save the bay and its nearshore habitats (see p. 187). Volunteer for education and clean-up projects.
- Follow local planning issues that have an impact on the shoreline.
- Contact your city, county, state, and federal representatives when bay and shoreline issues come up.
- If you think you see illegal filling along the shoreline, report it to one of the agencies or organizations listed on p. 186.

Alien Species

Although the alien species introduced into San Francisco Bay have increased the bay's biodiversity, they often harm natives by dominating habitats and competing for resources (see pp. 134–135). Never dump live bait fish or other foreign aquatic species—pet fish, turtles, salamanders, frogs—into the bay or nearby creeks, streams, ponds, or reservoirs.

Never feed feral cats or release cats into the wild—even if they are sterilized. Feral cat colonies

are now doing more damage to wildlife habitat than even the red fox (see p. 64), according to wildlife biologists. Cats not only eat birds, they can decimate rodent populations.

Keep your dog on leash or under voice control when visiting shorelines. Don't allow dogs to run through marshes or sprint down beaches chasing shorebirds. It may be good exercise for your canine, but shorebirds need a chance to rest and feed peacefully. There are ever fewer places where they can do so. Dogs can also damage marsh species and habitat.

If your home is on the bay, plant and cultivate your garden to prevent soil from washing into the bay. Consider planting natives and avoid invasive alien species, such as broom, pampas grass, ice plant, and eucalyptus.

Once established, native plants are both beautiful and beneficial, and most require minimal attention and watering. Many water-saving plants popular with nurseries are actually aliens; they may conserve water, but they are more likely than natives to die with the first cold snap. To find

out about natives appropriate for your yard, visit your local nursery and ask if it carries native plants. Another source for information and free literature regarding drought tolerant plants, most of which are natives, is your water company's customer service department. The East Bay Municipal Utility District sells an excellent book, *Water Conserving Plants and Landscapes for the Bay Area*. The California Native Plant Society will also gladly answer your questions (check your telephone book).

Bay Trail cleanup day at Candlestick Point

Adopt-A-Beach

The California Coastal Commission's Adopt-A-Beach program has volunteer groups cleaning up beaches, marshes, and shorelines year-round. During Coastweeks in September, a massive cleanup operation takes place. Join the crowds on a shoreline near you. To find out more about these activities, call 1-800-COAST-4U (1-800-262-7848).

When water that would naturally flow into the bay is diverted for human uses the bay's capacity to flush out pollutants is diminished.

"California is essentially a semi-arid region of the earth. Into this region of uncertain balance between wet and dry we have intruded the greatest system of dams and canals on earth to catch and store and deliver water to farms and cities. All this has been based on the idea that water that is allowed to enter the bay and estuarine system, and flow into the ocean, is 'wasted.' The great pumps that force the water into the canals that deliver water as far south as San Diego are causing a hemorrhage of the deltaic system."

Joel Hedgpeth, 1994

Park Day School in Oakland has adopted Damon Marsh.

Separately, the steps above may not seem very influential. But together, and with time, the individual actions of many inhabitants of the San Francisco Bay Area can make a powerful difference in the state of the bay, the health of its plant and animal species, and the well-being of the shoreline environments.

Look closely at life on the bay and around it. Every drop of water is an environment for many life forms. A microscope reveals worlds invisible to the naked eye, sometimes of great beauty. Explore with a magnifying glass or microscope and share what you see with others, especially children and young people. What may look like a streak of white on a rock or a shell may be a multitude of the *zooeicia* pictured here. Learning to see something is the first step toward caring for it.

Zooeicia, the vacated "houses" of zooids in a bryozoan colony. These tiny animals feed on plankton and can reproduce by budding. When dead, most colonies look like white lacework attached to boards, stone, or seaweed.

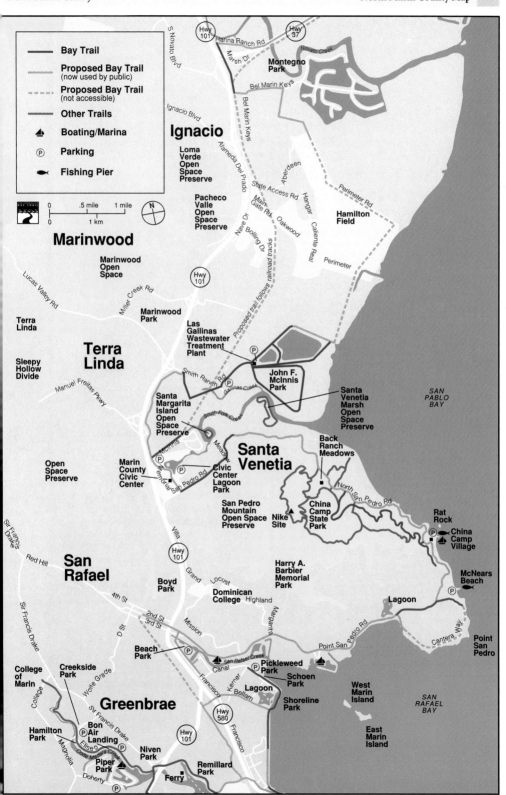

NOVATO CREEK TO GALLINAS CREEK

North Marin County's winding shoreline once sheltered and sustained many Indian villages. Today its expansive marshlands, stretching from Novato Creek through Hamilton Field to Gallinas Creek, offer excellent birdwatching and countless recreational activities. Parks are scattered along this shoreline, but are particularly numerous in the Gallinas Creek area.

Expansive marshlands and meadows around Hamilton Field

Hamilton Field

Hamilton Field was named in memory of Lt. Lloyd A. Hamilton, a pilot in World War I. It was dedicated as a military airfield in 1935, declared surplus in 1969, and deactivated in 1976. Ever since, its future has been the subject of heated controversy in Marin County. Voters turned down a variety of proposals over the years. Recently plans were approved for development on 400 of the 2,100 acres. About 700 acres of marshland may be reclaimed as wildlife habitat. Hangars and buildings stand empty throughout the base. Numerous toxic sites have been identified and will be cleaned.

Lt. Lloyd A. Hamilton

MARIN MEADOWS

Hamilton Field was built on a site once known as Marin Meadows, a name that still applies, in a sense. Surrounding the old military base are fields used for growing crops, particularly hay. Deer, mice, and other meadow wildlife work the edges of the fields. Hawks—and the occasional golden eagle—hunt from fences and electrical towers. Throughout the oak-lined residential areas of the old military base, acorn woodpeckers, red-shafted flickers, mockingbirds, and kestrels fill the air with chatter and song.

Hamilton Field

Las Gallinas Wildlife Ponds

South of Hamilton Field are the Las Gallinas Valley Sanitary District Wastewater Reclamation Project Wildlife Ponds. People don't normally associate sewage plants with wildlife, but Las Gallinas is a birdwatcher's paradise. The entrance, behind the sewage plant on Smith Ranch Road, has a kiosk with a listing of 187 bird species seen here, including white pelicans, barn swallows, Canada geese, and numerous shorebirds. In 1985, 385 acres of marsh, water treatment storage ponds, and irrigated pasture were

Canada goose

incorporated into a wildlife area. About 3.5 miles of public trails wind through the area. Las Gallinas is just one of several marshes on the bay either restored or created with treated wastewater. Others are in Palo Alto, Martinez, and Hayward.

McInnis Park

McInnis Park

John F. McInnis Park takes in 441 acres on the northern shore of Gallinas Creek, just off Smith Ranch Road and Highway 101. It offers piers for hand-launched craft, such as kayaks and canoes. It also has tennis courts, baseball diamonds, a golf course, driving range, miniature golf, soccer fields, and a restaurant. A 2.5-mile trail (mostly dirt) loops around this county park to the bay's shore. The sports facilities can be reserved by calling the Marin County Parks Department.

FRANK LLOYD WRIGHT

The Marin Civic Center building, last major project of architect Frank Lloyd Wright, is an object of pride for the county with its skylights, interior fountains, and tropical plants. It stands amid rolling green space, behind a lagoon circled by a trail and populated by ducks and geese. Docents lead tours of the building Monday through Friday.

Pickleweed

Santa Venetia Marsh

The Santa Venetia Marsh Open Space Preserve is dominated by stands of tough-skinned pickleweed, although bright yellow patches of brass buttons can be seen March through December. A dirt path circles the marsh for just over 1 mile, with no less than nine access points from the nearby community of Santa Venetia.

Santa Margarita Island

Santa Margarita Island Open Space Preserve is a small, beautiful island on the south fork of Gallinas Creek (end of Meadow Drive off San Pedro Road). A wide paved bridge, the only access, is a good spot to watch the tide work through the surrounding marsh. A 0.5-mile rough dirt path encircles the island, with several small trails leading to its oak-covered rocky summit. Warning: look out for large poison oak bushes; they are so big they don't look like poison oak!

Santa Margarita Island

PARALLEL PELICANS

Both white and brown pelicans frequent the bay. Both fly in flocks with heads pulled back on their shoulders, have similar outlines, and feed principally on fish. Aside from their differences in color, other features aid in their identification.

White pelican
The larger of the two species, the white pelican has a 9-foot wingspan and nests in the interior of the western U.S. It visits the bay from summer through winter, when large numbers can be seen circling high above the water. It is almost all white, except for black primary feathers and a yellow bill. White pelicans swim on the surface of the water scooping up fish, often in cooperative fishing groups.

California brown pelican
The brown pelican, with a 7-foot wingspan, nests off California's southern coast and into Mexico during the summer. During the non-nesting season it is often seen flying in formation inches above the surface of bay waters. This dusk-colored bird with a white or yellowish head plunges beak-first into the water in search of fish. The brown pelican was driven to near extinction by the pesticide DDT in the late 1950s and 1960s. Although still listed as endangered, the species has rebounded.

China Camp State Park, with marsh

Much of this shoreline is inaccessible. Short segments of Bay Trail are usable under the intersection of Hwys 101 and 37 as well as along Bel Marin Keys Blvd to the edge of Hamilton Field. Although Hamilton Field is open to the public, no developed public trails exist. To reach McInnis Park use streets. A dirt trail circles the park, and another dirt trail leaves the parking lot at Las Gallinas Valley Wastewater Treatment Plant and winds bayward through the wildlife ponds. The Bay Trail route continues south on Redwood Hwy Frontage Rd to the Civic Center, then moves onto North San Pedro Rd to China Camp State Park. The route divides at Back Ranch Meadow's entrance. One arm continues on North San Pedro Rd to McNears Beach; the other follows a dirt trail, merging with the paved road just north of McNears Beach.

DUCK BLINDS IN THE BAY

When waterfowl were more numerous on the bay, and duck hunting was more popular, elevated duck blinds dotted the nearshore. Not owned by anyone in particular, the wooden blinds were used on a first come basis by generations of hunters. Most have been removed, or have fallen down, but a few remain, particularly in the northern bay and the San Pablo National Wildlife Refuge. Look bayward from McInnis Park, or Hamilton Field, and you'll see a few weathered blinds rising above the bay on rotting pilings.

Duck blind

POINT SAN PEDRO TO SAN RAFAEL CREEK

The oak-studded peninsula separating San Pablo Bay from San Rafael Bay, known today as Point San Pedro, is largely undeveloped thanks to the creation of China Camp State Park and McNears Beach County Park. Numerous city parks offer welcome breaks in the midst of residential areas along the shores of San Rafael Creek.

Looking toward China Camp historic village and Point San Pedro

Swim, launch a boat, get a taste of history.

China Camp State Park

China Camp State Park's 1,500 acres include much of Point San Pedro and encompass miles of shoreline, salt marshes, grassland, coastal scrub, valleys shaded by oak and bay trees, and grassy ridgelines that afford unparalleled views of San Pablo Bay. Numerous day use areas are scattered throughout the park. There are 30 walk-in campsites (fee) at Back Ranch Meadows. Sixteen miles of trails wind past marshes, through woodlands, and along ridges. See trail map in historic village. (Parking fee.)

China Camp Historic Area

Once a Chinese fishing and shrimping village, China Camp Historic Area is now reduced to a few weathered buildings and one excellent museum. In 1870, 76 men—aged 12 to 62—lived in the China Camp region. Their families followed. By 1880, 469 people in villages at Point San Pedro exported a million pounds of dried shrimp to China annually.

Fan mill separated shrimp from shell.

Beginning in 1882, exclusion laws severely restricted Chinese immigration and denied Chinese residents the right to become citizens and own property. By the early 1900s restrictive legislation and outright hatred slowly brought an end to the Chinese villages (although there was a brief revival here in the 1930s). At China Camp only the Quong family remained, and thanks to their perseverance we have a taste for what life use to be like here. Today, the beach where shrimp boats once unloaded is a popular site for launching kayaks. The historic old store is next to the beach, still open on weekends. Nearby are the ranger's quarters.

Chinese settlement at Point San Pedro, ca. 1888

Shrimp

San Francisco Bay shrimp, which once supported this and numerous other fishing villages on the bay, are now collected exclusively for sturgeon bait. The shrimp spawn in the depths of the bay in winter and spring and the young migrate to shallow waters at the bay's edge in spring and early summer to avoid predators and to grow. Once mature, the shrimp return to the bay's deep channels in fall and winter.

> *Chinese Folk Song*
>
> I begin to work when the sun rises;
> I rest when the sun sets.
> I dig a well for my drinking water;
> I plow the field to provide my food.
> Powerful as the Emperors are,
> What has that power to do with me?

Chinese wall hangings, reproduced from a photograph found at China camp ca. 1887. From left to right the translations are:
"Safety on land and sea"
"Get what you wish"
"Peace and prosperity"

Pickleweed & Schoen Parks

Pickleweed Park is a 25-acre expanse of marsh, a grass field, and several boardwalks on the southern shores of San Rafael Creek. A 2-mile dirt trail with a parcourse circles this park. A Children's Center and the Pickleweed Park Community Center are in front of the park on Canal Street. A community garden next to the park overflows with flowers and vegetables year-round. A few yards eastward on Canal is the miniature Schoen Park, with a children's play area and lawn.

Pickleweed Park

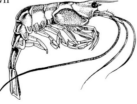

McNears Beach 🏕 🐟 ♿

This 52-acre park is named for John McNear, who manufactured bricks at Point San Pedro in the 1880s. McNears Beach is often bathed in sunlight when other portions of Marin are fogbound. With its large lawn, public pool, snack bar, pier, and mile-long beach, this park is a popular destination. (Fee.) A line of stately palm trees was planted when this was a private resort. Sturgeon, striped bass, and kingfish are caught seasonally off the large concrete pier. Just offshore are some rocky islands called The Sisters, covered by cormorants and guano. Rat Rock can be seen toward China Camp Park. Views of the Richmond refineries and San Pablo Bay define the horizon. The tip of Point San Pedro (outside the park) is an active rock quarry.

McNears Beach

Shoreline Park

Beach Park 🏕

Beach Park is behind several commercial lots off Francisco Boulevard East and Beach Park Road on the San Rafael Creek. The San Rafael Yacht Club is at one end of this small park. You will find a few benches and tables, and a small pier. Although San Rafael Park District employees clean the area weekly, there is a chronic problem here with homeless encampments and garbage.

Beach Park

Shoreline Park 🐦 🚶 🚲 ♿

Shoreline Park, which begins at Schoen Park and winds south along the bay's edge, offers parcourse stations (continued from Pickleweed Park) and spectacular views of West and East Marin islands. Although trails are in place, plans call for additional landscaping, construction of several observation platforms, and placement of interpretive signs. The trail here is wheelchair accessible for first 0.1 mile.

THE MARIN ISLANDS

The Marin Islands National Wildlife Sanctuary and State Ecological Reserve, established in 1992, takes in West and East Marin islands and surrounding tidelands. These two small islands, off-limits to humans, support one of the most important heron and egret colonies in northern California. Great egrets, snowy egrets, and black-crowned night herons can be seen with binoculars during the spring as they build nests, care for their young, and feed. Good viewing areas are Shoreline Park and the Loch Lomond Marina on the north side of San Rafael Creek.

Egrets and herons roost on Marin Islands.

GREAT EGRETS, SNOWY EGRETS, & BLACK-CROWNED NIGHT HERONS

Great egrets
Great egrets are all white with large yellow bills and black legs and feet. Standing over 3 feet, adults grow long plumes on the backs of their necks during breeding season. A slow methodical hunter, the great egret stands perfectly still in shallow water, looking for fish to grab with a quick jab.

Snowy egrets
About 2 feet tall and snowy white, snowys have slender black bills, black legs, and bright yellow feet that look like slippers. They walk briskly in shallow waters, stirring up food with their feet, and repeatedly jab at the water. Graceful head plumes made egrets targets of plume hunters at the turn of the century, who decimated their populations. Protection has since increased their numbers.

Black-crowned night herons
With their stocky 2-foot bodies and short necks and legs, these herons resemble stout old men in formal attire. Breeding adults have black heads and backs with wispy white head plumes. The young are brown. Although nocturnal, they can be seen by day roosting in trees and tall grass near marshes. When disturbed they emit a single loud *quok.*

Getting Around

From McNears Beach the Bay Trail moves on to Point San Pedro Rd and heads southwest into San Rafael. To get to Beach Park take San Rafael's 3rd St, then Beach Park Rd. To Pickleweed, Schoen, and Shoreline parks, farther south, take Bellam Blvd. Shoreline Park's paved trail becomes gravel then dirt, and continues south along the shoreline to the Marin Rod & Gun Club by the Richmond–San Rafael Bridge and San Quentin State Prison.

INFORMATION

China Camp State Park
415-456-0766

Marin Civic Center Tours
415-499-7407

Marin County Parks & Open Space Preserves
415-499-6387

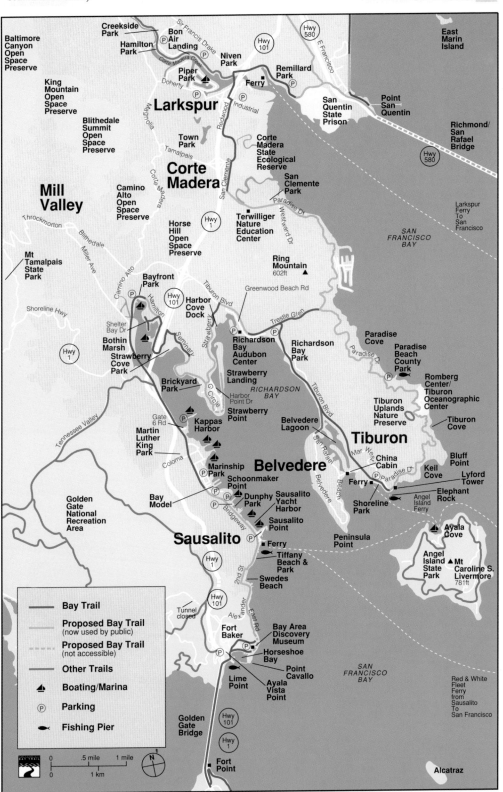

South Marin County

Baltimore Canyon Open Space Preserve

Creekside Park

Bon Air Landing

Hamilton Park

Sir Francis Drake

Corte Madera Creek

Niven Park

Hwy 101

Hwy 580

E. Francisco

East Marin Island

King Mountain Open Space Preserve

Piper Park

Doherty

Ferry

Remillard Park

San Quentin State Prison

Point San Quentin

Larkspur

Redwood

Industrial

Blithedale Summit Open Space Preserve

Town Park

Magnolia

Tamalpais

Corte Madera State Ecological Reserve

Richmond/ San Rafael Bridge

Hwy 580

Mill Valley

Corte Madera

Camino Alto Open Space Preserve

Corte Madera

San Clemente

San Clemente Park

Paradise Dr

Larkspur Ferry To San Francisco

Throckmorton

Horse Hill Open Space Preserve

Hwy 1

Terwilliger Nature Education Center

Westward Dr

SAN FRANCISCO BAY

Mt Tamalpais State Park

Blithedale

Miller Ave

Ring Mountain 602ft

Shoreline Hwy

Bayfront Park

Hwy 101

Harbor Cove Dock

Greenwood Beach Rd

Tiburon Blvd

Trestle Glen

Paradise Cove

Hwy 1

Shelter Bay Dr

Bothin Marsh

Strawberry Cove Park

Hamilton

Seminary

Strawberry

Richardson Bay Audubon Center

Richardson Bay Park

Paradise

Paradise Beach County Park

Romberg Center/ Tiburon Oceanographic Center

Brickyard Park

G Circle

Harbor Point Dr

Strawberry Landing

RICHARDSON BAY

Strawberry Point

Tiburon Uplands Nature Preserve

Tiburon Cove

Gate 6 Rd

Kappas Harbor

Tiburon Blvd

Belvedere Lagoon

Tiburon

Martin Luther King Park

Coloma

Marinship Park

Belvedere

China Cabin

San Rafael

Keil Cove

Bluff Point

Lyford Tower

Golden Gate National Recreation Area

Bay Model

Schoonmaker Point

Dunphy Park

Sausalito Yacht Harbor

Mar West

Ferry

Paradise Dr

Elephant Rock

Tennessee Valley

Bridgeway

Sausalito Point

Beach

Shoreline Park

Angel Island Ferry

Ayala Cove

Sausalito

Hwy 1

Ferry

Tiffany Beach & Park

Belvedere

Peninsula Point

Angel Island State Park

Mt Caroline S. Livermore 781ft

2nd St

Swedes Beach

Hwy 101

Tunnel closed

Alex

Easton Rd

Fort Baker

Bay Area Discovery Museum

SAN FRANCISCO BAY

Fort Point

Horseshoe Bay

Point Cavallo

Red & White Fleet Ferry from Sausalito To San Francisco

Lime Point

Ayala Vista Point

Golden Gate Bridge

Hwy 101

Hwy 1

Fort Point

Alcatraz

Legend

— Bay Trail

Proposed Bay Trail (now used by public)

----- Proposed Bay Trail (not accessible)

— Other Trails

⚓ Boating/Marina

Ⓟ Parking

🐟 Fishing Pier

0   .5 mile   1 mile

0   1 km

N

CORTE MADERA & LARKSPUR

These two cities are closely linked to the bay via Corte Madera Creek and the Corte Madera Channel. The creek's shorelines are graced by numerous popular parks. Corte Madera State Ecological Reserve is a model for marshland restoration, despite the fact that little of the original marshland remains.

Statue of Sir Francis Drake, with Larkspur Ferry Terminal and Mt. Tamalpais in the distance

Larkspur Ferry

The ferry between Larkspur and San Francisco's Ferry Building runs daily except on some major holidays. The futuristic terminal alone is worth a visit. Kiosks and posters throughout the building are full of historical information and details on local sights and activities. A pedestrian overpass from the terminal crosses Sir Francis Drake Boulevard and leads to the Larkspur Landing Shopping Center.

Larkspur Ferry Terminal

Piper Park ⛩

Larkspur's Piper Park, built on 30 acres of fill, has baseball diamonds, picnic grounds, soccer fields, a parcourse, and numerous pines and willows. A 0.75-mile dirt trail circles the park on the edge of marshland and Corte

Madera Creek. A small pier for hand-launched craft is on the creek. An organic community garden, fenced dog run, restrooms, and ample parking round out Piper Park.

Remillard Park

Remillard Park is on Sir Francis Drake Boulevard East, between the huge metal statue of Sir Francis Drake (some believe he landed here) and the windsurfing pull-out. Observation platforms and interpretive signs help you view the wildlife around two small ponds. Benches on the bayshore serve up a nice view of the Corte Madera State Ecological Reserve, the Larkspur Ferry Terminal, and Mt. Tamalpais in the distance. Across the street is the renovated Remillard Brickyard, a State Historic Landmark. Between 1891 and 1915 this brickyard produced 500,000 bricks a year. After the 1906 earthquake, much of San Francisco was rebuilt with Remillard bricks. The windsurfing spot next to the park is enormously popular.

Corte Madera Creekside Parks

The north shore of Corte Madera Creek is green with parks. Niven Park has a large grass area that extends to the creek and a scattering of benches. Bon Air Landing Park features benches, a small grass area, and a pier for hand-launched craft. Hamilton Park offers a nice view of the creek, a grass area, and benches. Ample parking throughout.

Bon Air Landing Park

Creekside Park overlooks the waterway and a small restored marsh that was once an Army Corps of Engineers dump site for dredged material from the creek. A boardwalk and observation deck provide good birdwatching. Gravel paths wind around the children's play area and an information kiosk. A multi-use trail, with parcourses, extends from Creekside Park to the College of Marin. A dirt path starts across the creek from the park and also leads to the college. The Marin Rowing Association maintains a facility on the shores of Corte Madera Creek. It offers lessons for beginners.

TERWILLIGER NATURE EDUCATION CENTER

The Terwilliger Nature Education Center offers classes, exhibits, and nature outings for children aged 3 to 7. Teaching techniques developed by Mrs. Terwilliger ("Mrs. T" to her many fans) invite children to explore the natural world while they learn about environmental issues and ecology.

Corte Madera Ecological Reserve

In the 1950s, 225 acres of salt marsh in Corte Madera were diked and slated for development. After 20 years—and no development—the desiccated wasteland became an outdoor laboratory for testing salt marsh restoration procedures. Dredgings from the construction of the Larkspur Ferry

Trail beside Shorebird Marsh, west of Corte Madera Reserve

Terminal were used to reconstruct the marsh. In 1976 dikes were breached to allow tidal waters to return. Pickleweed appeared quickly and was soon flourishing. Cordgrass followed, along with a healthy showing of shorebirds and other marsh plants and animals. Further experiments have increased biological diversity. Today, 125 acres of healthy salt marsh habitat survive as the Corte Madera State Ecological Reserve—a fantastic location for birdwatching (look for the red-tailed hawks on the electrical towers). With binoculars, you may also spot harbor seals resting on isolated shores. The reserve is accessible from the frontage road and San Clemente Drive. There is also good access and parking off Channel Drive, which runs off Harbor Drive and Yolo Street. A gravel parking lot is at the end of Industrial Way. Some 4 miles of dirt trails (many on the old dikes) wind through the marsh.

SAN QUENTIN STATE PRISON MUSEUM

An 1880s staff residence and inmate post office now serve as a unique museum. San Quentin Prison has been in operation since 1854. It began as a ship tied to the shore here. Historical photographs, documents, and artifacts make up the bulk of the museum's holdings. Drive to the prison's East Gate and tell the guard you are visiting the museum. Hours fluctuate, so call ahead. A donation ($2.00) is requested. The town of San Quentin, just outside the East Gate, has a small public shore accessible from a path through a eucalyptus grove off Main Street.

Getting Around

From San Quentin Prison the Bay Trail route moves southwest on Sir Francis Drake Blvd East toward Remillard Park, the Larkspur Ferry Terminal, and the Corte Madera Channel. A small paved trail leads under Hwy 101 and heads west up Corte Madera Creek to the College of Marin. The Bay Trail route continues on a pedestrian overcrossing at Rich St and south on the Redwood Hwy Frontage Rd. The trail borders Shorebird Marsh, a managed wetland, on the frontage road and San Clemente Dr, moving toward Paradise Dr and the Tiburon Peninsula.

INFORMATION

Larkspur Ferry 415-453-2100

Marin Rowing Association 415-461-1431

San Quentin Museum 415-454-8808

Terwilliger Nature Education Center 415-927-1670

TIBURON PENINSULA

The Tiburon Peninsula boasts some 17 miles of shoreline, a rich history, and a unique name. Punta de Tiburón is Spanish for "Shark Point." Whether an active shark fishery or frequent shark sightings lie behind the name is uncertain. Today's community began in 1884 when a small waterfront settlement formed around a spur of the San Francisco and Northwestern Pacific Railroad.

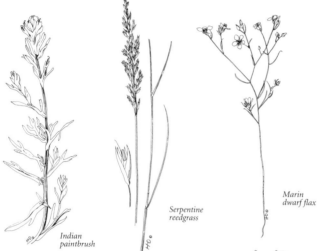

Indian paintbrush

Serpentine reedgrass

Marin dwarf flax

Paradise Beach County Park

Paradise Beach Park offers 19 acres of beautiful landscaping, generous facilities, and views of the Richmond/San Rafael Bridge, the Larkspur ferry, oil tankers, and San Quentin Prison. A large concrete pier, perfect for fishing and crabbing, juts out from a narrow beach. (Fee.)

Paradise Beach Park and pier

Ring Mountain

The Tiburon Peninsula's lower portions are wrapped in oaks, bay trees, and exotic grasses, while at higher elevations unique serpentine soils nurture some of the state's rarest plant species. The peninsula's serpentine cap is The Nature Conservancy's 400-acre preserve, Ring Mountain. (Park on Paradise Drive just east of Westward Drive. Look for the small sign and hike uphill.) Common native plants are joined here by uncommon and endangered companions: Marin dwarf flax, serpentine reedgrass, the Tiburon Indian paintbrush and the Tiburon mariposa lily (see p. 174). Many of these plants survive only within the boundaries of this preserve.

Tiburon Cove

About 3 miles out Paradise Drive from downtown Tiburon is a quiet stretch of shoreline where coastal Miwok people lived before successive waves of foreigners arrived. Like most California Indians they were either killed or expelled. Their home was given away as a Mexican land grant and eventually sold off and developed.

In 1877, a large codfish plant was established nearby to dry fish hauled here from the Okhotsk and Bering seas. In 1904 the Navy purchased the shoreline for a coaling station. In 1930 the tract was leased to the State of California for a nautical training school. In 1940 the Navy converted it into a submarine net depot (reactivated during the Korean War). In 1961 the federal government established the Tiburon Marine Laboratory, which preceded the current National Marine Fisheries Service. The buildings here are now occupied by the Romberg Tiburon Centers, a complex that includes public and private organizations. A 0.7-mile loop trail, which begins in some beautiful oaks and bays across the street from the Center, leads into the 24-acre Tiburon Uplands Nature Preserve.

Downtown

Tiburon's Main Street is lined with small shops and restaurants, including several with *al fresco* bayside seating. The Angel Island

Downtown Tiburon

ferry and the San Francisco ferries dock off Main Street, at separate piers. The old quarter of Main Street is a scant block long, ending at the Corinthian Yacht Club and a parking lot (fee). Public parking is available. Shoreline Park begins just off Main Street, at Tiburon Boulevard, where benches, grass strips, walking areas, and unimpeded views of San Francisco and Angel Island abound.

RICHMOND–SAN RAFAEL BRIDGE

Paradise Beach Park is the best place in the entire bay region for viewing the silvery Richmond/San Rafael Bridge, formally the John F. McCarthy Memorial Bridge. Opened September 1, 1956, it is 5.5 miles long, with major spans stretching 1,070 feet over dual shipping channels, 185 feet above the water. Some 44,000 vehicles cross its two decks daily.

Lyford Tower

Lyford Tower, a nationally registered historical site, was built about 1889 for Dr. Benjamin F. Lyford as the gateway to his planned utopian community "Hygeia" (Goddess of Health). Park by Shoreline Park and walk the short distance.

Angel Island State Park

This 758-acre island has served many purposes in the past 200 years. Don Manuel de Ayala set anchor in 1775 in what is now called Ayala Cove and named the island Isla de los Ángeles. His men exchanged gifts with the Miwoks. (Several Miwok middens remain on the island.) In 1839 Mexico

Historic Fort McDowell officers' quarters

gave the island to Antonio Maria Osio as a land grant. The U.S. military took over in the mid-1800s and expelled him. The oldest building on the island is a mule barn built in 1863 at Camp Reynolds, a recruit depot during the Civil War and the "Indian Wars." From 1898 through World War II, the island was the site of one of the world's largest military induction centers. From 1910 until 1940, an estimated 175,000 Asians were detained at Point Simpton waiting for permission to live and work in the U.S. Over a million immigrants of all nationalities passed through this "Ellis Island of the West."

Angel Island today

Today Angel Island State Park offers expansive vistas of the bay and nearshore communities. Two trails lead to 781-foot Mt. Livermore, a former Nike missile site. Another trail, about 5 miles long, circles the island. At Ayala Cove are the ranger's office, visitor center, historic buildings, and many picnic areas. There are excellent interpretive signs throughout. The ferries from San Francisco, Tiburon, and Vallejo dock in front of the snack bar and bathrooms. Campsites are available by reservation (fee). No dogs, skateboards, or skating is allowed on the island. Fee for ferry or docking.

Elephant Rock

Tiburon's Elephant Rock is "dedicated to all girls and boys under 16 years of age who love to fish." A short walkway leads to a small pier built atop Elephant Rock where you can drop a line or crab nets. (Even older people are welcome.)

Belvedere Peninsula

Belvedere

Belvedere, Italian for "beautiful view," was named by Thomas B. Valentine, who once owned the entire island. The Belvedere lagoon was much larger before the 1920s, when filling began to connect the island to Tiburon. Today best known for its exclusive homes (the average home price in 1990 was $1,165,000), Belvedere also has a community park and several public walkways on San Rafael Avenue.

MARIPOSA LILY

In 1971 Dr. Robert West was crossing the Tiburon Peninsula and happened upon a knee-high lily, with camouflaged foliage of light yellow-green petals flecked red-brown. Noticing it was an unfamiliar species, he snapped a photograph. He then looked for the lily unsuccessfully in several plant books. In fact, he had just discovered a new species—the Tiburon mariposa lily—a rare event in our heavily populated and well-explored state. In 1982 only 1,000 lilies were thought to exist. Now 30,000 are believed to exist, all within the Ring Mountain Preserve (see p. 172).

China Cabin ♿

The meticulously restored social saloon of the Pacific Mail steamship *China*, built in 1866 in New York City, now rests in Tiburon. William H. Webb designed the 360-foot SS *China*, a wooden side-wheeler also rigged for sail, for trans-Pacific passenger, cargo, and mail service. She came to San Francisco via the Strait of Magellan in 1867 for the first of 30 round trips to Yokohama and Hong Kong. By 1879 she was outdated by iron-hulled steamers and was slated for demolition. The social saloon was removed from the top deck and barged to Belvedere Cove, where it was used as a residence for 90 years. The Belvedere/Tiburon Landmark Society purchased the cabin and restored it in the late 1970s.

China Cabin

TIBURON GALLOWS

At the corner of Mar West and Tiburon Boulevard a pile of gigantic metal wheels hints of Tiburon's railroading past. They were part of the Northwest Pacific Railroad pier. Freight cars were rolled on and off barges that plied coastal waters between San Francisco and the "Redwood Empire" to the north. A mechanism called a gallows frame raised and lowered the ramp between the barge and pier with the changing tides. The wheels were part of the gallows frame. The railroad was built in 1884 and ceased operating in 1967. The pier was dismantled in 1974.

Getting Around

The Bay Trail route follows Paradise Dr to Trestle Glen Blvd, then cuts over to Richardson Bay. To continue on Paradise Dr you must use the road shoulder and pass downtown Tiburon, where Paradise Dr turns into Tiburon Blvd. The winding two-lane Paradise Dr is popular with bicyclists, but hiking is not advised.

INFORMATION

Angel Island State Park
415-435-1915

Angel Island/Tiburon Ferry
415-435-2131

China **Cabin**
415-435-1853

San Francisco/Vallejo Ferry
1-800-229-2784

The Nature Conservancy's
Ring Mountain Preserve
415-435-6465

RICHARDSON BAY

*Captain
William Richardson*

S ome 911 acres of shoreline and bay waters in the city of Tiburon form the Audubon Society's Richardson Bay Sanctuary. Together with the 55-acre Richardson Bay Park, these areas make up 1.5 miles of preserved shoreline. The bay was named after Captain William Richardson who in 1838 was given the 19,000-acre Mexican land grant Saucelito.

Richardson Bay

Richardson Bay Park

It may be long and thin, but Richardson Bay Park is big on recreation options. A visit any day will prove the point—runners, hikers, bikers, and roller-bladers work the shoreline path almost continuously. From the junction of Tiburon Boulevard and Trestle Glen Boulevard, where there is ample parking in the former "Blackie's Pasture" (look for an explanatory plaque in one corner of the lot), you can "workout" toward downtown Tiburon and Belvedere on a parcourse that begins near the parking lot. Look for the marsh by the parking area and the interpretive signs by the water treatment plant. A large grass playing field, McKegney Green, is a great place to relax and take in the views of the Strawberry Peninsula and Sausalito. Dogs must be leashed.

Richardson Bay Park

Richardson Bay Sanctuary

The sanctuary, established by the Audubon Society in 1957, encompasses one of the few remaining unaltered bay wetlands. About 80 species of waterbirds feed and rest here during fall migration and many resident threatened wildlife species can be seen, including harbor seals, brown pelicans, and great and snowy egrets. The sanctuary also takes in grasslands, woodlands, coastal sage scrub, and a freshwater pond. The Audubon Society's Education center and bookstore are on Greenwood Beach Road. An excellent 0.5-mile nature trail begins at the center. Sanctuary waters, closed to boats October through April, are patrolled by volunteers to prevent disturbance of migrating waterbirds.

Lyford House

The striking yellow Victorian on sanctuary ground is the Lyford House. It was constructed on Strawberry Point across Richardson Bay in the late 1870s and was the center of Lyford's Eagle Dairy. After Dr. Benjamin Lyford and his wife, Hilarita Reed, died in the early 1900s leaving no heirs, it stood empty for decades. In 1957 it was donated to Audubon, barged to its present site, and refurbished. It is open for tours on Sunday afternoons October through May, and rented for weddings and other events. (Fee.)

WATERFOWL OF RICHARDSON BAY

More than 80 species of migratory waterfowl have been observed in the sanctuary in numbers reaching into the thousands. Six of the more abundant, and therefore easier-to-spot, species are described in their winter plumage. During migration, however, various stages of plumage can be seen.

Western grebe
North America's largest grebe. Its striking black-and-white plumage, elegant neck line, and stunning red eye help identify this strong underwater swimmer.

Bufflehead
One of the smallest North American ducks, with oversized head, steep forehead, and short bill. Male is black above, white below, with large white patch on head. Female is duller, with a white patch extending on each side of head.

Lesser scaup
Two similar-looking species—Greater and Lesser Scaup—are found in the sanctuary (the greater, not surprisingly, is a bit bigger). Remember "black at both ends and white in the middle," and you'll know how to identify scaup.

Ruddy duck
A small compact duck, the male has white cheek pouches and a dull blue bill in winter, tail often pointing stiffly skyward. Its small stature and short wings give it a "buzzy" flight pattern.

Surf scoter
Informally known as the "skunk duck" (because of the male's black plumage and white head patches), the male scoter sports a wildly colorful bill. Scoters are tundra nesters and winter along the Pacific and Atlantic coasts.

Canvasback
This duck's sloping head profile and the whitish "saddlebag" across its back help classify the canvasback. The male has a rusty red head.

Getting Around

At the corner of Mar West and Tiburon Blvd, the Bay Trail route from Paradise Dr moves onto a paved path parallel to Tiburon Blvd. This piece of the Bay Trail leads to Richardson Bay Park, the Richardson Bay Audubon Center, and Strawberry Drive.

INFORMATION

**Audubon Center & Sanctuary
& Lyford House**
415-388-2524

STRAWBERRY POINT

Between Tiburon and Mill Valley hides unincorporated Strawberry Point. The peninsula leading to Strawberry Point provides grand vistas of the bay. Harbor Cove Dock, off Strawberry Drive, is a great place for hand-launching small craft. Landings

Looking from Strawberry Point toward Sausalito

and takeoffs of the only commercial seaplane operation on the bay can be viewed from the peninsula along Seminary Drive.

At the northern end of Strawberry Landing (a spit created by fill) a fenced wildlife preserve is one of only 12 harbor seal haul-out spots in the entire bay. A channel was dug to create an "island" at the tip of the landing, and a fence was erected to protect the reclusive seals from dogs, hikers, and runners. At the other end of the landing is a small grass area for viewing. There are water-level panoramas of San Francisco, the Bay Bridge, Belvedere, and Tiburon throughout. The Northwestern Pacific Railroad once operated a line from San Rafael along Strawberry Peninsula's eastern shore, crossing Richardson Bay via a trestle to Sausalito. San Francisco passengers transferred to ferries.

Brickyard and Strawberry Cove Parks

At the meeting of Seminary Drive and Great Circle Drive, a children's playground is tucked beneath a grove of shoreline-hugging trees. This is Brickyard Park, and the broken bricks strewn about the shore testify to the name's origin. Further along Seminary Drive, near the frontage road, is Belloc's Lagoon and small Strawberry Cove Park. The marsh is an even expanse of cordgrass nestled between De Silva Island (now a peninsula) and the park. A pathway follows Seminary Drive to a small exercise station. Stop on Seminary as it wraps around the cove and train your binoculars on the eucalyptus grove on De Silva Island. In spring you may see nesting pairs of great blue herons squabbling and caring for young here. A condominium development plan for the island includes a perimeter trail, two overlooks, and a shore access point.

Brickyard Park

HARBOR SEALS

Although present throughout the year in the bay, these seals are best seen on shore during the March-to-July breeding season. They give birth on land to one pup in early summer and can stay under water up to 20 minutes in search of fish, shellfish, and squid. Nearby construction and dredging have diminished the number of harbor seals here.

MILL VALLEY

Mill Valley was named after a saw mill built in 1836 by John Thomas Reed on Cascade Creek. Overlooking this community, and every inch of the Bay Trail here, is Mt. Tamalpais.

Saw mill on Cascade Creek

Bay Trail along Bothin Marsh, with Mt. Tamalpais to the north

Mt. Tamalpais

We will never know what the indigenous Miwok called their sacred mountain. To the Spanish it was Picacho Prieto—Dark Peak. Today it is Mt. Tamalpais. Most of the mountain is open space owned and managed by the Marin Municipal Water District and state and federal agencies. Some 200 miles of public trails weave a long tale of human use, including the "crookedest railroad in the world," which ran from Mill Valley to Tamalpais's East Peak from 1896 to 1930. The 2,571-foot summit is a fantastic perch for examining most of the central and northern bay. Numerous trails lead to Tamalpais, including those at the heads of Blithedale and Cascades canyons in Mill Valley, as well as from the Panoramic Highway en route to Stinson Beach.

Bayfront Park and Bothin Marsh

Whether you have two legs or four, want to run, walk, paddle, or just rest, Mill Valley's 14-acre Bayfront Park has something for you. On the western side of the park is a large dog-run area (elsewhere, dogs must be leashed) and a public pier for kayaks and canoes. A parcourse zigzags throughout. Crossing a bridge to the park's east side leads to a baseball diamond, more parcourse stations, soccer fields, and a large children's playground. Next to the park is Bothin Marsh, a 112-acre open

Bayfront Park

space preserve defined toward its southern and western fringe by the Bay Trail. Four small bridges along the trail rise over creeks and channels—great places to stop and watch for marine life when the tide surges in or out through these restricted waterways. Shorebirds abound. Dogs must be leashed.

Getting Around

The Bay Trail route turns off Tiburon Blvd onto Strawberry Dr and moves around the Strawberry Peninsula on roads. A 0.5-mile paved trail on Strawberry Landing can be reached via Harbor Point Dr. From the corner of Seminary Dr and the Redwood Highway Frontage Rd, the trail route crosses under Hwy 101 en route to Mill Valley. There is also a public overpass 0.25 mile north on the frontage road. A public pier and small-craft launch area are located about 200 yards west of Hwy 101 by some office buildings. The Bay Trail route weaves past restaurants, more office buildings, and condominiums to Bayfront Park, and the first of several bridges, via Hamilton Dr. The trail route moves down Shelter Bay Ave to the water's edge and some nice benches. The Bay Trail splits by the sewage treatment plant, with one arm circling around the Redwoods, a retirement complex, on roads, then paved trails; the other arm leads through the park. The two arms meet at Presidio Creek. At the last footbridge in Bothin Marsh, a trail leads southwest into Tennessee Valley, the Marin Headlands, and the Golden Gate National Recreation Area. The Bay Trail route, paved, crosses under the Richardson Bay Bridge toward Sausalito.

SAUSALITO WATERFRONT

I n just over two miles the Sausalito waterfront offers a wealth of colorful history, sites, sounds, parks, piers, restaurants, and shops. Sausalito's mellifluous name originates from *sausal*, Spanish for willow grove, which Spanish commander Juan Manuel de Ayala spied on its shores in 1775 and knew to be a sign of fresh water. Much of southern Marin, including Sausalito, was later encompassed in Rancho Saucelito, a Mexican land grant deeded to Englishman William Richardson. Over the past 150 years this stretch of bayshore has been used by Azorian whalers, brothels, railroads, gambling houses, massive shipyards, artist colonies, luxurious estates, and rickety houseboats. Today's explorer will find a bounty of parks and spectacular views. Except for Swede's Beach, the entire waterfront is wheelchair accessible to varying degrees.

Flotsam & Jetsam

Gate 6 Road, off the northern tip of Bridgeway (Sausalito's main drag), leads to Kappas Harbor and a small loop of public shore. Venture out onto the spit of land, find the bench, and take in the views or study contrasting lifestyles: to one side of the spit are Sausalito's famous houseboats; on the other side pricey yachts and sailboats glisten in their berths.

Hidden among Sausalito's numerous parks and walkways off Bridgeway are public shores and docks that require some searching to find. They are all great places to observe boats and maritime businesses. Flynn's Landing, for example, is a public dock stretching between Sausalito Point and Johnson Street. The end of Johnson Street also has a small unnamed public shore consisting of a dock and a few benches overlooking Pelican Harbor. At the bayside of Turney Street, another public pier with benches wraps around a restaurant and continues to Locust Street and another viewing spot.

Northside Commons

Shoreline Park has a nice grass area, benches, and a small marsh on its northern shore. It is also home to the San Francisco/Sausalito Sailing Club, which offers sailing lessons and rentals. As you move south to Marinship Park, look for the 204-foot *Wapama*, last of the coastal lumber carriers, on permanent display at the Army Corps of Engineers shipyard. Marinship Park has three

The Wapama

public tennis courts, with night lights, and a large grass field.

At Schoonmaker Point you can launch a kayak, spread a picnic, or just rest. A beautiful beach (no dogs allowed) grades into the bay. Lifeguard on duty (seasonally). If you drive don't be deterred by a "Permit Parking Only" sign. Smaller letters say public parking in green areas, and there are plenty of those.

A large lawn surrounded by weeping willows, with a refurbished gazebo, are the centerpieces of the 10-acre Carl Dunphy Park. A small

Dunphy Park

beach lets you cool off feet or watch for migrating shorebirds while children romp in the playground. Just offshore, a narrow gravel bar is a well-used resting spot for egrets and other shorebirds. (Parking and restrooms available.) Sausalito's Civic Center, library, and Historical Society are upslope from Dunphy, off Litho and Caledonia streets.

Along Sausalito's Bridgeway

Secret Southern Beaches

Don't blink or you'll miss Tiffany Beach and Park, a few square feet of sand just off Bridgeway. Several benches along the length of Bridgeway invite you to rest and watch. Note the Municipal Pier, good for fishing, watching sea lions, and studying Albert Sybrian's bronze sea lion sculpture 10 feet offshore. Moving south you can bounce along a public board-

Bronze sea lion

walk (it lines out in front of some private residences then wraps around a restaurant on the bay side of Main Street). Down a flight of wooden stairs, at the bayside end of Valley Street (just off 2nd), hides Swede's Beach. About 200 feet of narrow beachfront serves up exceptional views of Angel Island, Belvedere, the East Bay, and a confusion of old pilings.

SALLY STANFORD

A former San Francisco bordello madam, owner of the Valhalla saloon, and mayor of Sausalito in the mid-1970s, Sally Stanford left a spicy impact, best exemplified by the public drinking fountains erected in her honor by the ferry terminal. The fountain for humans is inscribed "Have a drink on Sally," while the one for dogs reads "Have a drink on Leland." Leland was Sally's dog.

Downtown Sanctuaries

Downtown is always busy, but three small parks offer rest. Gabrielson Memorial Park, just south of the ferry terminal, opens onto the water and is ringed with benches. Plaza Viña del Mar is next to the ferry terminal. It was built in 1904 and honors Sausalito's sister city, Viña del Mar, Chile. Two 14-foot-high elephants sculpted for the 1915 Panama-Pacific Exposition stand guard. To stretch your legs, and gain perspective, climb the Excelsior Lane steps directly across from the plaza and Bridgeway. Yee Tock Chee Park, named in memory of "Willie" Chee, owner of the Marin Fruit Company for 60 years, is a fascinating work of concrete and pilings tucked in between Bridgeway and the water's edge. Various levels of seating have been created with concrete and wooden platforms. This is a spot where ferries landed in the late 1800s.

MARINSHIP SHIPYARDS

A memo dated March 2, 1942, marked the end of the tranquil Sausalito waterfront: "It is necessary in the interests of the national emergency that the maximum number of emergency cargo vessels be completed prior to December 31, 1942." Marinship Shipyards were created to meet that goal, and shipbuilding began that year. More than 26,000 piles were pounded into the bay to create the yards, more than 24,000 feet of new railroad track were put down, and a rich tidal marsh was completely filled. A channel 300 feet wide and more than a mile long was dredged to accommodate oceangoing vessels. During three and a half years of production, 93 ships sailed out of the yards, as some 75,000 people worked around the clock, seven days a week. Marin City was constructed to house shipyard workers. The most rapidly built ship ever produced here took 28 days from keel to launching. Today the site of the shipyards is occupied by Marinship Park and the Army Corps of Engineers maintenance yard and Bay Model.

Marinship Shipyards, Sausalito, 1944

RICHARDSON BAY'S FLOATING COMMUNITY

Sausalito's houseboat community started slowly in the 1950s when artists and writers began arriving along the bayshore. By the 1960s scores of abandoned vessels had been converted to residential use. Today two distinct types of residential structures float on Richardson Bay: houseboats and live-aboard boats. Houseboats are of two basic types: boats that are no longer used for navigation and have been converted to homes,

Floating homes

and residences built on floating platforms (floating homes). Live-aboards are boats that are used for navigation but also function as the boat owners' homes. Most houseboats and live-aboards are moored at authorized marinas where houseboats are connected to sewers and utilities. However, some houseboats and live-aboards are illegally anchored offshore or moored along the shoreline. Some 450 authorized houseboats, 140 unauthorized houseboats and live-aboards, and an unknown smaller number of authorized live-aboards make up Richardson Bay's floating home community. Similar but smaller communities are at San Francisco's Mission Creek Harbor, Alameda's Barnhill Marina, and Berkeley's Marina. Richardson Bay's structures shelter fewer artists and more lawyers today than they did in the 1960s, yet this is still a community apart.

Ride a Ferry

The Red and White Fleet ferry leaves the Sausalito terminal and ventures out under the Golden Gate Bridge before looping back to San Francisco's Pier 43½ and Pier 41. On its return voyage it passes by Alcatraz and Angel Island before turning into Sausalito. The commuter ferry operated by the Golden Gate Ferry runs directly between Sausalito and San Francisco's Ferry Building at the foot of Market Street. Bicycles welcome.

LOVESICK TOADFISH

During July and August 1984, many people were puzzled by some loud and strange nocturnal noises coming from Richardson Bay. Speculations about their source ranged from low-flying B-17s to Russian submarines. In 1985, however, scientists discovered that the weird sounds were the call of the toadfish (*Porichthys notatus*), coming in once again from the Pacific Ocean for the mating season. Toadfish had been common in the bay until the 1960s, when pollution interfered with their migration. Their return in 1984 indicates that Richardson Bay is getting somewhat cleaner and healthier.

Getting Around

From Mill Valley's Bothin Marsh the trail passes under the Richardson Bay Bridge (where there are benches, a bike rack, and parking). East of the bridge a trail moves around an office complex fringed by marshes. The Bay Trail continues, paved, to Gate 6 Rd. From there a trail leads out to a small peninsula at Kappa's Harbor. Shoreline hikers and bikers can continue along Sausalito's main roads for about 3 miles, then follow East Rd toward Fort Baker.

INFORMATION

Bay Model
415-332-3871

Golden Gate Ferry
415-332-6600

Red & White Fleet
415-546-2628

BAY MODEL VISITOR CENTER

The Army Corps of Engineers' Bay Model (recently refurbished) is a 1.5-acre reproduction of the San Francisco Bay and Sacramento–San Joaquin River Delta system. Built to scale and capable of simulating currents and tidal action, it is used by the Corps to study the bay's ecology and to plan responses to industrial accidents. Exhibits highlight the bay's natural history, geology, wetlands, wildlife, and fishing and boat-building industry.

FORT BAKER

This old military post extends across quiet Horseshoe Bay, tucked under the northern expanse of the Golden Gate Bridge. Its sheltered waterfront and coastal bluffs have been actively used by the military since the 1850s when the Lime Point Reservation was established to guard the entrance to San Francisco Bay. In 1897 it was renamed Fort Baker after Civil War hero and transitory San Franciscan Edward D. Baker. Today the fort is part of the Golden Gate National Recreation Area and a great location to view historic military architecture, visit a gun battery, enjoy the dramatic underside sights and sounds of the Golden Gate Bridge, watch massive tanker ships, visit the Bay Area Discovery Museum, and fish off a concrete pier. Fort Baker's original military mission diminished after World War I with the invention of more sophisticated defense systems, but it served through World War II as both a Mine Command Headquarters (San Francisco Bay was spiked with 481 submerged mines by 1945) and an Air Defense Command Headquarters. Members of the Sixth Army still live and work at the fort and keep their pleasure boats at the Presidio Yacht Club.

Looking toward Fort Baker

Bay Area Discovery Museum &

The Discovery Boat, Salt Marsh, Underwater Sea Tunnel, and many other exhibits invite visitors to explore the natural wonders of the bay and nearshore. Other exhibits teach about architecture and design. Classes, tours, and presentations are offered. There is also a small cafe and gift store.

Bay Area Discovery Museum

Lime Point Lighthouse

The lighthouse stands at the western tip of Fort Baker on a rocky promontory that is part of the Bay Trail. It was built in 1883 to warn ships away from the Golden Gate's treacherous fog-shrouded shores with a duo of powerful steam whistles. In 1900, Lime Point's keepers mounted a flashing light on the tower. Both warning signals are still used today. Owing to lead contamination of the soil from bridge maintenance, some areas near the lighthouse are closed indefinitely to the public.

Juan Manuel de Ayala Vista Point

Named after the Spanish commander charged with the first official survey of the bay in 1775, this parking area displays an enormous cross-section of a redwood tree from Crescent City marked with important dates in California's history. When the redwood was 50 feet tall, in 1579, Captain Francis Drake sailed to the Point Reyes Peninsula and, some weeks later, to the Farallon Islands. Drake and his crew stayed 36 days in present-day Marin County repairing his ship, the *Golden Hind*, and stocking provisions. They then set sail for England, arriving some 14 months later, in September 1580.

"You always remember the first time you saw San Francisco Bay. It comes back to you in later years with vivid intensity: the sudden, breathtaking impact of that initial moment when the great Bay was first spread out before you, fresh and new and shining."

Harold Gilliam
San Francisco Bay, 1957

VITAL STATISTICS OF THE GOLDEN GATE BRIDGE

- Work began: January 5, 1933
- Bridge opened: May 8, 1937
- Length of span: 4,200 feet
- Length of suspension bridge: 6,450 feet
- Height of towers above water: 746 feet
- Depth of piers: 110 feet
- Diameter of cables: 36⅜ inches
- Number of wires per cable: 27,572
- Total length of wire: 80,000 miles
- Weight of bridge: 83,000 tons

HAWK WATCHING

Between mid-August and mid-December the largest concentration of migrating raptors in the Pacific states—10,000 to 20,000 birds—passes over the Marin Headlands. In an attempt to avoid water, hawks, eagles, falcons, vultures, kites, harriers, and osprey funnel through the headlands. September and October are the peak months. Most migrate when it's warmest, between 10 a.m. and 3 p.m. If it's foggy or raining, stay home: the raptors are resting. The best viewing is from Hawk Hill ("Battery 129"), 1.8 miles from Highway 101 on Conzelman Road. Pull off the road completely to park before Conzelman becomes one way, then hike up the ocean side of Hawk Hill to the summit. The record: approximately 2,800 birds sighted on September 21, 1984.

Northern harrier

MISSION BLUE BUTTERFLY

Hidden in the bluffs of the Marin Headlands and the chaparral-covered hills of Fort Baker, the mission blue butterfly is making a comeback from near extinction. This tiny endangered species, with sky blue wings that measure about an inch across, lays eggs exclusively on silver lupine plants. Recent efforts to protect its habitat and increase the number of lupine have helped the mission blue rebound. It survives in only four locations in northern California, so visits to its Fort Baker habitat are limited to ranger-led tours.

Mission blue butterfly

Getting Around

The Bay Trail route follows the shoulder of East Rd from Sausalito to Fort Baker —a scenic 2-mile trip with fabulous views of the bay. There are benches and tables along the way. The trail meanders by the fort's shore and in front of the Coast Guard's Station Golden Gate. From the Coast Guard station, one trail leads east toward Point Cavallo. On the edge of Horseshoe Bay there is a small accessible beach with good exposure at low tides, ample parking, and wheelchair access. The trail, paved, climbs westward to the northern tip of the Golden Gate Bridge and Ayala Vista Point. Hikers can connect with the Coastal Trail and the Marin Headlands through a cypress grove west of the bridge.

A walkway under the bridge joins Ayala Point with the western parking lot. Pedestrians can cross the bridge on the east sidewalk 5 a.m. to 9 p.m. daily. Bikers can cross at all times, using the west side 5 a.m. to 9 p.m. weekends and holidays, 3:30 p.m. to 9 p.m. weekdays, and the east side at other times.

Along the Bay Trail from Sausalito

Sea Floor Rocks

Chert can be seen in the cliffs along the Bay Trail between Golden Gate Bridge and Fort Baker, as well as on Lime Point Trail. This red-brown sedimentary rock is composed of the skeletal remains of microscopic single-celled animals, laid down on the ocean floor millions of years ago. The slow prodigious movement of Earth's crustal plates forced the Pacific floor under the western edge of the North American continent in a process called subduction, leaving behind contorted samples of chert at this monumental meeting ground. (For more on bay geology, see pp 2–3, 85, 114.)

INFORMATION

Bay Area Discovery Museum
415-332-7674

Golden Gate Raptor Observatory
415-331-0730

**Marin Headlands Visitor Center
Fort Baker**
415-331-1540

PUBLIC TRANSPORTATION

Buses & trains

AC Transit (Alameda-Contra Costa Transit) 800-559-4636
    TDD (for deaf callers only) 800-448-9790

BART (Bay Area Rapid Transit)
    San Leandro-Fremont 510-441-2278
    Oakland 510-465-2278
    Richmond 510-236-2278
    San Francisco 415-992-2278
    TDD (for deaf callers only) 510-839-2220

Benicia Bus Service 707-422-6378

CalTrain (San Jose–San Francisco rail service) 800-558-8661

Golden Gate Transit 415-453-2100
    (San Francisco–Marin & Sonoma)   or 415-332-6600

MUNI (San Francisco Municipal Transit) 415-673-MUNI
    TDD (for deaf callers only) 415-923-6366

Napa Valley Transit 707-255-7631

SamTrans (San Mateo County Transit) 800-660-4287
    TDD (for deaf callers only) 415-508-6448

Santa Clara County Transit 408-321-2300
    TDD (for deaf callers only) 408-299-4848

Sonoma County Transit 707-576-7433

Union City Transit (Union City only) 510-471-1411

Vallejo Transit 707-648-4666

West CAT (west Contra Costa County Transit) 510-724-7993
    (Crockett, Hercules, Montara Bay, Pinole,
    Port Costa, Rodeo)

Caltrans bicycle shuttle service

Bay Bridge 510-286-4444
    (MacArthur BART station, Oakland,
    to Transbay Terminal, San Francisco)

Benicia-Martinez Bridge 510-286-0589

Carquinez Bridge 510-286-0589

Ferry lines

Blue & Gold Fleet 510-522-3300
    San Francisco (Ferry Building & Pier 39)—
    Alameda (Gateway Center) & Oakland (Jack London Square)
    Bay cruise, dinner/dance cruise, charter 415-781-7877

Golden Gate Ferry Service 415-332-6600
    San Francisco Ferry Building—Sausalito   or 415-453-2100
    & San Francisco Ferry Building—Larkspur

Harbor Bay Maritime Ferry 510-769-5500
    Bay Farm Island—San Francisco

Red & White Fleet 415-546-2628
    San Francisco (Pier 43 1/2)—   or 800-229-2784
    Sausalito, Tiburon, Vallejo (& Marine World
    via shuttle), Angel Island, Alcatraz Island (tour);
    also Golden Gate/Bay cruise & San Francisco city tour

Tiburon Ferry 415-435-2131
    Tiburon—Angel Island

Information on road and traffic conditions

Caltrans (State Department of Transportation) 510-286-4444

MORE ABOUT TRAILS

To learn more about trails and trail organizations in
the San Francisco Bay Area and the state, contact:
    California Trails and Greenways Foundation 415-948-1829
    P.O. Box 183, Los Altos, CA 94023
The foundation maintains a library of information
on trails and organizations working on trails.

TOURS & NATURE STUDY TRIPS

Audubon Society:
    Richardson Bay Center and Sanctuary 415-388-2524
    Also call for information on other Bay Area
    chapters of the Audubon Society.

Bay Area Land Watch 415-467-6631
    Offers tours of San Bruno Mountain.

California Native Plant Society 916-447-2677

Cargill Salt 510-797-1820

East Bay Regional Park District 510-635-0135

Golden Gate Raptor Observatory (birdwatching) . 415-331-0730

Marine Science Institute, Redwood City 415-364-2760
    Offers a Discovery Voyage, mostly to school
    groups, six days a week, and occasionally has
    room for individuals.

Oakland Museum of California:
    Natural Sciences Department 510-238-3884
    Inside the museum, visit the Aquatic California
    Gallery and the Hall of California Ecology.

Point Reyes Bird Observatory (birdwatching) 415-868-1221

Refinery tours:
    Chevron, Richmond 510-242-5403
    For group tours, write:
    Chevron USA, P.O. Box 1272, Richmond, CA 94802-0272

    UNOCAL, Rodeo 510-245-4433

    Shell Oil, Martinez (museum) 510-313-3598

    Pacific Refining, Hercules 510-799-8000

    Tosco, Martinez 510-370-3370

Romberg Tiburon Centers 415-435-7100
    Small group cruises, with advance notice,
    on the research vessel *Questuary*

San Francisco Bay Bird Observatory (birdwatching) 408-946-6548

San Francisco Bay National Wildlife Refuge 510-792-0222

Save San Francisco Bay Association 510-452-9261

Terwilliger Nature Education Center 415-927-1670

Wastewater treatment centers often offer tours. Some include
wildlife ponds and wetlands (see information in chapters).

Also see museums and nature centers listed at end of chapters.

CAMPING & HOSTELS

American Youth Hostels:
    Golden Gate Hostel, Fort Barry, Sausalito 415-331-2777
    San Francisco International Hostel, Fort Mason . 415-771-7277

California Department of Parks and Recreation:
    Camping reservations for all State Parks 800-444-7275

East Bay Regional Park District:
    Camping information and reservations 510-562-CAMP

GGNRA camping and overnight information 415-331-1540

AQUATIC ACTIVITIES & INSTRUCTION

A Day on the Bay, San Francisco Marina 415-922-0227
    Sailing lessons & rentals

Bay Area Whaleboat Rowing Association . . . .*no phone*
    41 Sutter Street #1620, San Francisco, CA 94104

Bay Area Windsurfing Club, San Francisco 415-476-0417

Blue Waters Ocean Kayak Tours, Fairfax 415-456-8956
    Lessons & outings

Boater's Guide to Harbors & Marinas 415-826-8905
    Guidebook updated annually for
    San Francisco Bay, Delta, and Outer Coast

Cal Sailing Club, Berkeley 510-287-5905
    Windsurfing and sailing lessons and rentals

California Adventures, Berkeley 510-642-4000
Kayaking, sailing and windsurfing lessons,
rentals and outings

California Canoe and Kayak, Richmond 510-893-7833
River and sea kayak and canoe lessons, rentals . . 800-366-9804

Cass' Marina, Sausalito 415-332-6789
Sailing lessons

Club Nautique, Sausalito 800-559-2582
Alameda 800-343-SAIL
Sailing instruction and rentals

Dolphin Swim & Boat Club, San Francisco 415-441-9329
Rowing and swimming; members only

Lake Merritt Boating Center, Oakland 510-444-3807
Boating lessons, rentals, boat tours, and
programs for people with disabilities

Lake Merritt Rowing Club, Oakland 510-273-9041
Sweep and scull lessons

Marin Rowing Association, Greenbrae 415-461-1431
Sweep and scull instruction

North Bay Rowing Club, Petaluma 707-769-2003
Scull and sweep instruction

Olympic Circle Sailing Club, Berkeley 510-843-4200
Sailing lessons

Open Water Rowing Club, Sausalito 415-332-1091
Scull instruction and rentals

Outdoors Unlimited/Cooperative Adventures, SF . . 415-476-2078
Kayaking and windsurfing lessons and rentals

Sail Advancement Information League, Oakland . . . 510-834-1000
Information on sailing lessons and facilities

Sailing Education Adventures 415-775-8779
Oceanic Society, Fort Mason, San Francisco
Sailing and dinghy lessons and trips

San Francisco Boardsailing Association (windsurfing) . . .*no phone*
1592 Union Street, Box 301, San Francisco, CA 94123

San Francisco Estuary Project 510-286-0460
Call for a complete list of pump-out facilities.

Sea Trek Ocean Kayaking, Sausalito 415-488-1000
Classes, outings, and rentals

South End Rowing Club 415-776-7372

Spinnaker Sailing (Sailing and windsurfing lessons and rentals)
Mountain View 415-965-7474
Redwood City 415-363-1390
San Francisco 415-543-7333
San Mateo 415-570-7331

Tradewinds Sailing Club, Pt. Richmond 510-232-7999
Full sailing and navigation instruction,   or 800-321-8972
rentals to members

U.S. Coast Guard:
For information about navigation rules 800-368-5647
For free classes on navigation skills and rules . . . 510-437-3308

FISHING

California State Department of Fish and Game,
Yountville 707-944-5500
For seasonal fishing information around the Bay.
This office monitors SF Bay wildlife and administers
large tracts of state-owned wildlife habitat.

*Fishing licenses are not required for fishing from public
piers and jetties along the California coast, including the
Bay shoreline. Persons of age 16 and over must be licensed
for all other fishing in California.*

RIFLE RANGES

Coyote Point Rifle and Pistol Range 415-573-2557

San Leandro Rifle and Pistol Range 510-638-9605

EQUESTRIAN INFORMATION

East Bay information 510-672-5072
George Cardinet, Heritage Trails Fund

Golden Gate Park Stables 415-668-7360
Public stables and riding academy, offers
rentals and guided trail rides in GG Park,
reservations and fees required

Marin Horse Council 415-454-2923
Contact Connie Berto for bay-wide information

KITE FLYING

American Kiteflyers Association 510-525-2755
Tom McAlister, regional director
Also runs Highline Kites concession at Berkeley's
Cesar E. Chavez Park, site of the annual Berkeley
Kite Festival and West Coast Kite Flying Championships.
Call for information on best kiteflying sites, events, stunt
and sport kiting, team aerobatic kite ballet, kite buggying, etc.

BICYCLING, RUNNING, SKATING

Bicycle Trails Council of Marin 415-456-7512

California Adventures 510-642-4000
Organizes rockclimbing, camping and natural
history excursions, bike maintenance clinics,
equipment rentals, etc.

California Bicyclist - free magazine 415-546-7291
Northern California edition gives information and
events listings for Bay Area cycling.

City Sports - free magazine 619-793-2711
Information about organizations and activities
(no local or 800 #) involving running, biking,
skiing, tennis, in-line skating, etc.

East Bay Bicycle Coalition 510-530-3444

Golden Gate Race Walkers 415-493-2652
Organizes both competitive and non-competitive
events, offers instruction, newsletter.

Regional Bicycle Advisory Committee (REBAC) . . . 510-452-1221

San Francisco Bicycle Coalition 415-431-2453

Silicon Valley Bicycle Coalition 415-965-8456

DOG RUNS

Bayfront Park, Mill Valley
Point Isabel, Richmond

TO REPORT TROUBLE OR
PROBLEMS AROUND THE BAY

*To report pollution, oil or hazardous material spills,
toxic discharge, dumping:*

BayKeeper 800-KEEPBAY
or 415-567-4401

California Dept. of Fish and Game Hotline 800-952-5400
Poaching, creek pollution,
habitat destruction, fish or bird kills

Lindsay Museum Storm Drain
Pollution Hotline 800-LINDSAY

San Francisco Bay Regional Water Quality
Control Board 510-286-1255
Spills and water quality problems

U.S. Coast Guard 510-437-3073
or National Response Number 800-424-8802
Oil or hazardous material spills, 24 hours a day

U.S. E.P.A. Region 9 (emergency) 415-744-2000

Waste Alert Hotline 800-69-TOXIC
Environmental crimes and improper disposal
of hazardous materials in California

To report large submerged objects hazardous to navigation:
U.S. Army Corps of Engineers 415-332-0334

For information on toxic waste disposal:
California Integrated Waste Management Board
    Recycling Hotline 800-553-2962

To report suspected illegal shoreline and wetland fill or construction:
San Francisco Bay Conservation
    and Development Commission 415-557-3686

To report sick or stranded wildlife:
WildCare: Terwilliger Nature Education and
    Wildlife Rehabilitation 415-456-SAVE

California Marine Mammal Center,
Marin County 415-289-7325
    Marine mammals only

Lindsay Museum, Walnut Creek 510-935-1978

Local Humane Societies .... *check your local telephone directory*

To report a boat-related emergency, call 911

RIDGE TRAIL INFORMATION
Bay Area Ridge Trail Council 415-391-0697

BAY TRAIL INFORMATION
Association of Bay Area Governments:
    Bay Trail Project 510-464-7900

State Coastal Conservancy:
    Public Access Program 510-286-1015

SCIENTIFIC AND TECHNICAL INFORMATION
California Academy of Sciences:
    General information 415-750-7145
    Library 415-750-7102
    The Academy has an extensive library, including the Biodiversity Resource Center on the public floor, which also provides computer access to bibliographic databases, text sources, and interactive programs for youth.

Oakland Museum of California:
    Natural Sciences Department 510-238-3884

San Francisco Bay–Delta Aquatic Habitat Institute . 510-231-9539

San Francisco Bay Estuary Project 510-286-0460

VOLUNTEER OPPORTUNITIES
Bay Institute of San Francisco 415-331-2303
    Works to increase freshwater flow into the estuary, stop selenium pollution, etc.

BayKeeper (see p. 15) 800-KEEPBAY
                             or 415-567-4401

Bay Trail Project (see p. 5) 510-464-7904

California Academy of Sciences 415-750-7154
    Accepts volunteers for public services, special events, and qualified persons in research department.

California Coastal Commission:
    Adopt-A-Beach Program (see p. 157) 800-262-7848

California Department of Parks and Recreation:
    Marin District 415-456-1286
    Includes Angel Island and China Camp
    Long-term work includes docent-led historical tours, period dress presentations, visitor center staff; short-term includes trail building and maintenance, research, etc.

Citizens for a Better Environment 415-243-8373
    Urban environmental health organization works for clean air and water, and toxics-free communities.

Citizens for the Eastshore State Park 510-526-2629
    Nonprofit organization working toward the creation of a State Park extending from the Bay Bridge into Richmond)

GGNRA volunteer information 415-776-0693
    A wide variety of volunteer positions, from hawk watching to habitat restoration

Oakland Museum of California, Docent Office 510-238-3514
    Offers docent classes in ecology and volunteer opportunities.

Paint the Drain Campaign
San Francisco Estuary Project 510-286-0460
    Works to stop the pollution of the bay caused by dumping of toxics into storm drains.

San Francisco Bay National Wildlife Refuge 510-792-0222
    Welcomes volunteers for a wide range of jobs, from staffing the Visitor Center to guiding nature walks to clearing brush.

Save San Francisco Bay Association 510-452-9261
    Works to protect, preserve, and restore the bay's natural values.

Urban Creeks Council 510-540-6669
    Works to preserve, protect, and maintain the flow of natural streams in urban environments.

RESOURCES FOR TEACHING ABOUT THE BAY
Friends of the San Francisco Estuary offers *An Introduction to the Ecology of the San Francisco Estuary*, produced by the Save San Francisco Bay Association, and an activity and resource guide, *Estuarine Encounters*, for grades K–12. The guide is available through the Friends' educator workshops 510-286-0769

Golden Gate National Recreation Area offers interpretive progams, nature and bird walks, and historical tours, some of them on the bay. It also offers pier crabbing with a ranger at Horseshoe Cove and Fort Baker. Call the Western Region Information Center 415-556-0560

MARE (Marine Activities, Resources, and Education) is a whole-school, K–8, multicultural year-round ocean studies curriculum, offered by the Lawrence Hall of Science, University of California, Berkeley 510-642-5008

Marine Science Institute provides an elementary school program 415-364-2760

Project Ocean, a marine science program offered by the Tarlton Institute for Marine Education, includes a teaching program on bays and estuaries for grades 7–8, and one on marshes and mud flats for grade 3 415-433-3163

San Francisco Bay–Delta Aquatic Habitat Institute offers work-shops for teachers. It has published *Teaching About the San Francisco Bay and Delta: An Activities and Resource Guide*, intend-ed primarily for high school teachers 510-231-9539

San Francisco Estuary Project offers brochures and booklets on many issues that affect the bay, as well as a slide show and a video-tape about the estuary 510-286-0460

Save San Francisco Bay Association has a half-hour videotape, *Secrets of San Francisco Bay* 510-452-9261

Water Education Foundation offers a variety of educational materials designed to develop a broader understanding of water issues and resolution of water problems. Among these is *Layperson's Guide to San Francisco Bay* 916-444-6240

A WHEELCHAIR USER'S GUIDE
The State Coastal Conservancy's *A Wheelchair Rider's Guide to San Francisco Bay and Nearby Shorelines* is available (free of charge) 510-286-1015

A

ABAG. See Association of Bay
  Area Governments
Adopt-A-Beach, 157
Adventure Playground, 99
Agua Vista Park, 20
airports: Oakland, 77, 78;
  Palo Alto, 49; San
  Francisco, 30, 32
Alameda, 82–84, 88–89, 91,
  92, 93
Alameda Creek Regional Trail,
  68, 69, 71
Alaska Basin, 89
Albany Shoreline, 101
Alcatraz Island, 12, 13, 15,
  18–19, 95
Alemany Gap, 23
alien species, 134–35, 157
Alviso, 57–58, 60; Environ-
  mental Education Center,
  59, 60; Slough, 57
Amtrak, 57
Angel Island State Park, 12, 85,
  173, 174
Anza, Juan Bautista de, 11
Anza Lagoon, 32, 35
Apay Way Trail, 68
Aquatic Beach, 11
Aquatic Park, Berkeley, 100
Aquatic Park, San Francisco,
  10, 11, 15
architecture/historic buildings:
  Fremont/Hayward, 65;
  Marin County, 161, 165,
  173, 174, 175, 182;
  Napa/Sonoma, 142, 145;
  Northeast Bay, 122, 125,
  126, 127, 129, 131; Oak-
  land/Berkeley, 92, 96; Peta-
  luma/Novato, 153; Rich-
  mond/San Pablo, 107; San
  Francisco, 10, 11, 12, 14, 15,
  18, 21; South Bay, 53, 57, 60.
  See also bridges; lighthouses
Ardenwood Historic Farm/
  Regional Park, 65–66, 68, 71
Arrowhead Marsh, 79, 80
art: sculpture, 13, 43, 51, 77,
  79, 96, 98, 132, 180. See
  also architecture/historic
  buildings
Association of Bay Area
  Governments, 5
Avocet Marsh Trail, 68
avocets, 70, 83
Ayala, Juan Manuel de, 121,
  124, 153, 173, 179, 183
Ayala Cove, 173
Ayala Vista Point, 85, 183, 184

B

Back Ranch Meadows, 163,
  164
Bair Island, 38, 43
Baker Beach, 11, 14
Ballena Bay Point, 89
balloon rides, 140, 144
bass, striped, 127, 134, 141
Bay Area Discovery Museum,
  182, 184
Bay Area Ridge Trail, 1, 5, 54,
  129, 131, 142

Bay Bridge, 1, 12, 20, 23, 91,
  92, 98, 99
Bay Conservation and
  Development Commission.
  See San Francisco Bay Con-
  servation and Development
  Commission
Bay Farm Island, 76, 78, 82, 84,
  89
bayfill. See fill
Bayfront Park, Mill Valley, 178
Bayfront Park, North San
  Mateo, 31, 32, 35
Bayfront Park, South San
  Mateo, 43, 44
BayKeeper, 15, 24
Bay Model, 180, 181
Bayside Park, 32, 35
Bay Trail, 1, 5, 6; history of, 4;
  Project, 5. See also all maps
  and chapters for specific
  information, especially
  "Getting Around" sections
Bayview Trail, 68
BCDC. See San Francisco
  Bay Conservation and
  Development Commission
beaches: Alameda, 82, 84; arti-
  ficial, 82; Marin County,
  163–67, 172, 179, 180, 184;
  Richmond/San Pablo, 109;
  San Francisco, 11, 14;
  San Mateo, 30, 33
Beach Park, 166, 167
Bear Flag Revolt, 146
Belmont Slough, 38, 39
Belvedere, 174
Benicia: city, 129–30, 133, 144;
  Marina & Pier, 130, 133;
  State Recreation Area, 130,
  133
Benicia–Martinez Bridge, 126,
  127, 128, 131, 133
Berkeley: city, 85, 86–101;
  Marina, 99, 100, 101;
  Recreation Pier, 99
bicycles, 186; & BART, 7; &
  bridges, 7
bicycling. See every chapter
birds, 1–2, 7; endangered, 64,
  79, 89, 116, 150; Fremont/
  Hayward, 63, 64, 66, 68, 70;
  gulls, 80–81; Marin County,
  160–63, 166, 167, 171,
  175–79, 183; Napa/Sonoma,
  140, 141, 146, 147; Northeast
  Bay, 126, 130; Oakland/
  Berkeley, 89, 90, 96, 98, 101;
  Petaluma/Novato, 150, 151,
  154; Rescue Center, 100;
  Richmond/San Pablo, 2, 106,
  107, 109, 112, 115, 116; San
  Francisco, 23; San Lorenzo/
  San Leandro, 77, 79, 80, 82,
  83; San Mateo, 32, 38–43;
  South Bay, 50–54, 58, 59
blackbird, red-winged, 51
Black Point, 15; Public Boat
  Ramp, 152
Blue & Gold Fleet, 17, 19, 24
bluebird, western, 126
boating, 6, 136; Marin County,
  161, 170, 171, 177, 178, 179;

Northeast Bay, 121; Oak-
  land/Berkeley, 89, 93, 96,
  100; Petaluma/Novato, 151,
  152, 153; Richmond/San
  Pablo, 115; San Francisco,
  15, 17; San Lorenzo/San
  Leandro, 79; South Bay, 57,
  60. See also ferries; sailing
  boats: river, 140, 141, 151.
  See also houseboats;
  ports; ships
Bon Air Landing Park, 171
Bothin Marsh, 178, 181
Brewer's Island, 38
Brickyard Cove, 110
Brickyard Park, 177
brickyards, 110, 170
bridges, 7; Bay, 1, 12, 20, 23,
  91, 92, 98, 99; Benicia–
  Martinez, 126, 127, 128, 131,
  133; Carquinez, 125, 128,
  133; drawbridges, 20, 60, 93,
  132; Dumbarton, 43, 44, 48,
  63, 66; Golden Gate, 12, 85,
  111, 182, 183, 184; Richmond–San Rafael, 1, 112,
  117, 167, 173; San Mateo–
  Hayward, 1, 39, 70, 85;
  Sears Point, 132
Brisbane Lagoon, 27
Brooks Island, 106, 107, 110
broom, French, 72
bufflehead, 176
bulrush, 64, 123
Burlingame Recreation
  Lagoon, 32, 35
butterflies, 28, 65, 77, 183
Byxbee Landfill Park, 51, 55

C

California, birth of Republic
  of, 146
California Adventures, 99, 101
California Coastal Commis-
  sion, 157
California Maritime Academy,
  131, 133
California State Coastal
  Conservancy, 4, 116, 140,
  150
Calistoga, 142
Cal Sailing Club, 99, 101
campion, San Francisco, 11
Camron-Stanford House, 96
Candlestick Point Recreation
  Area, 10, 22, 23, 24
Cañizares, José de, 107, 121,
  133
Cargill Salt, 42, 48, 54, 57, 71
Carquinez: Lighthouse, 131;
  Park, 132, 133; Strait, 2, 102,
  120, 124, 127, 128, 129, 132;
  Strait Regional Shoreline, 85,
  126, 128
Carquinez Bridge, 125, 128,
  133
Castro Point, 113
Castro Rocks, 113
cats, feral, 157
Cesar E. Chavez Park,
  Berkeley, 100
Channel Park, 96
chaparral, 73

Charleston Slough, 52, 55
chert, 85, 114, 184
Chevron Long Wharf, 107,
  109, 117
Chevron U.S.A., 112, 113, 116,
  117
China Basin, 20, 22
China Beach, 11
China Camp State Park, 85,
  163, 164–65, 167
China Point, 30
Chinese shrimp camps, 23, 30,
  165
clams, Asian, 134, 135
Cliff House, 11
Coastal Conservancy. See
  California State Coastal
  Conservancy
Coastal Trail, 1, 11, 184
Coast Guard Island, 93
Connolly Ranch, 142
Contra Costa, 113
cordgrass, 53, 54, 64, 123, 135,
  171
cormorants, 1, 23, 39, 112
Corte Madera, 170; Creek,
  170, 171; State Ecological
  Reserve, 170, 171
coyote brush, 72
Coyote Creek, 59, 60
Coyote Hills Regional Park, 63,
  66–67, 68, 69, 71
Coyote Point, 33, 35
Crab Cove, 82–84
crabbing, 7
crabs, 41, 83, 135
Creek Junction, 79
creeks: Fremont/Hayward, 69,
  71; Marin County, 164, 166,
  170, 171; Northeast Bay,
  121, 122; Oakland, 93;
  Richmond/San Pablo, 116;
  San Francisco, 11, 20, 22, 23;
  San Mateo, 34, 42; South
  Bay, 50, 54, 59
Creekside Park, 171
Crissy Field, 12, 14
Crockett, 124, 125, 128
Crown (Robert) Memorial
  State Beach, 79, 82, 83, 84,
  88, 89
Cuttings Wharf, 142, 143
Cypress Point, 106

D

Damon Marsh, 79, 80
Davenport Mini Park, 98
deer, mule, 67
Deer Island Open Space
  Preserve, 154
Deer Park, 65, 71
De Silva Island, 177
Dillon Point, 130
dogs, 7, 101, 154, 157, 178
Dolphin Swimming & Boating
  Club, 15, 24
Doolittle Area, 79, 84
Dowrelio Pier, 125
Drake, Francis, 183
Drawbridge (ghost town), 60
drawbridges, 20, 60, 93, 132
dredging, 95, 150, 171, 177
ducks, 2, 51, 176

Dumbarton: Bridge, 43, 44, 48, 63, 66; Cutoff, 48; Pier, 48, 63

dumps, 3, 4; Oakland/Berkeley, 99, 100, 101; Oyster Bay, 2, 77; San Mateo, 34, 35, 43; South Bay, 51, 52, 57

dune restoration, 14

Dunphy (Carl) Park, 179

DUST (Demonstration Urban Stormwater Treatment) Marsh, 67

E

earthquakes, 12, 19, 95, 122

East Bay Regional Park District (EBRPD), 100, 101

East Brother Island, 115, 117

East Creek Point, 79, 80, 84

East Palo Alto, 49

Eastshore State Park, 98, 100, 101

East Waterfront Park, 19

Edgewood County Park, 85

egrets, 58, 167

Elephant Rock, 173

Elliot Cove, 131, 133

Elmhurst Creek Trail, 80

Embarcadero: Cove, 93, 96; Freeway, 19; Promenade, 19

Emery Cove Marina, 98

Emeryville: city, 97–98; Crescent, 98; Marina, 97, 98, 101; Pier, 97

Encinal Boat Ramp, 89, 96

endangered species, 2; birds, 64, 79, 89, 116, 150; butterflies, 28, 183; plants, 1, 172; salmon, 128; salt marsh harvest mouse, 64, 70, 116, 147, 150

Estuary Park, 93, 96

eucalyptus, 65, 117, 122, 143

Evans (Lucy) Baylands Nature Interpretive Center, 50, 55

Exploratorium, 12, 24

F

falcons, peregrine, 1, 64, 92

farms, 65, 66, 152, 155, 160

Fernandez Park, 122

ferries, 12; Harbor Bay Maritime, 78; Marin County, 12, 17, 19, 170, 171, 173, 174, 180, 181; Northeast Bay, 12, 17, 19, 126, 130, 131, 132, 173; Oakland/Berkeley, 1, 12, 17, 19, 89, 92, 96, 99; Richmond, 12, 109, 113; San Francisco, 12, 17, 19, 24, 173, 181

Ferry Building, 19

Ferry Point, 108, 109

Festival at the Lake, 96

fill, 1, 3, 53; Marin County, 174, 177; Oakland/Berkeley, 99; Richmond/San Pablo, 116; San Francisco, 10, 12, 19, 22, 23; San Lorenzo/San Leandro, 79; San Mateo, 38; South Bay, 51, 52, 56, 58

Fireboat Dock, 19

fish/fishing, 6, 7, 128; aliens, 134; dredging and, 95; Marin County, 166, 172, 173, 181; Napa, 141; Northeast Bay, 2, 122, 125, 127, 128, 129, 130, 132; Oakland/Berkeley, 89, 92, 95, 97, 99; Petaluma/Novato, 151, 152; pier piling, 21; Richmond/San Pablo, 109, 113, 114, 117; San Francisco, 16, 21, 23; San Lorenzo/San Leandro, 79, 82, 83; San Mateo, 27, 30, 34, 35, 39. See also piers; shellfish

Fisherman's Wharf, 16, 18

Fleming Point, 101

flood control, 116

Flynn's Landing, 179

fog, 28, 111

foghorns, 13

Ford Building, 107

Foreign Trade Zone, 19

Fort Baker, 182–84

Fort Funston, 11, 14

Fort McDowell, 173

Fortman Marina, 89

Fort Mason, 14–15, 24

Fort Point, 10, 13, 24; Trail, 11

Foster City, 38

Fourth Street Bridge, 20

foxes, red, 64

Franciscan Complex, 28, 85, 114

Fremont, 61–71, 85

Fruitvale Bridge piers, 82

Fruitvale Pier, 93

G

Gabrielson Memorial Park, 180

Gallinas Creek, 160, 161

Garretson Point, 79, 80

geese, Canada, 161

geology, 2, 28, 85, 114, 184. See also rocks

Giant Powder Company, 116

Gilliam, Harold, 111, 183

Glen Cove Marina, 131, 133

Golden Gate, 3; Bridge, 12, 85, 111, 182, 183, 184; Ferry, 19, 24, 181; fog, 111; International Exposition, 21; National Recreation Area (GGNRA), 10, 14, 19, 24, 85, 182; Promenade, 10, 11–15; tides, 12

Golden State Model Railroad Museum, 110

grain trade, 125, 126

Grand Street Boat Ramp, 89

grasslands, 67, 73

graywacke, 28, 85, 114

grebes, Western, 176

Greco Island, 43

gulls, 80–81

gumplant, 72

H

Hamilton Field, 155, 160, 163

Hamilton Park, 171

Harbor Bay Island, 78

Harbor Channel, 106

Harbor View Park, 34

Harbour Way, 107

harriers, northern, 40

hawks, 40, 43, 183

Hayward, 61–71, 85, 135; Regional Shoreline, 70, 71, 76

Hercules and Historic Clubhouse, 122, 128

herons, 58, 167, 177

high spots, 85

Hoffman Marsh, 106

horseback riding, 69

Horseshoe Park, 99

hot springs, 142

houseboats, 20, 179, 181

Hudeman Slough Boat Ramp, 146

Hunters Point, 23, 24, 30

hunting, 43, 147, 153, 163

Hyde Street Pier, 12, 15

I

icons, 6

India Basin, 23, 24

Indians. See Native Americans

industry: Fremont/Hayward, 70, 71; Northeast Bay, 120, 121, 123, 129; Petaluma/Novato, 151; Richmond/San Pablo, 106, 107, 108, 110, 112, 113, 116; San Francisco, 22, 24; San Lorenzo/San Leandro, 77; San Mateo, 30, 42; South Bay, 58

International Bird Rescue Center, 100

Islais Creek, 22; Bridge, 20

Island Park, 39

J

Jack London: Square, 91, 92, 96; State Historic Park, 145

Johnson's Landing, 70

Junior Center of Arts and Science, Oakland, 96

K

Kaiser Shipyards, 84, 107

Karkin, 102, 120, 124, 130. See also Native Americans

Keller Beach, 109

Kennedy (John F.) Memorial Park, 141, 143

King (Martin Luther, Jr.) Regional Shoreline, 79–80, 84

kite flying, 12, 13, 100

kites, black-shouldered, 40

L

Lake Merritt, 91, 93, 96

Lakeside Park, Oakland, 96

Lakeville Marina, 152

landfill. See fill

Lands End, 11

Larkspur, 170; Ferry Terminal, 170, 171

Las Gallinas Wildlife Ponds, 161, 163

lessingia, San Francisco, 11

lighthouses, 18, 93, 115, 131, 182

lily, mariposa, 174

Lime Point: Lighthouse, 182; Trail, 184

Littlejohn Park, 88

Lobos Creek, 11

Loch Lomond Marina, 167

London, Jack, 92, 145

Lone Tree Point, 122, 128

Lower Tubbs Island, 147

lugworm eggs, 41

lupine, 72, 183

Lyford: House, 175, 176; Tower, 173

M

McInnis (John F.) Park, 161, 163

McKinley Park, 88

McNears Beach, 163, 164, 166, 167

McNeer warehouse, 126

madrone, 73

Magnetic Silencing Range Building, 13

manzanita, 28, 73

Mare Island, 132, 133

Marina Green: Richmond/San Pablo, 107; San Francisco, 13, 24

Marina Park: Emeryville, 97; Richmond, 106, 107, 110; San Leandro, 76, 78

Marina Village Yacht Harbor, 89

Marina Vista Memorial Park, 132

Marin City, 180

Marin Civic Center, 161, 163, 167

Marin County, 85, 102, 115, 158–84

Marin County Open Space District, 153, 155

Marine World, 40

Marin Headlands, 85, 183, 184

Marin Islands, 167

Marin Meadows, 160

Marin Museum of the American Indian, 155

Marinship: Park, 179, 180; Shipyards, 180

Maritime National Historical Park, San Francisco, 15, 24

Maritime Service Officers Schools, U.S., 84

marshes, 3; DUST, 67; Fremont/Hayward, 64, 66, 67, 70, 135; freshwater, 123; Marin County, 161, 162, 163, 170, 171, 177, 178; Oakland/Berkeley, 97, 98; Petaluma/Novato, 150, 152, 153; plants, 53, 64, 72, 123; restored, 70, 135, 150, 161, 171; Richmond/San Pablo, 106, 116; San Francisco, 23; San Lorenzo/San Leandro, 80; San Mateo, 38; South Bay, 49, 50, 53

Martinez, 124, 127; Regional Shoreline, 127

Matadero Creek, 50

Mayfield, 44; Slough, 51

Meadowlands, 52

meadowlarks, 41, 43
Meeker Ditch, 106, 110
Meiggs Pier, 18
merchant marines, 84
merchant ships, 131
methane, 43, 52
Methane Recovery Plant, Menlo Park, 43
mice, salt marsh harvest, 64, 70, 116, 147, 150
Middle Harbor Park, 95, 96
Miller/Knox Regional Shoreline, 85, 108–10
Mill Valley, 178, 181
Mission Bay, 16, 18, 20
Mission Creek, 20
Mission Rock, 20
Mission San Francisco Solano, 143, 145
Miwoks, 102, 153, 155, 172, 173, 178
Moffett Field, 48, 55
Morgan Oyster Company, 31
Moth Ball Fleet, 126
Mountain View, 52, 54
Mount Burdell, 85, 153
Mount Tamalpais, 85, 170, 178
Mowry Slough, 59
mud flats, 41; Fremont/Hayward, 69, 135; Richmond/San Pablo, 106; San Francisco, 23; San Lorenzo/San Leandro, 82, 83; San Mateo, 32, 38, 40; South Bay, 54, 59
Muir, John, 55, 127, 128
Municipal Pier, San Francisco, 15
Municipal Pier, Sausalito, 180
museums: Fremont/Hayward, 63, 68, 70; Napa/Sonoma, 142, 145; Northeast Bay, 125, 127, 133; North Marin, 165; Oakland/Berkeley, 96, 99; Petaluma/Novato, 151, 153, 155; Resources, 185–87; Richmond/San Pablo, 110; San Francisco, 11, 12, 14, 15, 21; San Leandro/San Lorenzo, 82; South Bay, 50, 59; South Marin, 171, 173, 181, 182, 184; South San Mateo, 33, 43. See also nature centers
mussels, zebra, 135

N

Napa, 85, 102, 137–43; River, 129, 131, 132, 140, 141, 142
Natatorium, 108, 110
Native Americans, 3, 66, 102–3; and Alcatraz, 18–19; Mission San Francisco Solano, 145; Miwok, 102, 153, 155, 172, 173, 178; museum, 155; Napa, 142; Olompali, 153; Pomo, 145; Tuibun, 68; Vallejo and, 144; Wintun, 145. See also Karkin; Ohlones
nature centers: Fremont/Hayward, 63, 68, 70; Napa/Sonoma, 142; Oakland/Berkeley, 96, 99; Resources,

185–87; San Leandro/San Lorenzo, 82; South Bay, 50, 59; South Marin, 171, 182; South San Mateo, 33, 43. See also museums
Navy, U.S., 24, 55, 89, 113, 114, 133, 172
Neptune Beach, 84
Newark Slough, 60, 63, 68
Niles Community Park, 69
9th Street Park, Benicia, 129, 133
Niven Park, 171
North American Plate, 2
Northeast Bay, 85, 118–33
Novato, 148–55; Creek, 160; History Museum, 155

O

oak, 3, 73; poison, 162
Oakland, 86–101; Airport, 77, 78; downtown, 91; Estuary, 91; ferries, 1, 12, 17, 19, 89, 92, 96, 99; high spots, 85; Port of, 3, 88, 92, 94–95, 96, 150; waterfront, 91–92
Ocean Beach, 11
Ohlones, 102–103; Alameda, 88; Brooks Island, 107; Fremont/ Hayward, 63, 64, 66, 68; and shellfish, 31, 68; and tule, 64; village, 66; and yerba buena, 21. See also Native Americans
oil industry, 120, 123
Olompali, 153. See also Native Americans
Olompali State Historic Park, 85, 153, 155
owls, burrowing, 54
Oyster Bay Regional Shoreline, 2, 77, 78
Oyster Point, 30, 31
oysters, 30, 31, 134

P

Pacific Gas & Electric Company, 22, 23, 24, 43, 52
Pacific Marina, 89
Pacific Plate, 2
Pacific Steam Whaling Company, 20
Palace of Fine Arts, 12
Palo Alto, 44; Baylands, 50, 52, 55, 60; Duck Pond, 51
Panama-Pacific International Exposition (1915), 12, 180
Paradise Beach County Park, 172, 173
Parr (Carolyn) Nature Museum, 142, 143
Patterson House, 65, 67
pelicans, 162
Peralta Park, 96
Permanente Creek, 54
Petaluma, 2, 148–55; Adobe State Historic Park, 153, 155; Marina, 152; Marsh Wildlife Area, 153; River, 2, 150, 151–52, 155
Pete's Harbor, 42
pheasants, ring-necked, 52
phytoplankton, 123

pickleweed, 53, 64, 72, 116, 162, 171
Pickleweed Park, 165, 166, 167
pier biology, 21, 99; pilings, 99
piers: Alameda, 82; Benicia, 130, 133; Berkeley, 99; Crockett, 125; Dumbarton, 48, 63; Emeryville, 97; Oakland, 82, 92, 93, 95; San Francisco, 12, 13, 15, 17, 19, 22, 23, 24, 181; San Mateo County, 38, 39; Sausalito, 180; Vallejo, 132, 133. See also fish/fishing
Pinole, 121; Bayfront Park, 121, 128; Creek, 121, 122, 128; Shores Regional Park, 121, 128
Piper Park, 170
planned communities, 38, 40
plants, 3, 72–73, 157; coastal salt marshes, 53, 64, 72; coastal scrub, 72; coastal strand, 72; dune-colonizing, 14; endangered, 11, 172; Fremont/Hayward, 63, 64, 67; freshwater marsh, 123; grasslands, 67, 73; Marin County, 162, 171, 172, 174, 175, 183; mixed evergreen forests, 73; Napa, 142; Northeast Bay, 126; North Waterfront Park, 100; oak woodlands, 73; Petaluma/Novato, 153; Richmond/San Pablo, 116, 117; San Francisco, 11, 21, 23; San Lorenzo/San Leandro, 77, 79; San Mateo, 28, 29, 32; seasonal wetlands, 72; South Bay salt marsh, 53
playgrounds, 76, 99, 177, 178
Plaza Viña del Mar, 180
Point Bonita, 13
Point Emery, 98
Point Isabel Regional Shoreline, 97, 101, 106
Point Molate: Beach Park, 113, 117; U.S. Naval Fuel Depot, 113, 117
Point Pinole, 112, 116, 117; Regional Shoreline, 117, 128
Point Richmond, 108, 110, 117
Point San Pablo, 114, 115; Yacht Harbor, 115, 117
Point San Pedro, 164, 166
poison oak, 162
poke-poling, 13
pollution: Alviso, 57, 58; DUST Marsh and, 67; Hamilton Field, 160; Lime Point Lighthouse, 182; Moffett Field, 55; oil, 123; and oyster industry, 30, 31; Richardson Bay, 181; Roberts Landing, 77; South Bay water, 58; storm drain, 156. See also wastewater treatment plants
Port Costa, 2, 125, 126, 128
Portolá, Gaspar de, 3, 102
ports: Alviso, 57; Oakland, 3, 88, 92, 94–95, 96, 150;

Redwood City, 42, 49; Richmond, 107; San Francisco, 22, 115
Port Sonoma-Marin, 152, 155
Portview Park, 95, 96
Potrero de los Cerritos, 67
Potrero Hill, 22
Potrero Point, 106, 107
Presidio, 11, 24; Army Museum, 11; Historic Trail, 11
prisons: Alcatraz, 18; San Quentin, 167, 171

Q

Quarry Trail, 68
Quinn's Lighthouse, 93

R

Radio Point Beach, 98, 101
railroads, 44; Marin County, 174, 177, 178; miniature, 110; Northeast Bay, 121, 125, 130; Richmond/San Pablo, 108, 109, 117; San Mateo, 44; South Bay, 48, 57
rails, clapper, 64, 79, 116, 150
Rancho Petaluma, 144
Rancho San Pablo, 113
Rancho Saucelito, 179
Rankin Park, 127
Rat Rock, 166
rattlesnake grass, 73
Ravenswood, 49; Open Space Preserve, 44, 49, 55, 60; Pier, 44, 48, 49; Slough, 42, 43
rays, 35, 83
Red & White Fleet, 17, 19, 24, 181
Red Rock, 113, 117
Red's Java House, 19
Redwood City, Port, 42, 49
Redwood Creek, 42
Redwood Shores, 40, 41
Remillard Park, 170, 171
Rengstorff House, 53
restoration, 4; dune, 14; marsh, 70, 135, 150, 161, 171
Richardson Bay, 175–76, 181
Richmond, 2, 101, 104–17
Richmond Marina, 107, 110
Richmond Plunge/Natatorium, 108, 110
Richmond–San Rafael Bridge, 1, 112, 117, 167, 173
Ridge Trail, 1, 5, 6, 54, 129, 131, 142
Ring Mountain, 85, 172, 174
River Park, 132, 133
Roberts Landing, 76, 77
rocks, 28, 85, 113, 114, 166, 184. See also geology
Rodeo, 122, 128
Roemer (Elsie) Bird Sanctuary, 82, 83
Roosevelt (Franklin D.) fishing pier, 92
Rotary Nature Center, Oakland, 96
Rush Creek Open Space Preserve, 154
Ryder Park, 34

S

Sacramento River, 2, 124, 128
sailing, 53, 99, 115, 179. See also windsurfing
Sailing Lake, 53
salmon, 3, 128
saltbush, 72
salt ponds, 3, 38, 48, 59, 63; aerial, 71; Cargill Salt, 42, 48, 54, 57, 71; North Bay, 140; salt production, 70, 71; transformed, 70; wildlife, 49, 59, 71
salt wedge, 123
San Andreas Fault System, 2
San Antonio Creek, 93
San Bruno Mountain, 3, 23, 27, 28, 31, 77, 85
San Bruno Point, 27, 30, 31
sandcastles, 82, 83, 84
sandpipers, western, 50
sandstone, 28, 85, 114
San Francisco, 1, 8–24, 49; ferries, 12, 17, 19, 24, 173, 181; high spots, 85; naming of, 21; port, 22, 115; shoreline in 1850s, 18. See also bridges
San Francisco Bay Conservation and Development Commission, 3–4, 5, 38, 98
San Francisco Bay National Wildlife Refuge, 1–2, 38–44, 48, 56–60, 63–64, 66; Visitor Center, 63, 68, 71
San Joaquin River, 124
San Jose, 44, 49, 57, 58
San Leandro, 2, 74–85; Bay, 79, 91, 93; Marina, 71, 76, 78
San Lorenzo, 74–85; Creek, 71
San Mateo: city, 3, 25–44, 85; County Fishing Pier, 38, 39; Creek, 34
San Mateo–Hayward Bridge, 1, 39, 70, 85
San Pablo, 104–17
San Pablo Bay, 2, 115, 121, 123, 134, 137, 146–47, 150; Regional Park, 121, 128; Regional Trail, 123; National Wildlife Refuge, 147, 163
San Quentin State Prison, 167, 171
San Rafael Bridge, 1
San Rafael Creek, 164, 166, 167
Santa Clara Valley, 2
Santa Fe, 108
Santa Margarita Island, 162
Santa Rosa Ferry, 19
Santa Venetia Marsh, 162
sardines, 16, 114
Sausalito waterfront, 179–81
Save San Francisco Bay Association, 3
scaups, 2, 176
Schoen Park, 165, 166, 167
Schollenberger Marsh, 152
Schoonmaker Point, 179
scoters, surf, 176
Scottsdale Pond, 154
sculpture. See art
sea lettuce, 41

sea lions, 17
seals, harbor, 56, 59, 113, 147, 171, 177
Sears Point: Bridge, 132; Raceway, 146, 147
sea stars, 21
serpentine, 85, 114, 172
Seventh Street Pier, 95
sewage treatment. See wastewater treatment plants
sharks, 30, 34, 82, 172
shellfish, 30, 31, 41; alien, 134, 135; Chinese camps, 23, 30, 165; Crab Cove, 83; Ohlone, 31, 68; Oyster Point, 30; pier piling, 21. See also shrimp
Shimada Friendship Park, 106, 110
ships: building, 24, 30, 42, 84, 107, 108, 120, 130, 180; cargo, 24, 123, 125, 126; container, 94, 150; historic preserved, 14, 16, 20, 108, 174, 179; Liberty, 14, 84, 108; merchant, 131; schooners, 20, 42, 76, 151; submarine, 16; tankers, 21, 22, 106, 123. See also boating; ports
shipworms, 135
Shorebird Marsh, 171
Shorebird Park Nature Center, 99, 101
Shoreline Amphitheater, 52
Shoreline At Mountain View Park, 52–54, 55, 60
Shoreline Park: Alameda, 89; Bay Farm Island, 78; San Mateo, 32, 34, 35; San Rafael, 166, 167; Sausalito, 179; Tiburon, 173
shrimp, 165; bay brine, 49, 59; Chinese camps, 23, 30, 165; ghost, 41, 83; mud flat, 41, 83
Sierra Point, 27, 31
Silicon Valley, 56
Sisters, The 115, 166
Skyline Wilderness Park, 142
snails, 41, 71, 82
Sonoma, 85, 137, 143, 144–47, 150; State Historic Park, 145, 147
South Bay, 45–60, 102
South Beach Harbor, 19–20, 21
Southeast Shoreline, 93
South End Rowing Club, 15, 24
Southhampton Bay, 130
South Sailing Basin, 99
Sportsfield Park, 56, 60
squirrels, California ground, 54
Stanford, Sally, 180
State Coastal Conservancy. See California State Coastal Conservancy
Steinberger Slough, 40
Stevens Creek, 54; Shoreline Nature Study Area, 55
Strawberry Cove Park, 177
Strawberry Point, 177

Stremmel Mansion, 131
sturgeons, 2, 125, 132, 165
subduction, 2, 184
subsidence, 56, 58
sugar cane refinery, 125
Suisun Bay, 120, 123, 124, 134
Sunnyvale Baylands Park, 55, 56, 60
swimming, 11, 15, 82, 108

T

Telegraph Hill, 19, 85
terns, 64, 89, 90
Terwilliger Nature Education Center, 171
Third Street Bridge, 20, 22
Tiburon, 85, 172–74, 175
Tidelands Loop Trail, 63, 68
tide pools, 11
tides, Golden Gate, 12
Tiffany Beach and Park, 180
Tilden, Susan, 57
toadfish, 181
Towata Park, 82, 84, 96
toyon, 73
trails: Alameda Creek Regional, 68, 69, 71; coastal, 1, 11, 184; Fremont/Hayward, 63, 66, 68, 69, 71; Marin County, 161–78, 184; Napa/Sonoma, 142, 147; Northeast Bay, 121, 123, 129, 131; Oakland/Berkeley, 95, 100; Petaluma/Novato, 151, 152, 153, 154; Presidio, 11; Richmond/San Pablo, 116, 117; Ridge, 1, 5, 6, 54, 129, 131, 142; San Francisco, 11, 23; San Lorenzo/San Leandro, 76, 78, 80, 83; San Mateo, 40, 43; San Pablo Bay Regional, 123; South Bay, 49, 52, 54, 59, 60. See also all maps and chapters, especially "Getting Around" sections
trains. See railroads
Treasure Island, 21, 24
Tuibun, 68
tule, 64, 123
Turner (Matthew) Shipyard Park, 129, 133

U

UNOCAL, 123

V

Vallejo: city, 129, 132, 133, 144; Fishing Pier, 132, 133; Mill Historic Park, 69; Naval and Historial Museum, 133
Vallejo, Mariano Guadalupe, 129, 132, 133, 144, 145, 146, 153
Valley of the Moon Vintage Festival, 146, 147
Vicente Martinez Adobe, 127

W

Warm Water Cove Park, 22
Washington Park: Alameda, 84, 88; Richmond/San Pablo, 108
waste disposal, 156–57
wastewater treatment plants:

Fremont/Hayward, 69, 70; Marin County, 161, 163, 178; Northeast Bay, 121; Petaluma/Novato, 152, 155; Richmond/San Pablo, 116; San Lorenzo/San Leandro, 78; San Mateo, 30, 40, 43; South Bay, 50, 51, 56, 58, 60
water: issues, 123; recycled, 50, 152, 161. See also pollution; wastewater treatment plants
Wave Organ, 13, 15
West Brother Island, 115
West Frontage Road, 98, 101
Westwood Hills Park, 142
wetlands, 3, 57, 59, 66, 72, 157. See also marshes; mud flats; salt ponds
Whale Garden, 79
whaling, 20, 115
wheelchair access, 6, 33, 79, 83, 93, 96, 166, 179, 184
Whittell Marsh, 117
Wildcat Creek, 116
Wildcat Marsh, 2, 116, 117
wildlife, 1–3, 4, 7, 134–35, 157; Fremont/Hayward, 63, 64, 65, 66, 67, 70, 71; Marin County, 160, 175, 177, 183; Napa/Sonoma, 147; Northeast Bay, 2, 126; Petaluma/Novato, 150, 151, 153; Richmond/San Pablo, 106, 107, 109, 113; San Lorenzo/San Leandro, 77, 82, 83; San Mateo, 28, 38–43; South Bay, 49, 50, 56, 59. See also birds; endangered species; fish/fishing
Wilson/Lake Dalwigk Park, 132, 133
windsurfing: Marin County, 170; Oakland/Berkeley, 98; Petaluma/Novato, 152; San Francisco, 12, 23; San Mateo, 33, 38; South Bay, 53
wine, 114, 140, 143, 144, 146
Winehaven winery, 113, 114
woodpeckers, acorn, 154, 160

Y

Yee Tock Chee Park, 180
yerba buena, 21
Yerba Buena: Cove, 18, 21; Island, 18, 33, 92
Yosemite Creek, 23

Z

zooeicia, 157
zooplankton, 123

Black and White Photographs

Carol Arnold, p. 146

Richard Averitt, Baykeeper, p. 15 (Baykeeper)

Bancroft Library, University of California, Berkeley, p. 183

Bay Model Visitor Center, p. 180

Benicia Camel Barn Museum Collection, p. 130

Jennifer Bermon, pp. 11, 92 (cabin)

California Department of Parks and Recreation, p. 144

California Historical Society, San Francisco, p. 31

Coyote Point Museum, p. 33

Crockett Historical Museum, p. 126

East Bay Regional Park District, p. 65

Foster Enterprises, p. 38

Richard Frear, National Park Service, p. 15

Peter Grenell, p. 13

Jack Hearns, National Park Service, p. 127

Phoebe Hearst Museum of Anthropology, University of California, Berkeley, pp. 102, 103

Hercules Historical Area Restoration and Preservation Committee, p. 122

Dorothea Lange Collection, Oakland Museum of California, p. 88 (workers)

Mill Valley Public Library, pp. 175, 178

Chris Moser, Riverside Municipal Museum, p. 68

Department of the Navy, p. 133

Novato History Museum, p. 160

Oakland Museum of California, pp. 84, 88

Department of Parks and Community Services, Sacramento, p. 141

Petaluma Historical Museum, pp. 148, 151

Point Molate Winehaven files, US Navy Fuel Department, p. 114

Port of Oakland, pp. 91, 92 (*Potomac* & Jack London)

L.J. Quinn's Lighthouse, p. 93

Courtesy of National Maritime Museum, p. 18 (Meigg's Pier)

Richmond Museum of History Collection, pp. 108 (Point Richmond), 109, 113

Liza Riddle, p. 70

San Francisco History Room, San Francisco Public Library, pp. 3, 24, 27, 30

San Jose Historical Museum, pp. 49, 56, 57, 58

San Mateo County Historical Museum, pp. 42, 44

San Quentin Museum, p. 171 (ball & chain)

San Francisco Maritime Museum, p. 165 (fan mill)

San Francisco National Historic Park Collection, p. 76

Dewey Schwartzenburg, p. 171

Barbara Selke, p. 157 (cats)

Mark Snyder, Port of San Francisco, p. 22

C.H. Townsend, California Department of Parks and Recreation, China Camp, p. 165

Treasure Island Museum, p. 21

Tom Tutt, San Jose State University, p. 64

Vallejo Naval and Historical Museum, p. 131

Bob Walker/IDG Films, p. 111

Steefenie Wicks, p. 181

Color Photographs

Balloons Above the Valley, p. 140 (balloon)

Bay Area Discovery Museum, p. 182 (museum)

Brady Aerial Photography, pp. 8, 38 (Foster City), 97 (Emeryville Crescent), 112 (bridge)

Buena Vista Winery, p. 143 (winery)

California Maritime Academy, p. 131 (Academy)

Candlestick Point State Recreation Area, Bay Area District, p. 23 (Candlestick)

City of Benicia, pp. 129, 130, 131 (bridge)

City of San Jose, Department of City Planning & Building, p. 57 (house)

City of Sunnyvale Parks and Recreation, p. 56 (park)

Andrew Neal Cohen, p. 134 (J. Carlton), 135 (cordgrass)

Bob Colin, Caltrans, p. 48 (Dumbarton Bridge, page bottom)

Coyote Hills Regional Park, pp. 66, 68 (canoe)

Coyote Point Museum, p. 33 (bobcat)

Alice Cummings, pp. 49, 52 (slough), 53 (lake), 54 (Mountain View Shoreline Park), 55

Maurice Dockrell, Fort Mason Center, p. 14 (Fort Mason)

Juanita Doran, p. 142 (park)

George Draper/Bay Trail Project, back cover (gloved hand), p. 157 (cleanup)

East Bay Regional Park District, pp. 66 (park), 67 (Coyote Red Hill), 79 (aerial), 83 (Crab Cove)

Jerry Emory, pp. 67 (marsh), 78 (wastewater filter), 106 (Shimada Park , tankers), 107 (island, wharf), 112 (San Rafael Bridge), 113, 115, 117 (view from pier), 127 (pier), 165 (Chinese hangings)

K.T. Eugene, p. 58 (heron)

Stephen Evans, p. 174 (gallows, China Cabin)

Exploratorium, p. 12 (Palace of Fine Arts)

Phyllis Faber, pp. 170 (statue), 171 (park), 177 (Strawberry Point)

Nelia Forest, pp. 68 (platform), 83 (ramp)

Richard Frear, San Francisco Maritime National Historic Park, p. 10 (park)

Ken Gardiner, p. 50 (Baylands)

Phil Gordon, pp. 59 (refuge), 80, 81 (glaucous winged gull, Heermann's gull), 140 (mew gull)

Jim Hastings, pp. 144 (Sonoma Valley), 145, 150 (river)

Phoebe Hearst Museum of Anthropology, University of California, Berkeley, pp. 102-103 (historical photographs)

Scott Hess, p. 152 (turning basin)

John Inase, pp. 14 (dune), 16, 21, 22 (Islais Creek), 82 (snail), 167 (snowy egret)

Jay Jones, front cover (JFK Park), pp. 7, 40 (trail, marsh), 42 (harbor), 43 (Bayfront Park), 45, 51 (sculpture, pond), 52 (park), 53 (house), 57 (warehouse, Alviso), 58 (house), 60 (park), 69 (girl with horse), 76, 77 (shoreline, sculpture), 78 (park), 84, 89 (park), 92 (J.L. Plaza), 93 (park, pier), 97 (pier), 98, 99, 100, 101 (Fleming Point), 103 (family), 108, 110, 116, 121 (Pinole Bayfront Park), 122, 123, 125 (downtown), 126 (warehouse, Mothball Fleet), 131 (marina), 132 (pier), 137, 140 (Napa Valley), 141, 142 (downtown), 151 (downtown), 152 (Port Sonoma-Marin, recycled water, boat ramp), 153 (adobe)

Caroline Kopp, p. 135 (crab)

Ron Kukulka, pp. 11, 12 (Crissy Field, ferries), 13, 14 (meadow), 19, 20, 23 (India Basin), 24, 30 (Oyster Point), 32, 33 (Coyote Point Rec Area), 34, 35, 38 (Foster City), 39 (bridge, park), 89 (boat ramp), 93 (Embarcadero Cove), 160 (Hamilton Field), 161 (park, Civic Center), 162 (island), 163 (duck blind), 164 (China Camp), 165 (park), 166 (McNears Beach, Shoreline Park), 168, 170 (ferry terminal, park), 171 (trail), 172 (Tiburon, Beach Park), 173 (downtown, quarters, rock), 175 (park), 178, 178 (Mt. Tamalpais), 179 (park), 180, 184

Peter LaTourette, pp. 90 (Forster's tern), 81 (ring-billed gull), 176 (scaup), 126 (bluebird)

Jeff Lewis, p. 64 (fox)

Rob Lopez, Sears Point Raceway, p. 146 (raceway)

Lyford House, p. 175 (house)

Laurel Marcus, p. 150 (hayfields)

Marin Conservation Corps, p. 5

James A. Martin, p. 167 (islands)

Mia Monroe, p. 65

National Park Service, GGNRA, p. 182 (Fort Baker)

Larry Orsak, p. 183 (butterfly)

Joan Patton, p. 156

PG & E Spotlight, p. 173 (Angel Island)

Pier 39, p. 17 (ferry)

Gene Piscia, City of Napa Community Resources Dept., pp. 142 (wharf), 143 (vines)

Rich Poremba, p. 151 (*Petaluma Queen*)

Port of Oakland, pp. 88 (port), 89 (cranes), 91, 92 (village, saloon), 94, 95

Port of Redwood City, pp. 36, 42 (port)

Mark J. Rauzon, pp. 39 (birds), 70 (birds), 83 (sanctuary), 104, 112 (birds), 142 (birds)

Reineck & Reineck, pp. 85 (chert), 117 (Pier 39, sea lions), 181 (ferry)

Liza Riddle, pp. 86, 96 (kids at lake)

Thomas Rountree, pp. 81 (Bonaparte's gull), 90 (Caspian, California terns)

San Francisco Bay National Wildlife Refuge, front cover (terns), back cover (kids), pp. 40 (black-shouldered kite), 43 (island), 44, 63 (refuge), 147 (San Pablo Bay)

San Francisco Bay Trail Project, pp. 27 (exercise), 30 (peninsula), 33 (beach), 50 (boardwalk, Interpretive Center), 54 (owl), 59 (education center, creek), 60 (slough), 82 (Crab Cove), 120, 126 (shoreline), 132 (marina), 178 (Bayfront Park)

Save San Francisco Bay Association, pp. 64 (bird), 162 (pickleweed)

David Schooley, pp. 25, 27 (San Bruno Mountain), 28

Dewey Schwartzenburg, pp. 96 (Fairyland), 98 (Davenport Mini Park), 156 (kids)

Gordon Sherman/Audubon Canyon Ranch, pp. 23 (bird), 41 (bird), 51 (bird), 52 (birds), 81 (mew gull), 154 (bird), 167 (heron), 176 (bufflehead, ruddy duck, canvas back, surf scoter)

Shoreline at Mountain View, p. 52 (Meadowlands)

Doris Sloan, pp. 85, (sandstone, serpentine), 114 (rocks)

Sonoma Valley Visitors Bureau, Steve Phoffenberger, p. 146 (festival)

Ian C. Tait, back cover and pp. 40 (harrier), 61, 81 (herring